THE BOOK OF JACKS

THE BOOK OF
JACKS

CHARLES NEVIN

MAINSTREAM
PUBLISHING

EDINBURGH AND LONDON

First published in Great Britain in 2008 by
MAINSTREAM PUBLISHING COMPANY
(EDINBURGH) LTD
7 Albany Street
Edinburgh EH1 3UG

ISBN 9781845964054

All picture-section photographs
© Getty Images

A catalogue record for this book is available
from the British Library

Typeset in Goudy and Requiem

Printed in Great Britain by
Clays Ltd, St Ives plc

INTRODUCTION

J ack. You must have noticed, even if your name is not Jack, that there are a lot of them. Jack used to be the nickname given to a John. For the last 20 years or so, though, more and more parents have been choosing Jack as a first name in its own right. Jack has been the most popular name for boys in England and Wales for more than a decade. It has also regularly been the top choice in Scotland, Ireland, Australia and New Zealand, and is showing strongly in the United States and Canada.

Jack, you are everywhere. When Hollywood wanted a name for a pirate who is sassy, cool, naughty, and more than a touch wacky, what did it go for? Captain Jack Sparrow. The wild free spirit of nature doomed by proud Man's overweening confidence in his own powers? Jack Dawson of *Titanic*. The man who can save the free world? Jack Bauer of *24*.

Wondering about present Jacks led me to look at Jacks past. And, throughout history, you will find Jacks repeating such traits time and again. There have been fascinating, beguiling, eccentric, charming, rebellious men who have borne other names but not nearly so many, as you will see, who have been called Jack. Some of them, though, I am compelled to say, have not been nice, not nice at all. Machine Gun Jack McGurk is just one who comes to mind. And Black Jack Ketchum had his moments.

Most, though, are remarkably similar. A Jack tends to be generously gifted but attractively flawed, leading to mercurial careers and often sad ends. Quite a few of them, of course, have adopted the name Jack, which helps to explain it; others have been given it as a nickname, even though they were not christened John. And a John, it seems, only became a Jack if he showed such signs. What's in this name?

Well, for a start, it's mysterious: why should John be Jack? Other adaptations are much closer to their origin, even those such as Bob, Bill, Dick or Harry. And then there is Jack's powerful part in legend, fable and folklore. Jack is the nimble, quick-witted lad who outwits giants, witches and wicked fairies and lives happily ever after. Jack is Jack in the Green, the spirit of the forest and the wild, the fun of it, and the threat from it to our supposedly civilised ways. Jack figures in our festivals and rites of season, especially spring and autumn, the change from dark to light to dark, when the order is upset and mischief rules. Jack is the common man, who can get uppity if the higher orders cheat and mistreat him.

Can such a weight and freight of baggage and myth somehow be transmitted with a name and embedded into the personality? Being a Jack, Jack, you might think it all a load of old tosh that doesn't amount to a hill of beans. But your name matters. True, Shakespeare had Juliet doubt its importance in the matter of her Romeo, but we know what happened to them. Besides, Francis Bacon, a very resonant, not to say redolent, name in this context, thought there was 'much impression and enchantment' in names.

And first names are of especial significance. People react to them even before meeting their bearers, judging them by those they have known and not always loved. Parents agonise over their choice. Children agonise over it, too. Small wonder, when you remember the challenging time laid on by his dad for the boy named Sue. (And by theirs for the boys and girls named Warren Peace, Merry Christmas, Art Gallery and Moon Unit Zappa.)

Of course, we like to think that we base our judgements about people and things on far deeper considerations than labels and images. Tell that to the image-makers and the label-attachers. And to the researchers. They have found that reactions to names are based on unconscious associations of startling simplicity. So we will think someone is likely to be successful if he or she has a name used by royalty, that a girl or woman is likely to be attractive if she has a soft, feminine-sounding name, that a boy or man is likely to be attractive if he has a hard, masculine-sounding name.

For those who argue for the inspiring evolution of our species into rational sophisticates, it gets worse, I'm afraid. We think someone is likely to be lucky if their name sounds like 'luck' and has the same number of letters. I sense, Jack, that I now have your full attention. Yes, indeed, according to research carried out by the interestingly named Professor Richard Wiseman, Britain's only Professor for the Public Understanding of Psychology, Jacks are thought to be luckier than other men, while Lucy is the luckiest name for a woman. But there is something else, too, as while Lucy is thought only marginally more lucky than Katie, Jack is believed to be at least twice as lucky as the next man, Chris.

The something else, Jack, is that reputation which comes with your name: the mystery and the magic. That's also, perhaps principally, why we think you're lucky. Jack swapped the cow for a few beans, stumbled up a beanstalk and found the golden eggs. Lucky Jack managed to trick and kill the giant and live happily ever after. There is a term of art among anthropologists and psychologists for this kind of unconscious linking: associative magic, the hope that something might rub off. And the impulse shows no sign of lessening. Which is not so surprising: with daily reminders that our frail world is under any number of elemental threats, we have clearly decided that we still need all the luck we can get.

Does it work? Is there any evidence beyond my airy, if cogent, theorising that your name influences your behaviour as well as reactions to you? Certainly. To begin with, we are highly attuned to the sound of our own names. A French study, for example, found that people in a coma responded to their name, while Canadian psychologists have found that we prefer the letters that make up our names to any others. Further, work carried out at the State University of New York by Professor Brett Pelham has discovered that this 'implicit egotism' has remarkable effects. So people called Florence choose to live in Florida, and people called George go to live in Georgia (no data available on Scunthorpe). People are more likely to marry someone and even support politicians whose names begin with the same letter (yes, that's how George Bush did it, more Bs than Gs or Ks). They are also likely to go into jobs starting with the same letter as their name, or into jobs that have associations with their names. So, remarkably, it seems that all those names that make you chuckle are not a coincidence after all. There was a hidden impulse in the career paths of Miss Sharp the music teacher, Ms Herd, the spokesperson for the English Beef and Lamb Executive, Mr C. Ensor, the chairman of Bedford borough council's standards committee, Ms Sara Blizzard, the weather presenter, and Mr Peter Atchoo, the pneumonia specialist.

Jack, read and beware: even if all work and no play will make you a dull boy, and you wish to be Jack the Lugubrious rather than Jack the Lad, it is clearly going to require considerable effort. But I do have some consolations. Academic opinion is not all on the side of your perilous predestination. Professor Leo Hendry of the University of Glamorgan points out, not unreasonably, that there must surely be many unfamous Jacks throughout history who have not conformed to type, and thinks there are too many variables involved in my theory for it ever to be any more than that. Another study, cited by Professor Wiseman in his *Quirkology: The Curious Science of Everyday Lives*, has shown that some people react to preconceptions about their names by working hard and successfully to disprove them: the Boy Named Sue strategy works.

Peter McClure, a consultant on names for the *Oxford English Dictionary*, has light to shine on the mysterious origins of Jack. His research, published in a paper entitled 'The Kinship of Jack', shows that the name was formed in the twelfth century by mixing the Northern Old French Jan (our John) with the Middle Dutch ending, -ke, to form the nickname Janke, then Jakke. The name was then imported to Britain from Europe by the Norman conquerors. Fascinatingly, Peter McClure points out that Middle Dutch was considered socially inferior to Northern Old French, the court language of the Normans, and that they often used these mixed forms to mark out someone who was not as posh as they were. This would explain why Jack became the common, catch-all name for a peasant and a servant (and why mechanical servants came to be called Jacks, as in car jack). An alternative, of course, was knave, which had the same snobbish implications, and also mixed in the idea of the naughty, cheeky, saucy Jack of fairy tales.

The other explanation for Jack's early ubiquity is exactly that: there were an awful lot of them. From the middle of the fourteenth century until the middle of the twentieth century, John was the most popular name in England. By the late fourteenth century, three out of every ten people were called John, which comes from the Latin Johannes, itself derived from the Hebrew Johanan, 'God (Jah) is gracious'.

Peter McClure also follows E.W.B. Nicholson, the nineteenth-century Bodley's Librarian at Oxford, in dismissing the theory that Jack is related to the French and Latin for James, Jacques and Jacobus.

Those of us, though, with an obstinate impulse to the magical, mystical and mysterious persist in seeing something more in Jack than just another name for John. For there is another theory, of pleasingly misty origin, that Jack or Jakke is descended from Iacchus, or Bacchus, the ancient god of wine, revelry and mischief, of the emotional, unrestrained, uncivilised and fun parts of our existence.

This would further explain why so many Jacks, as you will discover, appear to have lived lives almost entirely devoted to his service. I have to report, though, that Peter McClure is unconvinced by this connection. In fact, his term of art for it is 'absolute rubbish'.

Ah, well. A good test of whether you are temperamentally a true Jack, Jack, will be whether you accept existing academic thought or follow your instinct and go your own way. In which case, you will also have to contend with those folklorists who refuse to see a line of clear and obvious tradition stretching back from our May Day and mumming Jacks to the Green Man, the carved and leafy and pagan symbol to be found lurking with the gargoyles as some kind of eternity insurance policy in churches throughout Europe, notably in places colonised by the Romans, one of whose gods was, of course, Bacchus.

Alternatively, you can just sit back, read and wonder at this remarkable collection of hell-raisers, handfuls, heroes, highwaymen, rogues, pirates, unruly squires, dashing fellows and relishable eccentrics. And the best of luck to every man Jack of you.

ADAMS (I)

Jack Adams was a famous diviner of the stars during the reign of Charles II. Astrologers today who complain about the lack of respect generally afforded to their activity should have a look at Jack's press. James Granger, the eighteenth-century Oxfordshire parson who compiled *A Biographical History of England*, reported him 'a blind buzzard, that pretended to have the eye of an eagle'. And more: 'When he failed in his prediction, he declared that the stars did not absolutely force, but powerfully incline; and threw the blame upon wayward and perverse fate!' Granger has a print of Jack showing him advising 'Joan, Queen of Sluts' of her future; the caption is a splendid precursor of the Latin invocations often found in *Private Eye* magazine: 'Magnifico Smokentissimo Custardissimo Astrologissimo, Cunningmanissimo, Rabinissimo Viro Iacko Adams, de Clerkenwell Greeno . . . Hobbedeboody, pinxit and scratchabat'. A 'cunningman' was defined as a man 'who pretends to tell fortunes, or teach how to recover stolen or lost goods'. In Captain Grose's *Dictionary of the Vulgar Tongue*, 1811, a Jack Adams is 'a fool'. Poor Jack. There again, perhaps he wasn't very good. But, like many other members of his calling, he was clearly hot on marketing: his *Perpetual Almanack* of 1662, promising 'an exact knowledge of all future things till the morrow after doomsday', bears the legend: 'to be sold by the Gingerbred-Woman in Clerkenwell Green'.

ADAMS (2)

This Jack Adams is another typically shadowy Jack, born some time in the late 1760s. On 28 April 1789, he was serving as an able seaman under the name of Alexander Smith on HMS *Bounty*. Although he later claimed, among much else, to have been asleep when Captain Bligh was seized, he followed Fletcher Christian on his doomed travels and settlement of Pitcairn Island. When, in 1808, an American merchant ship accidentally arrived at Pitcairn, Adams was found to be the only man of the nine mutineers, and the six Tahitian men who had accompanied them, left alive. The Americans were much impressed with his conduct, particularly his assiduous instruction of the remaining ten women and twenty-three children in a rudimentary Christianity with the help of the *Bounty*'s Bible. He told them the other mutineers, including Fletcher Christian, had been murdered by the Tahitian men and that the Tahitian men had then been murdered by the Tahitian women: he denied any part for himself. He was granted an amnesty but gave conflicting accounts to subsequent visiting naval officers and was always anxious to prevent any questioning of the surviving women. It is claimed that Adams was the instigator of much of the violence and that this explains his discovery of religion. Further, his use of a pseudonym and possession of a literacy unusual in an ordinary seaman has led to speculation about his true identity. Whatever, he is the only mutineer with a known grave, and he has another lasting memorial: the capital of Pitcairn is Adamstown, although what its name should really be can only be guessed at.

ALMACO

The Almaco Jack is a species of the Jack group of fish. As you would expect from a fish called Jack, it is a wanderer found in most of the world's oceans. In a further display of Jackish bravado, Almacos like to rub themselves against passing sharks to remove parasites. Yo!

AMEND-ALL

See the mysterious **Jack Cade**, 'Lord of London'.

ANAPES

Behind this satisfying insult, sadly no longer modish, lies a melancholy tale of fifteenth-century ambition outmatched by events and insufficiently supported by ability. Jackanapes is a corruption of Jack Napis, the nickname given to William de la Pole, fourth Earl and first Duke of Suffolk (1396–1450). It derives from the de la Pole crest, which features a collar and chain of the type favoured at the time for monkeys: thus n'apes and n'apis. You will have surmised, rightly, that it was not affectionate. For a few years in the mid-1400s, de la Pole was effectively England's prime minister, and he was as effective as he had been at taking on Joan of Arc, to whom he surrendered after the Maid raised the siege of Orleans in 1429.

To be fair to Jack, though, he was playing with a hand perhaps worse than any ever dealt to a British statesman. He had a weak king, Henry VI, following a great one, his father, Henry V, and a society going through one of its periodic convulsions of competing classes and interests as the feudal system continued its long stagger to extinction. Even larger upheavals across the Channel were making the impossibility of holding on to the French possessions ever more apparent and depriving the pressed administration of any distracting success: by 1449, the whole of Normandy had been lost. And the failures still had to be paid for. Jack, trying to disguise his king's impotence and his own influence while indulging in some fairly conventional nest-feathering, caught it in the neck, literally. At first, he seemed to have escaped with banishment, but his cross-channel voyage was halted by a ship named, ominously, *The Nicholas of the Tower*, on which he is supposed to have been tried and found guilty by persons still unknown. His execution on a small boat alongside took three or four blows. This is not surprising, as it must have been a bit rocky, and even executioners on dry land often needed more than one crack at it (see **Jack Ketch**). It was a vivid and lawless precursor to that summer's explosion of anger led by the equally mysterious **Jack Amend-All** (see **Jack Cade**).

Suffolk's body was left on Dover Beach for a month alongside his head before his wife, who was Chaucer's granddaughter, was permitted to take it for burial in Wingfield in his home county. He was further ill-used after his death by Shakespeare who, in *Henry VI*, for reasons of dramatic convenience, made him the lover of Margaret of Anjou and the murderer of another popular rival, Humphrey, Duke of Gloucester. There is no evidence for the first but some for the second. Lest we feel too much sympathy for Jackanapes, though, it should be noted that, the night before he surrendered to Joan, he defiled a nun. The ensuing daughter, named Jane, possibly in memory of the Maid, married into the Stonor family of Henley. Subsequent de la Poles tended to make a habit of backing the wrong side; the last one, Richard, died after doing it at the Battle of Pavia, 1524.

AND JILL

One of the most famous of all Jacks, the one who fell down and broke his crown. There are, as with all nursery rhymes, any manner of interpretations available, ranging from the fate of Louis XIV and Marie Antoinette ('Jill came tumbling after') to the inevitably sexual. This has 'going up the hill to fetch a pail of water' as an eighteenth-century euphemism for intercourse, which, while colourful, does make going to see a man about a dog seem positively straightforward. I prefer the more airy readings: the Reverend Sabine Baring-Gould, a nineteenth-century clergyman and prolific collector and expounder of folklore, argued that Jack and Jill are derived from Hjuki and Bil, two children who, according to Norse legend, can be seen in the full moon bearing a bucket of water on a pole. Have a look if you like, but bear in mind that Baring-Gould wrote 'Onward Christian Soldiers', kept a pet bat and once offended his young daughter at her birthday party by asking her who she was.

AND THE BEANSTALK

Ah, yes. This popular fairy tale stars what we might think of as the primest example of a Jack: cheeky, flighty, daring, resourceful, not beyond a bit of sharp practice, particularly with an axe. That, though, is but the half of it. There have, for instance, long been worries about how good an example this Jack is: disobeying, hiding, stealing, deceiving, killing. Some concerned adults have even contrived a back-story that has the giant robbing and slaying Jack's dad, and therefore deserving of retribution. Other concerned adults, including Freud and his followers, have sought to dig deeper and have come up with some remarkable interpretations. The beanstalk, as you might imagine them imagining, is phallic, a mighty awakening adolescent erection. Cutting it down, naturally, is all about castration fears, although a gentler reading sees its demise as Jack's acknowledgement that sex isn't everything. There are plentiful worries, too, about Jack's relationship with his mum, who remains worryingly single and appears to live happily ever after with Jack: concerned Victorians, as they would, conjured up a princess for Jack. In this connection, too, the cow's refusal to give milk signifies the trauma of weaning. The assertion of masculine control over menstruation also features, as does Jack's frequent hiding in such womb-substitutes as cupboards. Masturbation is frequently discussed: rarely have I enjoyed scholarly italics as much as in 'the magic harp that *plays by itself*'. There are also comparisons with Moses ascending Sinai for the Ten Commandments, and issues with the beanstalk itself: broad beans, which depend on puny stalks, were the only known variety in pre-Columbian Europe, and their puny stalks do not have the load-bearing and erectile potential of runners (funnily enough, the **jack-bean**, or Canavalia, is native to South America). Relief comes from pantomime, if one can ignore the cross-dressing.

ARANSON

Jack Aranson (1924–2008) was a British actor who inspired this splendid review in *Time* magazine: 'To devise a version of *Moby Dick* as a one-man theatre piece comes under the heading of "They said it couldn't be done . . ."' But Jack did it.

ARMSTRONG

Jack Armstrong, the All-American Boy. Jack was the hero of a US radio show that ran from 1933 to 1951. He was conceived by the great soap-opera pioneer Frank Hummart as a vehicle for selling the Wheaties breakfast cereal. Jack could do pretty much anything to a consummate standard, including playing football and baseball, flying aeroplanes, riding horses and catching spies. He was caught up in a real-life excitement when two children listening to him in Minneapolis heard a gunshot outside their home and found their father lying outside in a pool of blood, dead. As the children remembered what was happening to Jack when they heard the shot, the police requested a script to determine the time of death (programmes, of course, were live at the time). Afterwards, according to Scott Bruce and Bill Crawford in *Cerealizing America*, the makers of Wheaties, displaying interesting taste, presented the grieving children with a copy of the Jack Armstrong script autographed by the stars of the show.

ARNOLD

Jack Arnold (1916–92) was the Hollywood filmmaker who frightened the 1950s, directing such teaser titles as *It Came from Outer Space*, *The Creature from the Black Lagoon* and *The Incredible*

Shrinking Man. These are the last words from *It Came from Outer Space*, as the hero watches the aliens leave, and the girl asks if they've gone for good: 'No. Just for now. It wasn't the right time for us to meet. But there'll be other nights, other stars for us to watch. They'll be back.' The inhabitant of the Black Lagoon had gills and was horrible: 'I can tell you something about this place. The boys around here call it "The Black Lagoon", a paradise. Only they say nobody has ever come back to prove it.' And this is from the trailer for *The Incredible Shrinking Man*: 'Victim of weird mist! Day by day he shrinks! Science is baffled! Cat becomes monster! Terror at every turn! Deadly spider attacks! Lost in a flood's fury!' Jack's sure touch is also to be seen in episodes of *Gilligan's Island*, *Rawhide* and *The Love Boat*.

Ass

Jack is often used as a synonym for male. Preening, butch and vainglorious Jacks should, however, be reminded that Jack is also defined as 'an impertinent or silly fellow; a simpleton; a boor; a clown; also, a servant; a rustic'; and, of course, a knave, hence the playing-card Jacks. Further, in the robust world of electrics, the jack connection is termed female, because it gets the plug inserted into it. I'm not sure, either, just how good it is to be associated with 'jack off' (in which other connection, also see **Jack and the Beanstalk**, above). And then there's the Jackass itself, and most especially and lately, the television programme named after it, in which aspects of all of the above, plus the implacable stubbornness of the beast, are memorably on display as various young males subject themselves to dangerous, horrible and demeaning ordeals like stuffing live crayfish down their underwear. Some people are irritated or depressed by this; I applaud it as an important element of what I like to think of as Jackism, since it combines daring with dubious taste and a desire for fame, however fickle, fleeting or painful.

ASTOR

John Jacob Astor IV, known as Jack, was the great-grandson of John Jacob Astor I, a German who founded the Astor fortune on fur, property and opium. Born in 1864, Jack enjoyed an unfriendly rivalry with his cousin, William Waldorf Astor, which expressed itself in concrete fashion as they vied to see who could build the best hotel in New York. Thus, among others, the Astor and the Waldorf, next to each other on Fifth Avenue and eventually conjoined to become the Waldorf-Astoria (although corridors could be sealed should the uneasy truce between the cousins falter). Jack, when he wasn't pursuing numerous amours, also distinguished himself in the Spanish–American War, wrote a science-fiction novel, invented a bicycle brake and was a churchwarden. None of this saved him from the perhaps inevitable soubriquet Jack Ass; nor did it prevent his being dubbed, with his handsome wife, Beauty and the Beast (he was considered quite ugly). They divorced in 1909; two years later, to the scandal of New York society, Jack married an 18 year old, Madeleine Force. She was pregnant when, the next year, they decided to return from their extended honeymoon in Paris and Egypt on the maiden voyage of the *Titanic*. Jack found her a place in the lifeboat, asked if he might accompany her because of her condition, but was reminded of the priorities. He then threw his gloves to his wife and lit a cigarette. He went down with the ship and his Airedale, Kitty. His body was recovered seven days later; there was $2,500 in his pocket. There were other famous lost Jacks on the *Titanic*. **Jack Phillips** was the chief telegraphist, who stayed at his post. **Jack Dawson** was fictional and played by Leonardo DiCaprio in James Cameron's 1997 film. There was, in fact, a J. Dawson, a trimmer, on the *Titanic*, but he was a Joe, which is another thing entirely. **Jack Thayer**, who was 17 years old, survived and wrote a vivid account of the tragedy but killed himself after his son died in the Pacific in the Second World War. Madeleine Astor married and divorced twice more, the second time to a boxer. The embryonic son saved from the *Titanic* became a playboy. Jack's name has been borrowed by a chain of bar and grills. William Waldorf went to England, became Viscount Astor, bought the *Observer* and died on the lavatory in Brighton in 1919.

AUBREY

Jack Aubrey, Patrick O'Brian's Master and Commander, is an example of the bluff side of Jack. Throughout O'Brian's much-loved series of naval novels he is the forthright foil to Stephen Maturin, his half-Irish, half-Catalan ship's doctor, landlubber, naturalist, spy and cellist (often accompanied by Jack on the violin). O'Brian based Jack partly on John Byron – '**Foulweather Jack**', the storm-tossed grandfather of the poet, who sailed with George Anson, rounded the world, found the Falklands and lost Grenada – and partly on Thomas Cochrane – the tricksy and tricky Scot who commanded in the English, Chilean, Brazilian and Greek navies when he wasn't serving time as a fraudster or the rotten borough of Honiton as a radical MP, or conceiving of a scheme to free Napoleon and make him ruler of a united South America. Foulweather Jack should not be confused with '**Mad Jack**', his wastrel son who spent two fortunes, his wife's and his own, on foolish extravagances and harebrained (see **Jack Rabbit**) notions. Any shadowiness for this Jack comes from his creator: in 1998, just before the publication of the twentieth Aubrey book, in which Jack finally made Rear Admiral, O'Brian was found not to be an Irishman, as he had claimed, but an Englishman called Russ from Chalfont St Peter. He died in 2000 aged 85. Jack lives on, bluff, indefatigable, even surviving portrayal by a blond Russell Crowe.

AXFORD

Thomas Leslie Axford (1894–1983), known as Jack, is one of 22 bearers of the name to have been awarded the Victoria Cross. (Jacks are not the bravest; that is the Williams, with, by my count, no fewer than 117, nearly 50 more than any other first name.) An Australian soldier of the 1914–18 war, Jack was wounded twice before taking part in the attack at Vaire and Hamel Woods in July 1918. The citation reads:

> When the advance of the adjoining platoon was being delayed in uncut wire and machine-gun fire, and his company commander had become a casualty, Lance-Corporal Axford charged and threw bombs amongst the enemy gun crews. He then jumped into the trench, and charging with his bayonet, killed ten of the enemy and took six prisoners. He threw the machine guns over the parapet and the delayed platoon was able to advance. He then rejoined his own platoon and fought with it during the remainder of the operations.

Jack has a park named after him in a Perth suburb, which seems the least he deserves.

BACCHUS

Do you notice anything about Bacchus (Iacchus), the ancient god of fun and frolic, dance, drink and diverse other activities demanding the disengagement of caution, moderation, diligence and all the other boring stuff that is supposed to distinguish our species from the rest? Yes, that's right, it's exceedingly similar to Jack (Iacke, Iakke), a name whose bearers have customarily exhibited larger amounts of bacchic behaviour than has perhaps been good for them.

I am very much aware that etymologists and other serious scholars have been wary of the connection. In fact, as I have already noted, my respected consultant, Peter McClure, thinks it 'absolute rubbish'. But this is a book about Jacks, and so proceeds in their spirit. In any case, the origins and descents of Bacchus are so wrapped about in clouds of confusion that any theory has as much chance as the next of being correct, and ours has the beguiling persuasiveness of that indispensable friend of the speculator, coincidence. Bacchus, or Dionysus, might have originated among the Sumerians, the Minoans or the Greeks, for a few. This ubiquity is, I feel, best expressed by Ambrose Bierce in *The Devil's Dictionary*: 'Bacchus, *n*. A convenient deity invented by the ancients as an excuse for getting drunk.' And worse: the Romans also knew Bacchus as Liber Pater, or, freely, Slack Dad. The liberal gatherings in his name known as the Bacchanalia contained too much licence even for the Romans, which, you must admit, is going it some; permission for these raves had to be obtained from the Senate. The Bacchanalia were a Greek import, and had started out as wild all-women affairs in which participants achieved an ecstasy known as *eleutheria*, or liberation through wine, song and dance; things got worse, as usual, when men were allowed in. Bacchus, then, is our Id. His depiction with vine leaves has led to his identification with the Green Man, the lingering pagan deity of the forest, who also has links with Jack (see **Jack in the Green**). For further evidence of his influence on people named after him, simply read on.

BALMER

Jack Balmer was a legendary Liverpool centre forward who formed a formidable striking partnership with the far less euphonious Albert Stubbins. Balmer's goals fired Liverpool to the league title in the first season after the Second World War. He is the only man to have scored a hat-trick of hat-tricks, three goals in a game in three successive games, which should surely be called, in his honour, the Jack Trick.

BANNISTER

Jack Bannister is a former Warwickshire cricketer of the type most often described as stalwart. He took up commentating and journalism on retirement and is included here because in 1995 he wrote a newspaper article which he promised to eat if South Africa beat England in that year's series. So of course they did, and Bannister washed it down on camera with a good bottle of South African Chardonnay. The practice does not seem to have spread.

BAUER

Jack Bauer is the hero of the American TV series 24, in which each season, as its name suggests, unfolds over a day while Jack, a government agent, engages ruthlessly and routinely with death and torture to protect his country from twenty-first-century terror. Jack is a direct descendant of Dirty Harry and earlier men of the Wild West who were forced by the inadequacies of legal protection into doing what men had to do. Jack is widely admired in post-9/11 America; as a Justice of the Supreme Court put it: 'Is any jury going to convict Jack Bauer? I don't think so.'

This is a sharp Jack, a byword for the unrelenting application of right might. Bauer in German is, variously, a pawn, a peasant and the Jack in card games. There is a more mundane explanation offered for the choice of name – it was the name of a television executive that kind of seemed to fit – but we Jackites spurn it. It has also been pointed out that Jack shares initials with Jeremy Bentham, the eighteenth-century English proponent of the greater good justifying the means of accomplishment, and the architect of a prison system quite similar to that operating at Guantánamo Bay. You can also appreciate the power of names by trying to imagine Jack as Jeremy.

Admirers of sharp dialogue will like my favourite Bauerism: 'The only reason you're conscious right now is because I don't feel like carrying you.' Consideration of Jack's attributes and modus operandi are a favourite occupation in cyberspace, viz.: 'The city of Los Angeles once named a street after Jack Bauer in gratitude for his saving the city several times. They had to rename it after people kept dying when they tried to cross the street. No one crosses Jack Bauer and lives'; 'Some people see the glass as half full. Others see it as half empty. Jack Bauer sees the glass as a deadly weapon'; 'Jack Bauer never retreats, he just attacks in the opposite direction'; 'Once, someone tried to tell Jack Bauer a "knock knock" joke. He found out who was there, who they worked for and where the goddamned bomb was'; 'Jack Bauer can torture you into giving up information you do not possess'; '. . . and on the seventh day Jack Bauer said, "I'll take it from here"'; 'Jack Bauer could strangle you with a cordless phone'; 'Jack Bauer sleeps with a pillow under his gun'; 'Superman wears Jack Bauer pyjamas'; 'The Berlin Wall fell because Jack Bauer needed to get to the other side'; 'It's no use crying over spilt milk . . . Unless that was Jack Bauer's milk'; 'Jack Bauer named his cat "Chuck Norris". Why? Because he's a pussy'; 'If you wake up in the morning, it's because Jack Bauer spared your life'.

Jack is played by Kiefer Sutherland, son of Donald; 'Kiefer' in German can mean either pine tree or jaw, which must lead to confusion in both forest and dental surgery.

BEASLEY

Jack Beasley (1895–1949) was an Australian politician famed for his nickname, earned for an exceptional piece of floor-crossing political betrayal: Stabber Jack. Mind you, Australian legislators have always achieved a particularly high and imaginative standard of invective. The champ would be Paul Keating, Prime Minister 1991–6: 'You boxhead, you wouldn't know, you're flat out counting past ten'; 'You stupid foul-mouthed grub'; and, of his successor, John Howard: 'the little desiccated coconut'.

BENNY

Jack Benny (1894–1974) was one of the greatest ever comics, unsurpassed in both timing and deadness of pan. His first ever words on radio, in 1932, show the style that has been imitated, mostly less successfully, ever since: 'This is Jack Benny talking. There will be a slight pause while you say, "Who cares?"' He created a personality entertainingly foibled and flawed with meanness, weakness and self-regard, echoes and evolutions of which can be seen in such as Tony Hancock, Larry David and **Jack Dee** (qv). Benny was born Benjamin Kubelsky in Chicago to Lithuanian immigrants. Name-clashes with other performers saw him move to Ben K. Benny and on to Jack Benny, adopting the common nickname for a sailor (he served in the US Navy in the First World War). His most famous gag, playing on his meanness, was in response to a mugger demanding his money or his life. First, a perfect pause, then the challenge repeated by the mugger, followed by, 'I'm thinking it over.' My favourite, though, is in Ernst Lubitsch's marvellous *To Be or Not to Be* (1942), where Benny plays an insufferably vain Polish actor (Nazi: 'What he did to Shakespeare, we are doing now to Poland') reluctantly taking on, and beating, the German war machine. Playing Hamlet, he declaims the film's title, pauses, and is prompted. Bliss.

BLACK

Jack Black is one of those occasional Hollywood stars licensed to be irregular of feature, overweight and off-the-wall. His spoof music and other larks disguise a keen brain, which is not altogether surprising, as, key fact, he is the son of two rocket scientists.

Jack Black was also Victorian England's most renowned rat-catcher, operating from a house in Battersea which bore a plate announcing 'J. Black, Rat Destroyer to Her Majesty'. Jack was interviewed by Henry Mayhew, the great chronicler of London lives of the nineteenth century, who discovered that rat-catching was but one of Jack's many parts. He also bred from rarer examples and supplied them to the gentry for the sport of their terriers and to their ladies for pets: he is supposed to have provided Beatrix Potter with Samuel Whiskers.

Black was in addition a prodigious bird-catcher and song-trainer, and an employer of dogs, ferrets, weasels, stoats, badgers and polecats as his assistants, later stuffing them. He was also reputed to catch fish from the Thames with his bare hands using a secret method, which he divulged to Mayhew, who, though impressed, was, sadly, a gentleman, and stayed schtum. At one time Jack owned a public house in Regent Street, where his daughter dressed up as The Rat-Catcher's Daughter, and he wore his uniform of a fine topcoat, waistcoat and a belt bearing iron rats cast by himself, when it wasn't pawned. Jack, despite his prowess, clearly had money troubles, and although, once again, Mayhew is too polite to press the point, a possible clue is the most tremendous number of pubs mentioned by Jack in his account of his doings. I, meanwhile, was suprised to learn that rats can tread water for three days and that a female rat can mate as many as five hundred times with various males in six hours.

BLACKJACK

The basic casino game, based on achieving a score of 21, but lacking the glamour and éclat of roulette or baccarat, a game which, I was once told, was invented by a French count to amuse his idiot son, making my failure to make head or tail of it all the more shaming. Blackjack seems rather simpler, although you must not confuse it with *vingt-et-un*, which has a lower payout, or Spanish 21, which, apparently, is called Pontoon in Australia and Malaysia, and involves 48 cards rather than 52. Blackjack is so named because it used to pay out 10–1 if a hand was made up of an ace and one of the black Jacks, but they soon stopped that (see **Jackpot**). Still, we used to play Pontoon at home with 52 cards and only paid out matches.

BLANCHARD

Jack Blanchard is a country-and-western singer from Florida who sings with Misty Morgan. Aficionados of C&W titles will appreciate their 'Fire Hydrant #79' (1971) and 'The Legendary Chicken Fairy' (1972). Fit to rank, I should say, with some of my other country favourites, such as 'I'll Be Over You When the Green Grass Is Over Me', 'Walk Out Backwards Slowly So I'll Think You're Coming In', 'Since You Stole my Watch You've Been Living on Borrowed Time', 'Here's a Quarter (Call Someone Who Cares)', 'Did I Shave my Legs for This?' and 'I Still Miss You but my Aim Is Getting Better'.

BLOODY JACK

Bloody Jack was the nickname of Hone Tuhawaiki, a paramount Maori chief during the early settlement of New Zealand. You might imagine he gained his sobriquet for his warlike deeds, but it was, in fact, given to him by whalers because of the frequency with which he swore in English. Even so, shocking whalers with your bad language surely deserves respect.

BODELL

Jack Bodell was one of many undistinguished British heavyweight boxing champions who fought in the shadow of Henry Cooper in the 1960s and '70s and lost. But he was distinguished by his home town, Swadlincote, Derbyshire, whose previous greatest excitements had been the visit of the Domesday commissioners in 1086 and Gene Vincent in 1963. And by managing to lose his title to 'Dangerous' Danny McAlinden, a fighter more often a danger to himself.

BOND

A Jack of the steady kind (there have been a few), Jack Bond was the sound, rather than spectacular, cricketer who used that steadiness and soundness to captain a lively Lancashire side to a spectacular string of successes in the newly introduced one-day competitions in the late 1960s and early 1970s. Perhaps the most memorable victory came in 1971, in the semi-final of the one-day competition, against Gloucestershire, when David Hughes came out to bat in the Manchester gloom at 8.45 p.m. and hit 24 runs in an over to leave Lancashire one run short of the final and the second of their hat-trick of titles. Steady Jack then blocked four balls before hitting the winning single. Earlier, he had complained about the light. 'What's that up there?' asked Arthur Jepson, lugubrious even by the refined standards of cricket umpires. 'The moon,' replied Jack. 'Well,' said Jepson, 'how far do you want to see?'

BOOT

Jack, as we shall see, is something of a catch-all word, especially with objects, although it now seems to have been overtaken by thingie. This has lent it some undeserved associations. Jack was, among many other things, a generic name for servant; consequently, many labour-saving devices have come to be called jacks. Thus the Jack who used to pull off his master's boots became the jack that pulled off its master's boots. Throw in the heels of the boot and the idea of something being jacked up and you begin to approach the complicated etymology behind what is now the symbol of dictatorial oppression. That, of course, is mostly thanks to the German habit of rather emphasising their footwear in that exaggerated and concentrated ballet of fierce boot-waving, the goose-step. Not for the first time, the short, snappy sound of 'ck' proved a useful way of expressing something nasty in English. And, to boot, the word was handy, having been used as an insult since at least 1754, when Pitt the Elder, complaining about the appointment by the Duke of Newcastle of Thomas Robinson as Leader of the House of Commons, said, 'the Duke might as well have sent his jackboot to lead us'. You might not know that the Prussians were the first to adapt the marching step to the heartbeat, taking 72 paces to a minute; or that half an hour of the goose-step has the same effect on the legs and abdomen as half a day's route march. The German for jackboot, by the way, is *Boot*.

BOUVIER

Some Jacks seem far better suited to wide paperbacks with big words on the front than to real life. John Vernou Bouvier III was descended from a French cabinet-maker who had taken Napoleon's defeat at Waterloo particularly badly, leaving for the New World forthwith. He took to making cabinets in Philadelphia, some of them for Napoleon's brother, Joseph, the former King of Naples and Sicily and King of Spain who, unlikely as it may seem, at one point spent some time farming in New Jersey. As his Roman numerals indicate, John's family rose rapidly after the cabinet-maker realised there was more money to be made in property than in props. John was handsome (known as Black Jack on account of his dark good looks), rich and charming; he married well and had two beautiful daughters. The elder daughter, Jacqueline, named after him, was particularly striking and went on to live a life composed of capital letters: JFK, First Lady, Camelot's Queen. As if all this were not enough, Black Jack was a textblockbuster womaniser and heavy drinker who told his daughters that 'all men are rats' but groomed them, in the words of Gore Vidal, a relation by divorce, to be geishas. The girls, naturally, adored him, despite the philandering, gambling and gulping which ended his marriage to their mother. Further confirmation that we are in High Society comes with the wedding day of Jackie to another handsome womaniser called Jack, when Black Jack failed to turn up to give his daughter away because he was drunk at the nearby motel whither he had been ostracised. That would be the last high point, buster-wise, although the arguments still go back and forth as to how drunk he was and who'd plied him with it, the Kennedys or his ex-wife. All of them, I'd guess. I suppose we should also mention that he is supposed to have been bisexual, although it's a mystery how he got the time, and to have coached Jackie's style. By one of those inelegances of real life, the riderless horse that followed poignantly behind President Kennedy's funeral cortège was also called Black Jack.

BRABHAM

Sir Jack Brabham (born 1926), the Sydney grocer's son who won three Formula One world driving championships and set up his own racing team, is, despite his dashing calling, not a Jack of the cheeky, devil-may-care sort. Indeed, one of his most noted characteristics is thrift, which inspired this unusually vivid quote (for a sportsperson) from Dan Gurney, his American teammate: 'Jack was tighter than a bull's ass in fly season.' Hyperbole, of course: Gurney seems more of a Jack than Jack, being not only the son of a singer with the Metropolitan Opera, but also the man who invented the habit of wasting expensive champagne on the winner's podium.

BRADLEY

There had to be a Jack among the six American soldiers who so famously raised the US flag on Iwo Jima, and this is he, Pharmacist's Mate Second Class John 'Jack' or 'Doc' Bradley. The rank and title suggest to the uninitiated someone who hands out pills. Wrong: the Navy Hospital Corpsmen landed alongside the Marines across the South Pacific and had to do their best to patch up their comrades' appalling injuries on the battlefield. After he had helped the five marines erect the flag on top of Mount Suribachi, Jack rescued a fallen marine by reaching him, treating him with a blood infusion, and then dragging him 30 yards to safety, waving away help, all the time under heavy fire.

The raising of the flag – it was a second, larger replacement for the first foreign flag ever to fly over Japanese territory – did not mark the end of the battle for Iwo Jima, during which three of the flag-raisers were later killed, and two more Jacks, **Lummus** and **Williams**, were awarded posthumous Medals of Honor for acts of startling bravery. Another, **Jack Lucas**, just 17, survived being blown up by one of two grenades he had dived on to protect his comrades (see **Jack Osborn**). Bradley and the other two surviving flag-raisers were fêted, and fated ever after to be symbols of victory. One took to drink, the other to fame, which came and went and soured. Bradley shunned celebrity and survived.

Collectors of macabre and ironical conjunctions should know

that Bradley's ambition from an early age, which he fulfilled after the war, was to run a funeral parlour. Collectors of something deeper should know that he raised a family and earned respect in his small town in Wisconsin. He didn't tell anyone that he had been awarded the Navy Cross for his heroism on Iwo Jima. He rarely talked about the battle at all, and when he did, he said, 'the heroes of Iwo Jima are the guys who didn't come back'. His son, James, wrote about all of it in *Flags of Our Fathers*, which was made into a film by Clint Eastwood (Bradley had earlier repeated his feat in the John Wayne film *The Sands of Iwo Jima*, in 1949). When Jack died in 1994, the editor of his local newspaper wrote, 'John Bradley will forever be memorialised for a few moments' action at the top of a remote Pacific mountain. We prefer to remember him for his life. If the famous flag-raising at Iwo Jima symbolises American patriotism and valor, Bradley's quiet, modest nature and philanthropic effort shine as an example of the best of small-town American values.'

BRAG

Jack Brag is the hero of the book of the same name by Theodore Hook, published in 1837, a man who comes from nothing to a prominent place in society. Those seeking easy contemporary comparisons should note that Jack is pretentious, boastful and vulgar, and that Lord Bragg takes a second g.

BROUGHTON

Jack Broughton (*c.* 1703–89) was the bareknuckle heavyweight champion of England for 24 years. He also introduced the first formal rules, which included not hitting a man when he was down. A boxer who relied as much on skill as on force, Broughton was nevertheless clear about his trade, which he described as the most successful method of beating a man deaf, dumb, lame and blind. He was also something of an entrepreneur, opening an 'ampitheatre' which featured bull-baiting and armed mock battles as well as boxing, a sport much attended and often practised by the aristocracy of the time, for whom Broughton provided the first boxing gloves, or 'mufflers', to protect them from the 'Inconveniency of black Eyes, broken Jaws, and bloody Noses'.

He became a Yeoman of the Guard, threatening to take on enemy regiments one by one between breakfasts, and was with George II at the Battle of Dettingen (1743), the last occasion on which an English monarch took to the field. In 1750, though, setting a precedent unfortunately much followed since, he came out of retirement for one last fight, tempted by the taunts of, naturally, another Jack, **Jack Slack**, a Norwich butcher, whose punching closed both Broughton's eyes, much to the disgust of his patron, another famous butcher, the Duke of Cumberland, the bloody victor of Culloden. The duke had had a lot of cash riding on the result and cried, 'What are you about, Broughton? You can't fight! You're beat!' Broughton replied with the (obviously paraphrased) raw bravery that has always been both the best and the bedevilment of boxing: 'I can't see my man, your Highness; I am blind, but not beat; only let me be placed before my antagonist, and he shall not gain the day yet.'

But he did, Jack was stopped, and the duke and his patronage were gone for good. Broughton continued to teach boxing, but, in a relishable contrast, spent most of his time as an antique dealer. In a possibly unique treble for a fighter, he died aged over 80, wealthy, and was buried in Westminster Abbey, where the dean objected to the inscription of 'Champion of England' on the gravestone, a gap finally filled in 1988.

BRUCE

Jack Bruce, supergroupster, of Cream and Scotland, produced, as befits a classically trained musician, the most literately punning song title in the pop canon, 'Weird of Hermiston', a play on *Weir of Hermiston*, Robert Louis Stevenson's last book, curtailed by his death, chronicling the life of Archie Weir, a romantic young laird. Note, too, the implied pun in the lyrics: 'I'm going to the river' – river: weir. All right, all right, but it certainly beats 'Chirpy, Chirpy, Cheep, Cheep', and, for that matter, this, from acclaimed singer-songwriter Carole King's 'Home Again': 'Snow is cold, rain is wet.'

BUCHANAN

The British Astaire. Not so much remembered now, Jack Buchanan was an arch exponent of what used to be judged the English virtue of effortful effortlessness, the belief that to be seen to be trying too hard was bad form. Naturally, he was a Scotsman. With unrelenting concentration and much slog, Jack breezed through a career of more than 40 years as a singer, dancer and light comedian of the charmingly rueful variety. His dancing disguised polished professionalism as amiable artlessness. He lent its timing to his singing, which was as distinctive and appealing as the voices of those two other great dancers, Astaire and Kelly. He shared a lot with Astaire: the elegance, the ease in top hat, white tie and tails, the attention to detail, and an excellent film (*The Band Wagon*). And, as the critic Allen Saddler has written, a curious asexuality. Jack lost his father early, and (apart from a very brief early marriage to a difficult Bulgarian singer) lived with his mother until she died, when he was 46. One of his most popular numbers, sung without any apparent irony, was 'And Her Mother Came Too'.

Despite this, or perhaps because of it, he had a devoted following. 'Jack's Gallery Girls' were to be seen at his performances sitting in 'languishing rows', as another critic put it. 'I would wander into Jack's dressing room, where silence reigned,' wrote Vivian Ellis, his friend and composer. 'There, while removing his stage make-up, he would be regarded in soundless ecstasy by worshipping Gallery Girls whom he entertained out of sheer kindness or policy, probably both. Meanwhile, Jack's mind would be miles away – thinking out a new piece of stage business – with an occasional meaningful glance, when he remembered, at his silent audience.'

Different days. His fellow matinee idols with their own female followings, Ivor Novello and Noël Coward, were both, of course, gay, or 'musical' as it was often and aptly known then. Jack himself was wonderfully camp as Jeffrey Cordova, the deliciously pretentious theatre director in *The Band Wagon*. He made the film in 1953, when he was in his 60s; but he had been as big a star on Broadway as in the West End since the 1920s, appearing with Gertrude Lawrence and Beatrice Lillie (aka Lady Peel, and author of that splendidly entitled memoir, *Every Other Inch a Lady*; when a waiter spilt soup on her at Buckingham Palace she told him never to darken her Dior again). They stayed at the Algonquin, taking up with Dorothy Parker and the rest of the Round Table. Later, Lawrence and Lillie moved into a large apartment with a piano, where played Kern, Rodgers, Gershwin and Berlin. Different days indeed.

Coral Browne partnered Jack for some time on and off stage before he suddenly and surprisingly married an American divorcee 25 years younger than himself in 1949. A few years after Jack's death in 1957, a drunken Englishman arrived unannounced in her theatre dressing room in Moscow, where she was playing in *Hamlet* with Michael Redgrave. The man had just thrown up in Hamlet's sink; he now bummed cigarettes and soap off Gertrude. He was Guy Burgess, the defected (and defective) British spy. He invited Miss Browne to lunch in his small and miserable flat and revealed the purpose of the meeting had been to get her to go to his tailor in Savile Row. The food was not good. Burgess played her a record, one of the two things he had brought with him when he fled London. It was a selection of Jack's stuff.

'There I was, two days before Christmas, it was snowing and one couldn't have felt more miserable to be away from home. What made it all the more poignant was sitting there in the most unlikely place in the world listening to Jack's voice forever perpetuating a light-hearted and carefree land of make-believe.'

Alan Bennett re-created the scene consummately in his play *An Englishman Abroad*, using 'Who Stole my Heart Away', which, irony upon irony, appears essentially and evocatively English, but was in fact written by Jerome Kern and Oscar Hammerstein. Ms Browne later married Vincent Price, and was fabled for her ripe wit, as when she urged a friend to desist with a piece of gossip as they stood outside London's Brompton Oratory after mass since she was 'in a state of fucking grace'.

Jack loved golf but was erratic. Most days, he lunched off cold rare roast beef, salad and champagne. He liked little better than crossing the Atlantic by Cunard. He was a determined producer, theatre owner and businessman but not wildly successful, some said because he would keep giving his money away. He became very conscious of his age, but could be teased, especially by his satellite chums, Jack's gang, who were there mostly to keep him amused, in the later style of Sinatra. One of Jack's biggest hits was the title song of his British film, *Good Night, Vienna*, a light operetta, as you might imagine, featuring a general's son and a shopgirl. When he asked one of his gang, **Jack Prendergast**, a Yorkshire film distributor, how well it was being received in Huddersfield, Prendergast replied, 'Probably as well as *Good Night, Huddersfield* would be received in Vienna.' And Jack laughed. His last two big performances were taking over in *King's Rhapsody* on the death of Ivor Novello and a show spoofing his successors, the new pop singers. Jack's day was done. And so, in 1957, his timing as perfect as ever, he took his Last Bow.

BUETEL

Jack Buetel was an insurance clerk turned Hollywood actor whose big moment – the title role in a major movie – was overshadowed, almost literally, by the most famous double act in film history, Jane

Russell's breasts. Yes, Jack was 'The Outlaw', Billy the Kid, playing against Russell's Rio McDonald and her twin peaks, the obsessions of Howard Hughes, the outstandingly eccentric and more than a little crazed billionaire who directed the film in 1943. Besides making films and before turning into America's most famous recluse, Hughes was a pioneer flier, owned TWA, suffered from OCD, liked his lettuce shredded on the bias, kept a slide rule to measure the size of his peas, slept with, among many others, Jean Harlow, Katharine Hepburn, Bette Davis, Yvonne De Carlo, Rita Hayworth, Linda Darnell, Ginger Rogers, Kathryn Grayson, Ava Gardner and Lana Turner, and banned his stable of starlets from being driven at more than two miles per hour in cars over bumpy roads because the sudden motion might tear at their breast muscles. Poor Jack never stood a chance, and anyway it was a lousy film, even if the publicity was inspired ('How would you like to tussle with Russell?'). To add insult to the mammaries, they even spelt his name wrong (Beutel). I don't know why he didn't stick to his real name, Warren Higgins.

BUNSBY

Jack Bunsby, mariner chum and valued confider of advice incomprehensible to anyone but Captain Cuttle in *Dombey and Son*. This Jack finds Dickens at the very top of his very considerable game, being described magnificently as having 'one stationary eye in the mahogany face, and one revolving one, on the principle of some lighthouses'.

BUTLER

Jack Butler (1901–86) was the last native speaker of Jiwarli, an Aboriginal language of Western Australia which had been slowly dying out since the 1920s. For eight years before his death, he helped an Australian professor of linguistics compile a record of Jiwarli. The Jiwarli word for 'camera' is mangarn manaji; 'mangarn' is the soul, 'manaji' means 'it grabs'. There were probably 250 or so Australian Aboriginal languages at the time of the European invasion; about 160 of them are now extinct. In another of the Western Australian languages, a boomerang is a kylie. When Captain Cook asked an aborigine what the strange-looking marsupials were called, the aborigine replied 'Kan Ga Roo', which translates, freely, as, 'I haven't got the foggiest what you're on about, whitey.' There are spoilsports who doubt, with documentation, this story: I would point them in the direction of South America and the strange coincidence between the name for the indigenous woolly pack animal and 'como se llama?', the Spanish for 'what's it called?' And to show my unquestionable impartiality in such matters, I would point you to jackaroo, Australian for a young stockman, and the fantastic theory that it derives from dhugai-iu, a supposed north-eastern aboriginal word for 'wandering white man'. *The Cambridge Guide to Australian English Usage* doubts it, going instead for a hybrid of Jack and kangaroo, but nevertheless omitting the obvious conclusion that the Jack bit is in tribute to **Jack Donohoe** (qv), the original Wild Colonial Boy.

CADE

Here is an early model for popular Jack, cheeky Jack, shadowy Jack. All that can be said for certain is that in 1450 a man who appeared from nowhere very nearly became King of England by dint of little more than the force of his personality, placing himself at the head of a discontented, disparate, desperate and disorganised few thousand who for a few heady summer days that year held London.

Jack's followers were from what we now know as the Home Counties. They seem mostly to have come from the yeomanry, and they were extremely fed up with the ineffectual and corrupt administration of Henry VI, which, when it wasn't robbing them, was losing France (see **Jackanapes**). With Jack, now dubbed Jack Amend-All, at their head, they surged, straggled and skirmished their way from Kent to the capital, forcing their way over London Bridge. In Cannon Street, Jack raised his sword and smote the famous London stone, ancient symbol of the city, declaring himself 'Lord of London'. Henry, as he was prone to do, panicked and fled north. Jack took up easy residence in Southwark, at the White Hart, an inn bearing the sign of another ineffectual monarch, Richard II, who, 70 years before, had faced his own people's revolt (see **Jack Straw**).

At first, Jack kept himself and his men under control, but soon lost it, and them. There were ransackings and worse, whereupon the Londoners, always dismissive of people from south of the river, drove them back over the bridge into Southwark. Then came bishops offering to take petitions and grant pardons. Jack was done, on the run and alone with a price of around £750,000 in today's money on his head. He was captured after a fierce, short fight near Heathfield in the village known today as Cade Street, and died from his wounds on the way back to London. The body was taken to the White Hart, where it was identified by the wife of his recent mine hoste, and thence to Newgate, where it was beheaded. The head was placed above the late scene of his triumph, London Bridge, and the quarters were sent for display at Blackheath, Norwich, Salisbury and Gloucester.

Who was he, this self-styled Captain of Kent, Lord of London? Impossible to say now, an insoluble mystery, lost along with the ruthless force and fierce charm that must have allowed his brief accomplishment. Some said he was an Irishman, others a clothier, that his father was a plasterer or bricklayer, his mother a midwife or pedlar of lace. Others claimed he was a physician, or a soldier of fortune fresh from France, or even, and understandably, a magician, a sorcerer. He himself further muddied matters by assuming the name of John Mortimer and claiming kinship with the Duke of York, Henry's rival.

Shakespeare, nodding to the Tudor fierceness for law and order, takes his usual liberties, making Jack some kind of Kentish Caliban, commanding the fountains of London to run with wine while the land descends into a nasty, brutish, ignorant anarchy. Why, he even has Jack agreeing with that famous call, which, for some reason, has resounded down the centuries, the one about killing all the lawyers. What would we give for a true account of Jack, by Jack; until then we are left with the Bard's dying words for him: 'Tell Kent from me, she has lost her best man.'

Intriguingly, in a very similar revolt 100 years before, in France, the peasants were known as the Jacquerie, after their leader's *nom de guerre*, Jacques Bonhomme, the French generic name for a peasant. But his real name was Guillaume Cale, about whom also next to nothing is known. Cale, Cade: coincidence? You will also be wondering about Jack and Jacques being the English and French nicknames for the common man, especially as Jacques Bonhomme was translated as Jack Goodfellow. But Peter McClure, my consultant (see the Introduction, and under Bacchus) says it is no more than John and Jacques being the most common first name in their respective countries. We Jackists say: hmmm.

CALICO JACK

Clearly, one might feel differently if one were the trepidatious captain of a small coastal vessel or fishing boat plying between Jamaica and the Bahamas in the early eighteenth century, but at this remove it's easy to have quite some sympathy for John Rackam, or Calico Jack, as he was better known on the Spanish Main. He has become a bit of a byword for bloodthirsty, brutal piracy: I myself well remember the shiver that went through the timbers of *The Sultana* when Captain Dan Tempest (Robert Shaw) screwed his eye round the telescope and announced ominously 'Calico Jack!' in that fondly remembered epic TV series of my youth, *The Buccaneers*.

But, in truth, as far as that is possible with pirates, Jack seems to have been a reasonably civilised sort of fellow. The *Dictionary of National Biography*, for example, mentions report of 'a tall, dark-eyed, handsome man whose swashbuckling manner was matched and supported by his theatrical dress: striped calico shirt, jacket and trousers'. But it also confides that Jack was 'essentially a small-time and not particularly bloodthirsty pirate'. And not a particularly successful one, either, even without his inevitable end. My thoughts move towards a combination of Captain Jas. Hook, Cut-throat Jake of the *Flying Dustman*, sworn enemy of Captain Pugwash, and, of course, **Captain Jack Sparrow** (qv). He was popular with his crew, but that wouldn't have been difficult, as the previous incumbent, set adrift in a small sloop after they voted for Jack to take his place, was the notorious Charles Vane, not only legendarily cruel even for a pirate but also – far worse – no respecter of the Pirate Code, which demanded equal pieces of eight for all. It seems, too, that Jack was pretty lax, leaving most of the running of his ship, the *William*, stolen from Nassau Harbour under the eyes of the governor, to his two formidable lieutenants.

These were, even more famously, Anne Bonny, who was his mistress, and Mary Read, her great friend. Both dressed as men and were far harder than anything usually found in trousers. When the *William* was eventually captured, Anne and Mary were the only ones to put up a fight; they attempted to stir their comrades into action by shooting at them, but succeeded only in killing one and injuring a few others. Jack was drunk. All three were sentenced to hang; two of them were reprieved when they were found to be pregnant. Anne visited Jack to bid him farewell, telling him 'that she was sorry to see him there, but if he had fought like a man, he need not have been hanged like a dog'. Poor Jack. His body was hung in irons from a gibbet on Deadman's Cay at the entrance to Port Royal harbour, Jamaica, as a deterrent to others. Today the spot is called Rackam's Cay. Mary died shortly afterwards, but Anne, by accounts, was taken by her father back to South Carolina, where she married a local man, had eight children and died at the age of eighty-four, much respected. But you wouldn't have wanted to jump the queue in front of her at the general store.

CARDIFF

Jack Cardiff (born 1914) is a master cinematographer, responsible for the look of such classics as *A Matter of Life and Death* and *The Red Shoes*. But I like most the eccentrically eclectic achievement of his having directed *Sons and Lovers*, *Girl on a Motorcycle* and that triumph of Smell-o-Vision, *The Scent of Mystery*, starring Denholm Elliott, Peter Lorre, Elizabeth Taylor and a machine in cinemas that could pump out aromas crucial to the plot, such as those of wine, bread and pipe smoke. This was the publicity: 'First they moved (1895)! Then they talked (1927)! Now they smell!' Sadly, it stank.

CARTER

This Jack is the hero of *Get Carter*, the fine gangster movie made by Mike Hodges in 1971, which prodded us into remembering back beyond the Carry Ons to a tradition including *Brighton Rock* and anything involving Dirk Bogarde not playing Dr Simon Sparrow. The cast included such diverse and unusual perfomers as John Osborne and Bryan Mosley (taking a rare but well-deserved break from playing *Coronation Street* corner-shop owner and bore Alf Roberts). It also had Michael Caine giving a performance as Jack Carter which managed to convince us that northerners could talk like that, too. The scene with a naked Caine, a shotgun, the street and the drum majorettes is a special joy. The most quoted dialogue is Jack to an angry Bryan, as loan shark Cliff Brumby: 'You're a big man, but you're in bad shape. With me it's a full-time job. Now behave yourself.' I also like: Eric (a shifty Ian Hendry): 'So, what're you doing then? On your holidays?' Carter: 'No, I'm visiting relatives.' Eric: 'Oh, that's nice.' Carter: 'It would be if they were still living.' Despite an impassioned campaign, fans of the film and of Owen Luder, the brutalist architect (rather fewer), have failed to stop the demolition of the car park in Gateshead from which Jack hurled Bryan/Cliff to his death (Bryan was, in fact, if surprisingly, an accomplished stunt man and fight arranger).

CASADY

Jack Casady is probably the leading bass guitarist of the rock era, performing with Jefferson Airplane, Jimi Hendrix and Hot Tuna. He also pioneered that most derided rock feature, the bass solo, cue for any number of jokes about how you get people to talk. My favourite, though, is this: 'How many bass players does it take to change a light bulb?' 'Never mind. The piano player can do it with his left hand.' Still, you've got to hand it to Jack for best ever group name: Jack Casady and the Degenerates.

CHARLTON

This Jack is a lad, a character, almost a caricature of the plain-talking, non-doffing Geordies, fetching folk with an affecting faith in the ability of their no-nonsense accent to lend an intrinsic wit and wisdom and interest to anything they might care to say (another is **Dr Jack**, now Lord, **Cunningham**, former Labour minister, fixer and regular radio fireman for any passing flare-ups). This Jack, Our Jack, is a World Cup-winner whose footballing career was a triumph of will over ability, a successful manager of rude and simple method, an after-dinner speaker of often intimidating stamina, a socialist, a countryman, quick to anger, quicker to forget, so often contrasted with his more talented player of a brother, Bobby, whose gift for vivid expression is, or was, in his feet rather than his mouth, which is where Jack sometimes puts his. Bobby was a dazzler; Jack is a Jack.

Even so, he sometimes gets called Jackie, in the manner of another, yet more fabled Geordie footballer, Jackie Milburn, 'Wor Jackie', of Newcastle United, a quicksilver striker from the days when most centre forwards had centre partings and were most often described as 'uncompromising'. Jackists, though, as a rule, take a firm line on Jackies, believing them generally to have been so called because they lack the essential quality, indescribable but instantly recognisable, that makes a Jack. But we do, as you will see, make the odd exception.

CHERTOK

Jack Chertok (1906–95) is one of the Jacks we have to thank for the first great western television serial, *The Lone Ranger*. Jack, a veteran Hollywood man, was the show's first producer. People of a certain age who were once, mostly, boys, still thrill for their own special reasons to the sound of Rossini's *William Tell* Overture, the serial's theme tune, over which this, interspersed with hoofbeats and gunshots, would be sonorously intoned: 'A fiery horse with the speed of light, a cloud of dust and a hearty "Hi Yo Silver!" . . . With his faithful Indian companion Tonto, the daring and resourceful masked rider of the plains led the fight for law and order in the early west. Return with us now to those thrilling days of yesteryear . . . The Lone Ranger rides again!' Marvellous. The Lone Ranger, sole survivor of a cowardly ambush, used his astonishing marksmanship to disarm rather than kill anyone with his unique silver bullets, and only ever kissed Trigger. He was most played by Clayton Moore, born **Jack Carlton Moore**, who had previously appeared in *The Gay Amigo*, a film featuring another early TV legend, *The Cisco Kid*; the role of Tonto was taken by Jay Silverheels, a Canadian Mohawk whose real name was Harold Smith (this might be the place to note that the Iroquois actor who starred as Kicking Bird in Kevin Costner's *Dances with Wolves* is called Graham Greene). Fran Striker, the Ranger's writer, wrote the Lone Ranger's Creed, Article 3 of which was: 'That God put the firewood there but that every man must gather and light it himself.' Despite a row over rights, over which we shall draw, well, a veil, Moore continued making personal and masked appearances well into his 70s. 'It's my symbol, it's Americana,' he said, of the mask. 'I guess when I go up to the big ranch in the sky, I'll still have it on.' His favourite song was: 'My Heroes Have Always Been Cowboys'. Hi Yo!

CHURCHILL

Lieutenant-Colonel Jack Malcolm Thorpe Flemington Churchill, DSO and Bar, MC and Bar (1912–96), no relation. Certain British, and particularly English, soldiers, including the poet **Siegfried Sassoon** (qv), have earned the nickname 'Mad Jack' on account of their eccentricities, which have always included a startling disregard for safety during battle. Jack Churchill began halfway there, already having part of the name, but his astounding exploits make him possibly the nonpareil. There have been soldiers as brave, but none last century accustomed to fighting with a bow, arrows and a sword. You will imagine the consternation this caused among the enemy, especially, as with the German advance into Normandy in 1940, when slain comrades were discovered felled by an arrow (Churchill had shot for England before the war).

Although English, Churchill was also a great lover of the bagpipes, and was accustomed to playing them as he led Commando raids throughout the Second World War, often dressed in nothing more than a kilt. In 1941, at Vaasgo, Norway, he stood in the lead landing-craft playing 'The March of the Cameron Men'; in 1944, the last commando alive holding a position on the Adriatic island of Brac, he took up his pipes and began to play 'Will Ye No Come Back Again' until knocked unconscious by a grenade explosion. In between, he had led an attack at Salerno screaming 'Commando', going on to capture nearly fifty Germans with the help of one corporal. He escaped from German confinement twice, and was disappointed to arrive in Burma just after Hiroshima and Nagasaki: 'If it hadn't been for those damned Yanks we could have kept the war going for another ten years.' After the war, and after appearing as an archer in the film *Ivanhoe*, he faced down a group of Arab terrorists in Jerusalem: 'I grinned like mad from side to side,' he said afterwards, 'as people are less likely to shoot at you if you smile at them.' He died in his bed nearly 50 years later, having spent the remainder of his time war-instructing, building model ships, running a steam-launch business on the Thames, surfing the Severn Bore and entertaining rail passengers by flinging his briefcase out of the window before getting off at the next station and walking home, where it would be lying at the bottom of the garden.

COHEN

For obvious and other reasons, many bearers of the Jewish name Jacob have ended up being called Jack; most of them have brimmed with the native cheek and charm known as chutzpah. Sir Jack Cohen (1898–1979), founder of Tesco, the mighty supermarket chain, was born Jacob Kohen, in Whitechapel. First apprentice tailor (to his father), then canvas-maker (to the Royal Flying Corps), Jack became, quite literally, that sneered-at but envied social and business phenomenon of the late twentieth century: a barrow boy.

He spent his demob money in 1919 on surplus army stores, which he sold from an increasing number of market stalls. The Tesco brand name was created in 1924 from the first two letters of his name and the initials of his tea supplier. He opened his first two shops in 1931; eight years later, there were a hundred. After the Second World War, he pioneered self-service in Britain and continued to practise the business philosophy he had acquired on his stalls, 'pile 'em high, sell 'em cheap'. Jack always liked a deal: they still talk of how he snapped up a consignment of tinned milk from a ship wrecked on the Goodwin Sands and then sent it round his shops with the note, 'Managers are allowed to use Duraglit to remove any rust from the tins.' Jack's nickname, 'Slasher Jack', referred to both his way with prices and his way with employees, from the bottom to the board, where sat two sons-in-law. Jack forced one son-in-law out and attacked the other several times, once while he was driving along the A3 after he, not Jack, had been presented with a carriage clock, and once with a ceremonial sword hanging in the boardroom (this son-in-law, Leslie, was married to Jack's daughter, Shirley, later Lady Porter, a Conservative politician with similar views to her father on democratic process). It couldn't last, of course; the barrow boy was eventually sidelined while the operation moved to the superior, slicker end of the market. At the check-out, whither you have been smoothly manipulated with heavily laden trolley, you might amuse yourself with the memory of the tieclips Jack would hand out to visitors, inscribed 'YCDBSOYA'. Jack used to say it was Yiddish; in fact, the letters were the initials of 'You can't do business sitting on your arse.'

COMER, COLMORE, COMACHO

Another Jewish Jack, but this one wasn't nice at all. Better known as Jack Spot, this Jack was a villain and a thug from London's East End who claimed in the early 1950s to be Britain's leading criminal. Handy with his fists, handier with a chiv, or cut-throat razor, Spot profited from the problems caused by outdated legislation struggling to control gambling, drinking and the like. His favoured methods included running illegal gambling operations and taking protection money from others doing the same, or working in easily targeted monopolies, such as the bookmakers at racecourses, the only ones then permitted.

Spot, so called because of a large mole on his cheek, had the suits and the shoes and the sidekicks with names like Moisha Blueball and Sonny the Yank; but his career now seems even more petty and hyped than that of the Kray Twins, his younger contemporaries, who, though not more noticeably competent, were clearly yet nastier. Large chunks of Jack's income appear to have come from the fees paid to him by popular newspapers for his colourful and unsubstantiated claims to power and influence. But you should never underestimate the potency of a name (cf the Kray Twins), and Jack Spot has exactly the right ring to it, as well as being able to fit neatly into headlines. Like the Twins, he also had the old villains' bind of being driven by a need for attention combined with a penchant for leaving public areas littered with bleeding bodies, a mistake not made so often now, although the exploitation of failed attempts at social engineering still continues, most noticeably with drugs. Jack's éclat never really recovered from a knife confrontation with a rival villain in a fruiterers in Old Compton Street which swung against him when the irritated lady proprietor hit him over the head with her scales. He died poor and forgotten in an Eastbourne nursing home in 1996. He told fellow residents he was a retired butcher.

CORNWELL

Poor Jack. The Battle of Jutland, the greatest naval engagement of the First World War, failed to be conclusive in the matter of British or German sea supremacy, but was fatally so for more than 6,000 British sailors and more than 2,000 Germans. Jack was one of them, only a few months over 16. Boy First Class Cornwell, very lately East End delivery boy Cornwell, was a member of the crew of a 5.5-inch gun on the forecastle of HMS *Chester*, a light cruiser. He was mortally wounded in the chest at the beginning of the battle, but remained standing, with the rest of the gun crew dead and wounded all around him, quietly awaiting orders amid the madnesss and mayhem until the end, which preceded his by but a little. He had been at sea for a month. British prestige, as holed as the Navy's three battleships and three cruisers, was looking for one of those glorious consolations it so regularly retrieves from setbacks. Poor Jack was seized upon, literally, after he was mentioned in dispatches by Admiral Beatty, author of that famous judgement on Jutland, 'there seems to be something wrong with our bloody ships today'. Jack was praised in parliament and press, hailed as 'the imperishable boy Cornwell', and proposed for a posthumous Victoria Cross: 'An honour paid to Cornwell's memory would be an example to the boys of the Empire at their most susceptible age.' His body was then exhumed from its common grave with other Jutland dead at Grimsby and re-interred with much pomp in East Ham. He was awarded the VC two months later. His father died five weeks after that, and a brother was killed in action in August 1918. Poor Jack: he is not even the youngest holder of the VC; that is either Andrew (or Arthur) Fitzgibbon, a medical orderly severely wounded tending to the injured at the capture of North Taku Fort, India, in 1860, or Thomas Flinn, a drummer boy who took on two Indian mutineers in hand-to-hand combat at Cawnpore in 1857. Both were aged fifteen years and three months. But Jack is still remembered, most recently on a Royal Mail stamp, and a boy was given the first names Travers Cornwell as late as 1955. Should you wish to see the gun, it is on display at the Imperial War Museum.

CRAPP

Jack Crapp (1912–81), the first Cornishman to play cricket for England, never forgave himself for dropping Bradman twice at slip as the greatest Australian batsman made 173 not out to secure a win against all the odds in the Fourth Test at Headingley in 1948. Many tales are told of Jack, including his purchase in 1936 of a five-guinea pair of cricket boots which he then wore for the next forty-three years as a player and first-class umpire. But the most famous story concerns Jack arriving at the England hotel before that Headingley Test. 'Bed, sir?' enquired the receptionist. Jack, thinking she was referring to his teammate, Alec Bedser, replied, 'No, Crapp.' 'Through those doors and first on the left,' said the receptionist.

CRAWFORD (I)

The story of Jack Crawford (1775–1831) might be instructive. A previously unremarkable seaman from Sunderland, he was serving under Admiral Duncan on HMS *Venerable* at the Battle of Camperdown in 1797 when part of the ship's mast was felled, taking with it the Admiral's standard and so signalling surrender to the rest of the fleet. Jack shinned up the mast under withering gunfire and nailed the colours back, saving the day and allowing Duncan to defeat the Dutch fleet, then allied to France. He was hailed 'The Hero of Camperdown', taken to London to meet the King, and granted a pension of £30 a year. Some, though, have claimed that Jack was either ordered up the mast or was too drunk to know what he was doing. Nor is it clear whether he volunteered to join the Navy or was press-ganged. Whatever, after stalwart service during the rest of the French wars, it seems that a liking for drink contributed to his death in poverty, the first man to die in the cholera epidemic that struck Sunderland in 1831. There was a pub named after him in Monkwearmouth, but it was knocked down in a German bombing raid in the Second World War.

CRAWFORD (2)

This Crawford was, in the Jack way, a reverse of the accepted. Australian sportsmen are meant to be hard-living, hard-playing larrikins, contemptuous of anything but winning. But this was Gentleman Jack Crawford, an elegant tennis champion of the 1930s, who used to pour himself a cup of tea from his tray when changing ends. Jack was impeccably mannered; the only betrayal of emotion on court was when he carefully rolled up his long sleeves if the game was going against him. But they were rolled down and buttoned up again as soon as the crisis was resolved, which it invariably was. Gentleman Jack's nemesis was Fred Perry, the son of a mill-worker from Stockport, a man as untypical of his milieu as Jack was supposedly of his. Fred horrified the English tennis establishment with a will to win that went as far as playing on his opponent's weaknesses. When he'd done that to Jack to win Wimbledon in 1934, a high-ranking Wimbledon official told the Australian, 'Bad luck, old chap. This was one day when the best man didn't win.' And they wonder why Fred is the last Englishman who did.

Daniel

The distiller, of Lynchburg, Tennessee, made legendary by his company's advertising, which has whiled away many a moment spent waiting for public transport – most instructively in the manner of his death, allegedly caused by blood poisoning after he damaged his toe kicking his safe because he had forgotten the combination; and most entertainingly by his grave, which has two chairs next to the headstone, allegedly placed there to comfort the many local ladies who mourned his passing (Jack never married). A later Jack, **Jack Weil**, the oldest ever working CEO in the United States, reportedly had a glass of Jack's twice a week to keep his blood thin. Jack, who founded the western clothing company Rockmount Ranch Wear, died in August 2008, aged 107. He gave up smoking at 60, drinking any other liquor at 90, and red meat at 100. Vale, Jack.

Dash

They are gone now, but politics in twentieth-century Britain were much enlivened, and certainly agitated by a breed of mostly self-educated working-class activists who upset the complacencies of traditional social superiors with their wit, intelligence and, most irritatingly of all, their sparky refusal to defer in the manner to which all were accustomed. This was Jack Dash, unofficial Cockney

Communist tribune of the London dockers and quasi-official middle-class bogeyman during the 1960s, cited in the House of Commons in 1966 by the exasperated Labour prime minister, Harold Wilson, as one of a 'tightly knit group of politically motivated men' responsible for the seamen's strike of that year. Jack's nature matched both his names: a wiry Londoner with a gift for a phrase and an eye for publicity, in the 1930s and '40s he was a hod-carrier, boxer, unemployed and a fireman, fought Mosley in Cable Street and took the unemployed to ask for tea at the Ritz. After the war, he took to the docks and the fight to preserve dock labour, which was as hopeless as the Communism he was able to die believing in before it was finally exposed by the people who had to live under it. But, as with many another radical Cockney populist (see Livingstone, Ken, and **Wilkes, Jack**, qv), he had a chirpy charm that those who thought they knew better – the Oxford Union, Conservative dining clubs – found impossible to resist. On retirement, he organised a rent strike at his council accommodation and became a London tour guide. He is commemorated by Jack Dash House in Docklands and in Cockney rhyming slang for the function once memorably described by Barry Humphries as 'pointing Percy at the porcelain': Jack Dash: slash.

DEE

A traditional figure among his more outré and experimental peers in early twenty-first-century British comedy and so a master of the crafts – drollery, point, timing, punchline – often sacrificed by them in favour of some wacky but safe surreality and repetition. A fine stand-up and an accomplished actor, straight or sitcom, where his **Jack Benny** (qv) and Larry David misanthropy is slightly undermined by a niceness that insists on coming through. It can work well, though, as with this early stand-up gag: 'I read in my local newspaper, they had this advert, "Please look after your neighbours in the cold weather", and shall I tell you something about that? I live next door to this 84-year-old woman, do you know, not once has she come round to see if I'm all right yet. The lazy cow hasn't even taken her milk in for a fortnight!' Well, I liked it.

DELLAL

Black Jack Dellal is all a rich Jack should be. Worth over £500 million, Jack made his money from secondary banking, the stock exchange and property. Now in his 80s, he has been married twice, to a former Israeli air hostess and to a Miss South Africa runner-up who is 33 years his junior. At the last count, he had nine children, two of them born since he was seventy-five. His nickname is said to come from his love of gambling. To top all this Jackishness, and to give you a warm glow, I ought to mention that in 1995 he won £67,000 on a National Lottery scratchcard.

DEMPSEY

A man revered, this Jack. Not only an example of that prime male, the world heavyweight boxing champion, but a wild force of nature at a time – the 1920s – when America, fresh and relatively unscathed from its First World War experience, saw itself as the same: big, unstoppable, unbeatable. Dempsey lived the American Dream, complete with obstacles to be obstinately overcome, a tale writ outrageously large: 'Has there ever been a fighter quite like the young Dempsey? – the very embodiment, it seems, of hunger, rage, the will to do hurt; the spirit of the Western frontier come East to win his fortune,' as Joyce Carol Oates put it.

The third son of a struggling family from Manassah, Colorado, he was named William Harrison Dempsey after the American President, but followed his two unsuccessful boxing brothers by calling himself Jack in tribute to **Jack Dempsey**, an earlier and stylish Irish fighter who finished poor and drunk. This Jack didn't. Hundreds of thousands watched him shatter the bones and knock the sense out of bigger men with his will to do hurt. 'The Manassah Mauler' had the style of a Mike Tyson and the popularity of a Muhammad Ali. Like Ali, he refused to fight in a war (for less honourable reasons, earning him another name, Slacker Jack). He also took the title unexpectedly, handing the giant Jess Willard a terrible beating. And he came into real affections late, after his defeat by Gene Tunney, the unstoppable halted by a thinker, a more sophisticated fighter: 'It's a set-up,' reported back a spy sent by the Dempsey camp to watch Tunney training before the fight. 'I seen the lug readin' a book!'

Tunney won the rematch, too, after the controversial 'long count' when Dempsey knocked him down but failed to retreat to a neutral corner. But Jack made no excuses – 'Honey, I forgot to duck' was his famous quote to his wife, later repeated by Ronald Reagan after the 1981 assassination attempt – and he was loved for it. He retired soon afterwards, in 1928, just before the Depression set in and relieved him of most of his money. He fought endless exhibition matches and opened up a restaurant in Broadway which he would keep open until 1974. During the Second World War, remarkably, given his record in the First, he served as a Morale Officer and landed at Okinawa. He died at the age of 87 in 1983. This last glimpse from his biographer, Roger Kahn: 'When he was coming back from the restaurant one night, they got out of the cab and a couple of people jumped him. There was this man, now white-haired, expensive topcoat, and they jumped him for his wallet. And Dempsey turned, he gave them a couple of body punches, and these guys would not get up until the police came to protect them.'

DIAMOND

Ah, yes: Jack 'Legs' Diamond, the big Jack gangster of the 1920s. There could have been another, but John Dillinger, the Public Enemy Number One and bank robber regarded by many as a Robin Hood/

Jesse James figure, remained just John, although he did acquire the minor nickname of Jackrabbit for his ability to vault bank counters (which he claimed he copied from gangster movies). Diamond was a fairly ineffective bootlegger and protection racketeer, with a knack of making other hoodlums want to kill him. He became a popular hero, mostly thanks to that nickname (awarded for his speed in getting away from said other hoodlums) and to the yellow press, especially after claiming that 'The bullet hasn't been made that can kill me.'

You will guess what happened soon afterwards. This is from the *Daily News* of 18 December 1931:

> Jack (Legs) Diamond, laughing in alcoholic glee at his latest victory over the law, marched from the arms of titian-haired Kiki Roberts into the fatal revolver blast of Manhattan underworld assassins, detectives determined tonight . . . Three times in the last four years his enemies tried to put him on the spot. Each time Legs went to a hospital. Each time he cheated death. But after his last miraculous recovery it was declared that his body was so full of lead that it would sink in Salt Lake.

Jack's life, with liberties taken, was later made into a Hollywood film and a Broadway musical, which also tempted fate with this line: 'Only a critic can kill me.' They did, after 64 performances. Moving In Mysterious Ways Note: the musical's failure resulted in the sale of the theatre to the Times Square Church.

DONOHOE

Another bold bad Jack of the Hood (Robin, that is) variety. Jack Donohoe, shipped out from Ireland in 1825, was the last of the transported convicts, or 'convict bolters', to flee life-servitude and become an Australian bushranger, or highway robber. A successful escape between gaol and court in Sydney and any number of attributed robberies in the infant New South Wales started up the legend of Bold Jack, who was reputed always to rob the rich, no matter that he sold, rather than gave, the goods to the poor settlers. Contemporary accounts noted that Donohoe and his gang were 'remarkably clean' bushmen. Bold Jack was described as fitted out in a black hat, a superfine blue cloth coat lined with silk, a pleated shirt and laced boots. He further fanned his fame by dying with them on after throwing the hat into the air and shouting 'Come on, you [expletive expletives], we're [expletive] ready!' when challenged by troopers (the local art of sledging has a long history). Jack's young and lithe body was sketched at the morgue by the Australian Surveyor General, no less, and these lines from Byron were added: 'No matter; I have bared my brow/Fair in Death's face – before – and now.' Songs of praise followed for the first People's Hero of a People's Country, chief among them 'Bold Jack Donohoe', and, even more famously, 'The Wild Colonial Boy', the country's first unofficial anthem ('There was a wild colonial boy, Jack Donohoe was his name'). Attempts were made to ban it, but in usual robust style, they just changed the name to Jack Doolan, or Jim Doolan, or John Dowling, and sang it anyway.

DOUGLAS

I know I was a little disobliging about the Carry On films earlier (see **Jack Carter**) but you will never understand the famous English sense of humour without them. Older people will smile indulgently at their memory, but are advised not to watch them again. Relish instead such names as Sir Sidney Ruff-Diamond, The Khasi of Kalabar, Private Widdle, Bungdit Din, Doctor Nookey, Rodger De Lodgerly, Detective Sergeant Sidney Bung, Big Dick Turpin, Sir Rodney Ffing, Lord Darcy Pue, Citizens Camembert and Bidet, and, from, of course, *Carry On Jack*, Midshipman Albert Poop-Decker, and others proving that 'there's nothing like a Jolly Roger on the

Seven Seas with the Carry On Team'. Jack Douglas, large, gormless and given to twitching, followed Bernard Bresslaw in providing the grotesque figure popular in English comedy (see also Ken Dodd, Bernie Winters, Max Wall, Dan Leno and **Sir John 'Jack' Falstaff**, qv). His catchphrase was 'wahey' rather than 'whoar'. Nor should we forget his other large, gormless, twitching stage creation, Alf Ippititimus.

DOYLE

Another roaring boy, another Irishman, another boxer. To complete the set, this one was also a tenor, an actor, a womaniser, a gambler and a drinker, but, familiarly and poignantly, realised his full potential only in the last three activities. Jack Doyle (1913–78), known as the Gorgeous Gael, stood six foot four, starred in two Hollywood movies, married a future wife of Marlon Brando, and wanted a crack at the world heavyweight title. But the drink did for him, and he became another lost Irish legend, dying in Paddington of his liver, on borrowed beds. In late interviews, he attributed his decline to fast women and slow horses and denied any regrets: 'None at all. 'Twas never a generous man went to hell.'

DRUM

Giving someone Jack Drum's Entertainment is an obscure and now obsolete phrase defined by Brewer as 'turning an unwelcome visitor out of doors'. It is also the title of a play from 1600 written by John, sometimes Jack, Marston (1576–1634), a descendant through his mother of Balthasar Guarsi, the Italian physician who had the mixed privilege of being physician to Katherine of Aragon. Marston offended his lawyer father by rejecting a legal career and instead writing erotic poetry and satires. Notably argumentative, he had a special feud with Ben Jonson (mocked in *Jack Drum's Entertainment*), but he made it up, briefly, to collaborate with Jonson and George

Chapman on *Eastward Ho!* (1605), a satire on just about everything in early Stuart Britain, including the Scots. Jonson and Chapman were imprisoned for it; shortly afterwards Marston gave up the stage, married a royal chaplain's daughter and became a country parson for the next 25 years, returning to London only to fight to have his name removed from a collection of his plays. The inscription on his tomb is 'Oblivioni Sacrum': Blessed in Oblivion. Clearly not a man for our age.

DRUMMOND

Sir Jack Drummond, the *Dictionary of National Biography* tells us, 'was small, neat, sprightly, and gay, abounding with energy'. He was knighted in 1944 for his work in ensuring that the diet of wartime Britain, complete with its rations of rosehip and blackcurrant syrup, was the healthiest ever achieved either before or since. Such is celebrity, however, that he is remembered more for having been brutally murdered, along with his wife and ten-year-old daughter, one August night in Provence profonde in 1952. Those intrigued by the workings of Fate will note especially that the man convicted of the family's murder was a Mediterranean peasant farmer of the type whose diet is said by nutritionists to prolong life. Conspiracy theory aficionados will know that Sir Jack was more likely a spy bumped off by the KGB or an irritant executed by the big food manufacturers or the agrochemical industry because he would insist on promoting healthy eating and criticising excessive use of fertilisers. Whatever, many unanswered questions and a grandson convinced of the farmer's innocence have sustained attention on the sad affair, poignantly and still marked by a shrine of cards and cuddly toys where poor little Elizabeth Drummond died.

DUCKWORTH

This Jack, occasional cabbie, window cleaner, cellarman, landlord, pall bearer, lollipop man and cabaret artiste (as Vince St Clair), is, nonetheless, a Jack of the idle kind, rewarded for his heroic fecklessness by a son, Terry, whose spermal irresponsibility is matched only by his fertility, and a wife, Vera, with whom he took the northern matrimonial comedy of love and hate to new heights of enjoyment, for watchers. More is best told in lines written by those modern Martials, masters and mistresses of the epigram, the *Coronation Street* scriptwriters: Vera on Jack's attitude to healthy eating: 'He think's brown bread's white that's gone mouldy'; Jack on his mother-in-law: 'She's like Boris Karloff after a busy night at the graveyard'; Bet on Jack's light-fingered tendencies: 'They say the midwife that delivered him is still looking for the scissors'; Jack on buying a new car: 'The nearest I've got to a deposit is when I'm cleaning the pigeons out'; Jack trying to seduce Bet: 'I can't help it. I'm drawn to you. It's like magnetism. I'm like a little nail drawn to a lump of iron.' Ah, yes, but my favourite, after all these years, is still Ena Sharples, over a milk stout in the Rover's: 'I'd like to go like my mother went . . . she just sat up, broke wind and died.'

DUPREE

Some rich Jackness here. Champion Jack Dupree was the last of the barrelhouse pianists, learning his trade in a hard school for blues players pretty similar to the bar in Leadville where Oscar Wilde observed a sign reading, 'Don't shoot the pianist. He is doing his best.' Marvel at the names with which Jack is associated: Tuts Washington, Drive 'em Down, Scrapper Blackwell, Big Bill Broonzy and Tampa Red. Marvel, too, at the legend assembled around and by Jack. He didn't know which year he was born in, 1908, 1909 or 1910, let alone the date, so, like Louis Armstrong, he chose 4 July.

Like Armstrong, he was sent to the New Orleans Home for Colored Waifs. He was orphaned at two: his father was from the Congo; his mother was a Cherokee Indian who gave him the gold which later filled his teeth. They died when their house was burnt down by the Ku Klux Klan. Jack called himself Champion Jack on account of a triumphant 170-bout boxing career. Jack served under John F. Kennedy in the Second World War. Jack had a half-finished tattoo on one arm, started by a fellow-prisoner when Jack was serving 30 days in the Indianapolis Penitentiary. Unfortunately, the tattooist was executed before he could finish off Jack's arm. How much of all this is true? Well, most remarkable for me was that he lived for many years in a council house in Halifax: a Yorkshire girl was one of his three or four wives, and he was often to be seen driving round Yorkshire in his Lincoln Continental. That's a Jack. He influenced Fats Domino and the Rolling Stones, and appeared alongside the Beatles. His stage patter, unchanged from the barrelhouse, was heroically obscene; I prefer this more subtle lyric: 'Mamma, move your false teeth, Papa wanna scratch your gums.'

E

EARLE

This Jack was a giant. Born Jacob Erlich in Denver in 1906, he was over six foot tall by the age of ten; by seventeen he was appearing in the first of twenty-five Hollywood silent movies. His career was halted by a fall from a ladder caused by his failing eyesight; doctors treating him discovered a tumour in his pituitary gland. The tumour was removed, ending his growth at the height of seven foot seven, or, in top hat and big-heeled boots, eight foot six. The top hat and boots followed a trip to the Ringling Bros circus while he was convalescing in El Paso. If we were running a circus, we might be somewhat discomfited if a member of the audience turned out to be a touch taller than our current attraction; but not this manager, who asked Jack, 'How would you like to be a giant?' Jack stayed with Ringlings until 1940, billed as the Texas Giant, and often appearing with Clarence Howerton, 'Major Mite', just two foot tall. The Major later became a Munchkin in *The Wizard of Oz*, and, unsurprisingly, could be truculent. Steve Willis, writing in *The White Tops*, the magazine of the Circus Fans Association of America, put it this way: 'He would march into a tavern in full top hat regalia, kick the shins of the nearest person, and order, "Set me up on the bar, you bastard!" If he felt really mean, he would run the length of the bar, drop-kicking anything in his path.' Jack, in classic contrast, seems to have been a gentle, wistful giant, who painted, sculpted and published poetry (a volume entitled *The Long*

Shadows). He left the circus when he was offered a job as a salesman with the Cribari Winery in Fresno, California, making his calls in a specially designed car and billed as the 'largest man in the world working for the world's largest winery'. He died in a crash in his car in 1952 and never got to move into the house he was having built in El Paso with nine-foot-high ceilings and a shower head fixed eight feet above the bath.

EDMONDSON

Jack Edmondson was the first Australian to be awarded the VC in the Second World War, at Tobruk. Corporal Edmondson, five privates and an officer fixed bayonets and charged German infantry who were firing at least six machine guns, mortars and two small field pieces at them. Already badly wounded in the neck and stomach, Jack killed one of the enemy and then went to the aid of his officer, killing two more and saving his life. He died before dawn, aged 26. In her poem, 'Edmondson VC', Dame Mary Gilmore, often criticised for doggerel, nevertheless achieved this powerful effect:

> All night he lay waiting the end maybe
> Remembering Parramatta oaks,
> Where as a boy he played, or heard the sea
> Of Sydney beat with silken strokes.
>
> Maybe he thought of home, dreaming he saw
> His mother stand beside the door,
> Watching his father rake the windlestraw –
> And then he saw no more.

Some, though, might prefer this, from his mother: 'Of course I am proud of him. I have always been proud of him. In a way, this great honour seems futile. I would rather have my son.'

ELAM

Once upon a time in the west, the good guys wore white hats, the bad guys wore black hats, and the movies were no worse for it. Most often, too, the bad guys looked bad. And Jack Elam looked the baddest. Jack's was not just a wolfish, chilling leer: it was a wolfish, chilling leer involving one good eye and one very bad one, with a crazed sense of direction all of its own. Many tried to describe Jack, from the 'archetypal ornery varmint' to 'rather like Dr Jekyll stuck in mid-transformation into Quasimodo'. If you've never seen him, watch the opening of Sergio Leone's *Once Upon a Time in the West*, which I won't spoil for you. Before he was an ornery varmint, Jack was an accountant and, even more entertaining to imagine, the manager of the Bel Air Hotel. He did the books for various Hollywood companies, and got his break by offering to raise the finance for a series of films in return for parts as the heavy. His first big hit was *Rawhide*, in 1951: 'I was pretty bad in that movie,' he said. 'I shot a baby to make it dance, and I killed everybody in the picture except Tyrone Power and Susan Hayward. That's bad.' As you can see, Jack had a good sense of humour. Because of the numbers, he was also pretty good at cards, too. He had never ridden a horse before he made films, but he spent a lot of time in the saddle thereafter, before being inevitably gunned down. The eye was the result of a scrap with a fellow boy scout armed with a pencil. 'I don't control it at all,' said Jack when complimented on what he could do with it. 'It does whatever the hell it wants.' Later on in life he played winningly on his looks and past outings in several comedies, but remained as refreshingly unimpressed by it all as ever. This is Jack on the stages in the career of a character actor: 'Who's Jack Elam? Get me Jack Elam. Get me a Jack Elam type. Get me a young Jack Elam. Who's Jack Elam?'

ELLIOTT

Ramblin' Jack Elliott is an excellent example of the wonders that can attend the name Jack, whether it's given or chosen. Ramblin' Jack, born in 1931, is a folk singer in the style of Woody Guthrie, his early mentor. Ramblin' Jack can also claim much influence on Bob Dylan, whom he met when Dylan first arrived in New York, at Guthrie's hospital bed. But Jack can also claim to have inspired another, somewhat different, legendary figure: Rambling Syd Rumpo. Anyone unfamiliar with the oeuvre of this English folk singer, created in emulation of Jack by the late Kenneth Williams, will find recordings online. I defy you not to cry with laughter from Syd's opening 'Hello, my dearios', which prefaces such sad songs as the one in which a young cordwangler is hung by the postern and has his moolies nailed to the fence; other featured unfortunates have their woggle irons twisted or their nadgers hit by a bosun's plunger. And there is more: like Dylan, Jack is Jewish, born Elliott Charles Adnopoz in Brooklyn, part of the Jewish cowboy tradition which also includes Kinky Friedman, from Chicago, founder of the country-and-western band Kinky Friedman and the Texas Jewboys, whose most noted number was 'They Ain't Makin' Jews Like Jesus Anymore'. Kinky also ran for Governor of Texas, paying tribute to a recent incumbent with the slogan 'How hard can it be?' He lost. Ramblin' Jack, meanwhile, won a Grammy in 1995 and has been awarded a National Medal of Arts, which Rambling Syd would undoubtedly have hailed with a 'Well, rollock me futtock and griddle my nodes!'

F

FAIRMAN

We have already noted the most famous Jack racing driver, Brabham; Jack Fairman is the most Jack racing driver, not least because he wasn't all that successful, wins-wise. But Jack was a handsome fellow whose moustache made him look like Ronald Colman: Jack looked like a racing driver should. Jack was 'Jolly Jack' or 'Fearless Fairman', the chap who escaped a career in the Surrey family laundry business, took his Alvis along to Brooklands for a spin and went on, with an interruption while he drove tanks, to become a test driver and partner to the great Stirling Moss in promoting the exceptional Jaguar XK120 at Le Mans and elsewhere. Later, this time in an Aston Martin DBR1, Moss and Fairman fought off the Ferraris to win the 1,000-kilometre sports car challenge at Nürburgring in 1959 and spark one of those periodic fits of national pride. The victory was achieved through the exceptional skill of Moss and a most Jack-like contribution from Fairman: baulked by a slower car, the Aston spun off the track and landed in a ditch with its nose in the air, one wheel off the ground. The rules forbade any outside assistance; Moss, in the pits, assumed the jig was up. But Fairman, displaying equal amounts of sangfroid and strength, simply heaved the car up, out and onto the track, climbed back in and kept on driving. He took up Formula One when he was past forty and kept at it for another ten years; third place was his best. He retired, but lost his precision-tool business and spent the last years of his working life variously as a driving instructor and delivering special cars to customers, which is how it can be with Jacks. Nürburgring, Le Mans, Jags, Astons, the 1950s and that tache, though, remain Jolly Jack's memory.

FALSTAFF

Was there ever another such a Jack as sweet Jack Falstaff, kind Jack Falstaff, true Jack Falstaff, valiant Jack Falstaff, plump Jack Falstaff? Keep reading. But Falstaff – rollicking, leery, braggarty, lewd, cunning, weak, cowardly, lovable and loving – must be one of the finest realisations of a true and rounded (in every way) character, even in Shakespeare. The magic in making us like him despite everything is the magic that makes us like humanity despite everything. In his rueful but fleeting acknowledgement of his failings is ours of our own. This, with wit, is the difference between a rogue and a villain, and the distinction that marks many a bad Jack. There is a sigh for good intentions foundered upon bad luck, overpowering temptation, an unsatisfactory world and the need for a robust realism. And there is a wink, which may come before or after. Mistress Quickly's moving, poetic description of Falstaff's death is instantly followed by a discussion about whether he cried out for a woman as well as drink, and by a bad joke. The Bard, I feel, is trying to tell us something. Ah, yes, that's right: 'banish plump Jack, and banish all the world'. Meanwhile, there is the fat old fellow's letter to Prince Hal, with its advice and sign-off giving guidance on Jack usage: 'Repent at idle times as thou mayest; and so, farewell. Thine, by yea and no, which is as much as to say, as thou usest him, Jack Falstaff with my familiars, John with my brothers and sisters, and Sir John with all Europe.'

FERTIG

Jack Fertig, until he left the order to become a full-time astrologer, was a member of the Sisters of Perpetual Indulgence, the clever, jokey but successful gay rights activists who, according to their founding myth, emerged in San Francisco in 1979, three years after a convent in Cedar Rapids, Iowa, lent some of its habits to a group of young men who were putting on *The Sound of Music*. They have been outraging the staid ever since. Fertig's nun name was Sister Boom-Boom (other sisters have been called Sister Roz Erection and Sister Phyllis Stein the Fragrant). In the early 1980s, Sister Boom-Boom ran for public office in San Francisco under the slogan 'Nun of the Above'. She did rather well; San Francisco then introduced a measure – known popularly as The Sister Boom-Boom Law – obliging candidates to use their real names. Spoilsports. In an interesting note on his website, starjack.com, Fertig, promoting the claims of Uranus to be a gay planet, points out that its first five moons – Titania, Oberon, Umbriel, Miranda and Puck – are named after fairies. Boom, boom.

FIDDLER

Zhauwuno-geezhigo-gaubow, meaning 'He who stands in the southern sky', was a late-nineteenth-century shaman of the Sucker tribe in what is now north-west Ontario. European traders, for obvious reasons of brevity, and because the Suckers were most taken with the fiddles the strangers brought with them, called him Jack Fiddler. Jack was renowned as an adept in dealing with windigos, humans possessed by evil spirits once seemingly prevalent in the North American forests but now mostly confined to horror films. His method was to strangle them, which, as you might expect, eventually brought him into conflict with the Royal Canadian Mounted Police, who got their man: Jack was charged with murdering a young woman member of the tribe. His response was to slip away from captivity and strangle himself (by hanging). A sad tale of clashing cultures: one is reminded of the robust response of Sir Charles Napier to the Indian practice of suttee:

> You say that it is your custom to burn widows. Very well.
> We also have a custom: when men burn a woman alive, we
> tie a rope around their necks and we hang them. Build your
> funeral pyre; beside it, my carpenters will build a gallows.
> You may follow your custom. And then we will follow ours.

Napier is also renowned for the one-word telegram reporting the pacification of the province of Sindh during the Indian Mutiny in 1843: 'Peccavi' (I have sinned). Reluctantly, I have to reveal that a *Punch* cartoonist made it up shortly afterwards (see also: Lord Clyde, Lucknow, 'Nunc fortunatus sum', 'I am in luck now'; and Lord Dalhousie, Oudh, 'Vovi', 'I vowed'). The earliest example, before *Punch* even, is attributed to Drake after the Armada: 'Cantharides', the Latin name for the drug Spanish fly.

FINDLAY

Another Jack racer. This one, the Australian motorcyclist, changed his name from Cyril to get a racing permit at the age of fifteen, two years under the limit, and then raced for the next twenty-eight years, travelling from race to race in Europe, living on the small amount paid to start, and going on to compete with the big boys on an elderly bike which he serviced himself and had acquired after the death in a crash of its owner. He fractured his skull twice but eventually won the Isle of Man Senior TT and the F750 world championship on better machines before dying at the age of 72 from emphysema as a result of all those years inhaling exhaust fumes.

FLASH

Jumping Jack. This, from the Rolling Stones website Time Is On Our Side, is how to write some of the most time-conjuring, strut-summoning (if admittedly not extensive) lyrics in pop music. Keith Richards: 'Mick and I were in my house [laughs] in England in the country . . . and we'd been up all night and it was six thirty in the morning, a dismal day, you know, English, grey. And we were just both crashing, Mick was on the couch and I was in an armchair with a guitar and we were, like, on the verge. And suddenly this sound of these boots [laughs] went by the window, clump clump clump – really, I mean, you had to be there to hear it – and woke Mick up, and he said, "What was that?" And I looked out the window and I thought, Oh, that's Jack, that's jumpin' Jack . . . But I mean, really, we were sort of virtually woke up out of a stupor by this guy's boots, he was my gardener, he was a great guy but he's another story. And I just said, "That's Jack." And Mick said, "Well, he's leaping about a bit." "Yeah," I said, "it's jumpin' Jack", and then Flash came and suddenly we were wide awake and we started to work, you know. You never know when they're going to come.' And here's Keith telling that 'another story': 'Jumpin' Jack Flash comes from this guy Jack Dyer, who was my gardener. He'd lived out in the country all his life. I'll put it this way: Jack Dyer, an old English yokel. I once said, "Have you ever been to town?" And town, to an Englishman, means London, right? And he says, "Oh, yeah, I was up there VE Day, when the war finished. That cathedral is something." He meant Chichester, the local big town, seven miles away . . .' Terrific. The only other thing I have been able to find out about Jack is that he had big feet.

FLAVELL

At first sight a yeoman Jack, this Worcestershire fast bowler's England appearances were limited by the embarrassment of riches during his time, including those of the long-term partnership of Yorkshire's Trueman and Lancashire's Statham. Renowned for line and length and lack of show and fuss, he was a keen whist player, captain of his golf club, noted exhibitor of vegetables, possessor of the flat tones of his native Black Country, enthusiast for amateur opera and keeper of a guest house in Barmouth. Show me, though, a fast-bowling Jack with red hair who doesn't have his moments. Jack's bouncers were as feared as the sustained ferocity of his attack on a green pitch. When Jack lost at whist, his teammates found the cards likely to exit through the coach window. I like, too, the story **Jack Bannister** (qv) tells of him at the Ashes centenary dinner at Lord's in 1980: 'As we stood for Grace, he looked around the room at cricketers such as old timers Arthur Morris, Bill Lawry, Richie Benaud, the Chappells, Lindsay Hassett, Keith Miller, Ted Dexter et al. And then he muttered to me, albeit grudgingly, "You know, there's a few here who could bat a bit."'

FM

A radio station that doesn't have any disc jockeys or anyone at all talking and just plays hit music of any type from the last 40 years in no particular order? That must be a Jack station, a franchise reflecting the true Jack spirit, even if was created by an American called Bob. Jack is named after the fictitious **Cadillac Jack Garrett**, 'a hard-living radio cowboy who decides he's going to play whatever he wants'. All right for Jacks, of course, but it might be a bit strong for Simons and Tims.

FORD

Jack Ford was the leading character in the BBC television series *When the Boat Comes In*, a drama of the 1920s and 1930s set in the North-East. The series rose above the ordinary Catherine Cookson and 'now, bonny lad/lass' social climbing and falling largely because of Jack, an ambitious amoral charmer who uses trade unionism and, as my late father would have put it, 'any bugger he can' to rise. He falls, of course, but is redeemed by a late fit of loyalty and an attachment to the right side in the Spanish Civil War which kills him (in Spain, or, in reality, the beach at Formby doubling for Spain). Jack was played by James Bolam as a stylish interpretation and extension of his famous earlier character, Terry Collier, the Jack the Lad of *The Likely Lads*. Bolam himself is a rather more reserved character, at least where personal publicity is concerned: his interviews are rarer than a Geordie character on television who doesn't say 'pet'. I was extremely fortunate to be granted one many years ago; sadly, the weekend this hinny's tooth was to be published was the weekend the printers decided to go on strike (they used to do that sort of thing, you know), so it never appeared. Moreover, my editor said it was 'a bit dull', a contention I am now unable to refute as I've lost it. Bolam's many later roles include that of **Jack Halford**, the retired chief superintendent in the engaging *New Tricks* television series, featuring the talents of three ex-policemen and written by Roy Mitchell, a West Bromwich Albion fan who has named them after Albion's Halford Lane Stand. The anal-omni-retentive Brian 'Memory' Lane is played by the excellent and equally ubiquitous Alun Armstrong, another north-easterner, who had his first film part in *Get Carter* (qv). My favourite memory of him is from the set of the Granada adaptation of A.J. Cronin's Geordie coal-mining drama *The Stars Look Down*, during a particularly intense camera rehearsal. Armstrong, playing the upwardly mobile Joe Gowlan, carefully perused a letter, paused, and then told his secretary: 'I think you'll find, Miss Smith, that there are three "n"s in "cunnilingus".' Dennis Waterman, who was also George Carter, the sidekick of **Jack Regan** (qv) in *The Sweeney*, plays the third policeman, Gerry Standing.

FROST

Many mysteries surround our icy old friend, Jack Frost. For example, if he is derived from the Norse names Jokul (icicle) and Frosti (frost), how is it that his first mention, according to the *OED*, came not in some early medieval maunderings but in 1826, in a hearty sporting connection: 'Jack Frost, however, put a veto on our morning's sport'? Another perplexer is why he inspires such uniformly mediocre films (honourably excepting – but only for the title – *Jack Frost 2: Revenge of the Mutant Killer Snowman*). Another is quite why the David Jason vehicle *A Touch of Frost*, starring DJ as, naturally, Inspector Jack Frost, has been quite so successful. But any investigation of that would lead us into wondering contemplation of the mystery of the enduring appeal of the TV murder mystery, and, in particular, the greatest mystery of them all, *Midsomer Murders*.

FRUIT

The jackfruit grows on jackfruit trees, which are spreading. Native to India, they are now also to be found in Brazil and parts of Africa. As you would expect, the jackfruit is a very good grower – the largest tree-borne fruit in the world, in fact: up to eighty pounds, three foot long, and nearly two foot wide. Mention that to your children next time they baulk at an apricot. Sadly, academic rigour obliges me to reveal that jack in this instance derives from *chakka*, the word for the fruit in Malayalam, the language of Kerala. But you should try one, if you haven't already, as they are excellent in curries and cakes. Shopping tip: it's ripe if you can hear a dull, hollow sound when you tap it.

FULLER

All times are distinguished by characters mostly known for being characters. A certain eccentricity and a liking for attention joined to a reckless disregard for reputation: these things guarantee notice but conspire against any real achievement. And so characters are more quickly forgotten than any other public figures. Consider: Sir Gerald Nabarro, Gilbert Harding, Lady Docker, Farmer Ted Moult, Derek Hatton, Quintin Hogg, Magnus Pyke.

Such, too, was Mad Jack Fuller (1757–1834), a man better known then for the above sort of thing than for his patronage of J.M.W. Turner and endowment of two professorial chairs at the Royal Institution, and hardly known at all now. But Mad Jack has his monument, or rather monuments, scattered all round the family estate, at Brightling, Sussex. For Mad Jack was a folly-builder of major proportion. He took it up after retiring from a parliamentary career most noted for a forced removal from the chamber, heckling and general mischief, powered by a twenty-two-stone frame and three bottles of port a day.

He built an observatory, designed by Sir Robert Smirke, of British Museum fame, used by Jack to study the heavens and by his servants to spot their squire's carriage on its way home. He built an obelisk, 646 foot high, which might or might not be to commemorate Trafalgar, or Waterloo. He built a 35-foot-high cone, which might or might not be a replica of the packets then used for selling sugar, source of the family fortune, or of the spire of Dallington Church, six miles away, which, he had wagered, largely and unwisely, he could see from Brightling. He was buried beneath a 25-foot-high pyramid in Brightling churchyard. Once again, respect for truth and balance requires me to mention that one of his purposes in all this was to provide work for local people in pressed times, and that he was not, as reputed, placed in the pyramid beside a table with his usual bottle at hand, dressed for dinner.

FUNCTION

According to the ubiquitous and indispensable Wikipedia, the Jack function, introduced by **Henry Jack**, the late distinguished Dundee mathematician, in a paper to the Royal Society of Edinburgh in 1970, is a homogeneous, symmetric polynomial which generalises the Schur and zonal polynomials, and is in turn generalised by the Macdonald polynomials. I should also mention the brainchild of **Prof. Jack Morava** over at Johns Hopkins University in Baltimore, Morava's K-Theory, a matter of cohomology, algebraic topology, double indexing, ring spectra and homotopy. No, after you.

G

GARDNER

And some achieve Jackness by marrying one. This is Isabella Stewart Gardner, Mrs Jack L. Gardner, or, simply, Mrs Jack, the pride, shock and awe of Boston at the turn of the twentieth century. Belle was the granddaughter of a Brooklyn bar owner who married the reserved (for a Jack) son of a wealthy Boston family and developed her own style, which allowed her to cock a snook at snobbish Bostonian society by outspending and outsmarting it. So Mrs Jack built a mock Venetian palazzo, a museum to live in, and stocked it with efforts of Titian, Tintoretto, Veronese, Tiepolo, Raphael, Mantegna, Botticelli, Velázquez, Manet, Degas, Matisse, Holbein, Durer, Vermeer, Rubens and Rembrandt.

Mrs Jack toured Europe with Jack in tow and befriended Henry James and James Whistler, who painted her, as did, even more famously, John Singer Sargent. Bernard Berenson helped her collect; George Santayana visited. But Mrs Jack also drank beer, played backgammon, smoked Turkish cigarettes, arranged boxing matches, and at the age of 71 went to a Boston Symphony Orchestra concert wearing a ribbon that said, 'Oh, you Red Sox' (they had just won the World Series). Perhaps the best model is Lorenz Hart's 'The Lady Is a Tramp' ('I get too hungry for dinner at eight; I like the theatre but never come late').

Legends have amassed around Mrs Jack: that she once walked a lion cub down Tremont Street; that every Ash Wednesday she would arrive by limousine with a bucket and mop to wash down the steps of the Church of the Advent as her penance. Of the anecdotes, I like best her claiming descent from the royal house of Stuart, and telling some Boston dowager who was banging on about antecedents that could be traced back to 1776, 'Ah yes, they were much less careful about immigration in those days, I believe.' Mrs Jack died aged 80 in 1924; Jack had gone before some 25 years earlier, leaving his widow the wherewithal for her museum, still a wonder of Boston today. She also had the distinction of being summed up by Henry James, who likened her to 'a locomotive – with a Pullman car attached'.

GLASS

The late Irish comedian Dave Allen, who was far more of a Jack than a Dave, had a story about a Protestant preacher working himself up into a fine state as he outlined the horrors of Hell, where, he thundered, there would be 'weeping, wailing and gnashing of teeth'. Whereupon a disrespectful old man interrupts, 'But what about me? I haven't got any teeth.' 'Teeth,' replies the pastor, 'will be provided.' Time has conferred the tale upon the Reverend Ian Paisley, a liberty which nevertheless emphasises that there is something inescapably ridiculous as well as threatening about extremism and bigotry. And so to Pastor Jack Glass, leader of the Zion Sovereign Grace Baptist Church in Glasgow, the man who thought Paisley was too liberal. He was certainly as loud: one less fierce Scottish cleric remarked that an encounter with Jack left him with 'Protestant tinnitus for at least three days'. I myself heard him clearly from at least 150 yards when he protested against Pope John Paul II's visit to Britain in 1982.

The Pope, of course, was a top target: Jack is renowned for marching round St Peter's Square in 1966 with a placard proclaiming 'No Popery here!' Other targets, apart from the usual, included comedy, particularly that of Billy Connolly, whom he picketed over a period of some 30 years after taking exception to Connolly's conceit of setting the Last Supper in a Glasgow pub. Connolly responded by leading a counter-demonstration to Glass's church with a banner proclaiming 'Jack is a wee pastor'. As you will have gathered, Jack's performances were as outrageous as those of any comedian: he once interrupted an opening ceremony being conducted by Bishop Desmond Tutu's wife by shouting, 'Hang Mandela!' Wearing a crown of thorns, he also picketed an Edinburgh Fringe production in which he claimed Christ was being 'spoofed as a poof', hurling a bag of money at one of the actors with the cry: 'There's your 30 pieces of silver, you Judas!' When the coins were counted, there were found to be only 29. I particularly enjoyed his characterisation of the urbane Roy Jenkins, then a local MP, as 'the Herod of Hillhead'. Jack had a typically ringing response to his recovery from lung cancer: 'An amazing miracle . . . I've lived to see the Devil run away. I'm like Lazarus, who rose from the grave.' Suspicions that Jack's was an ironic God were strengthened by the cancer's resurgence and fatal spread to his brain. Privately, and when not discussing religion, Jack was said to be a charming, affable man. 'I don't hate anyone,' he once said. 'I'm just trying to bring people to Christ. Glasgow has turned its back on God. Sadly, God will have to punish it.'

GOOD (I)

Jacks often star in fables, and this Jack is a fine example of a modern one. Jack Good is from Palmers Green, North London, a post-war grammar-school boy of the kind fabled by Alan Bennett, one himself. Jack got to Oxford at around the same time as Bennett, after national service, became president of the Oxford University Dramatic Society, and ended up as a BBC producer. But Jack was not a tweedy man. Jack got a second at Oxford after conducting his oral exam using the voice of Billy Graham. Jack was one of the first of those clever, fierce and unsnobbish consumers of pop culture who have produced such snappy, crackling television.

Jack made 6.5 *Special* for the BBC and *Oh, Boy* for ITV, showing for the first time the studio, cameras and audience enjoying itself, and introducing all those popsters with the confected names, Cliff Richard, Marty Wilde, Billy Fury, Vince Eager and Dickie Pride. Jack got Gene Vincent to wear leather and play on his gammy leg: 'Limp, you bugger! Limp!' That's a Jack. Next, he moved to America and did the same thing. But Jacks are rarely simple. He also tried, and failed, to become a great movie actor (although he did get to appear with Elvis). And he had converted to Catholicism. A fabled moment was his appearance on *This Is Your Life* in 1969. 'My old tutor Russell Meiggs came on and he said, "Jack could have done anything", and I thought to myself, "If I could have done anything, what the hell have I done? I haven't become a great Shakespearean actor. My whole life has revolved round rock and roll." And I did not like the pop culture . . . I had had a hand in corrupting the youth of this country.'

Since then, Jack has taught himself to paint, thought about becoming a monk and lived on his own for 12 years in the New Mexican desert, painting religious murals, including one of the Devil as a TV screen. But, being Jack, he has also started the genre of musicals based around pop lives, and put his own on stage. Now back in Britain, he says, 'I'm a self-indulgent pig who drinks too much and doesn't do anything valuable except pray. But I just can't help believing, as Elvis used to sing.' Good man, Jack.

GOOD(2)

There is another Jack Good. This one was named Isidore Jacob Gudak in 1916 by his father, a Polish émigré who had taught himself to repair watches by watching a watchmaker through a shop window, and whose name on his antique jewellery shop near the British Museum was changed to Good by a challenged signwriter. Young Jack changed his first name after the success in London of a play called *The Virtuous Isidore*. Young Jack also worked out the irrationality of the square root of two, based on a parity argument, at the age of nine while in bed with diphtheria. Unsurprisingly, he read maths at Cambridge, graduating in 1938, and thereafter, equally unsurprisingly, found his way to Bletchley Park, where he broke codes with Alan Turing and others. He worked for the British government in the same line after the war, and celebrates this part of his career with a personalised number plate reading 007 IJG. He has worked in the United States since 1967. In all, he has written some 800 papers and made significant contributions in mathematics, computer science, philosophy, physics and statistics, and has popularised the game 'Go'. The following review further points up an important part of Jack's approach:

> Botryology is an obscure term which was meant as a dignified label for the discipline of cluster analysis, meaning 'the theory of clusters'. It is formed from the Greek *botrus*, meaning 'a cluster of grapes'. In the article 'The Botryology of Botryology', the author I.J. Good puts in an heroic effort to lift the term into mainstream usage, though his argumentation seems somewhat humorous.

GRAYBURN

Lieutenant John Hollington 'Jack' Grayburn was the man who found himself at the very sharp end of that dashingly conceived but practically doomed Allied operation towards the end of the Second World War, Operation Market Garden. The plan was for an airborne invasion to seize a series of eight bridges across canals and rivers on the German–Dutch border, thus allowing a dagger-thrust into the heart of the failing Third Reich. It required too much luck, too few determined defenders and became, famously, a bridge too far. That was the one, at Arnhem, which Jack Grayburn found himself trying to take with insufficient support. In common with so many of his comrades, he was wounded; the paratroopers withdrew to defend their end of the bridge; Jack was the last man off, covering his men. For three days, the Germans tried to force the British back before their reinforcements arrived.

Somewhere in the middle of all this was Jack's superior officer, Major Allison Digby Tatham-Warter, carrying an umbrella. This was because, as he explained, he could never remember passwords and the brolly would make it perfectly clear that he was British. He also used it on one occasion to disable a German armoured car by poking it through a slit and blinding the driver. (Also present was Father Bernard Egan, chaplain to the Second Parachute Battalion, who was taking shelter from mortar fire when the major came to help him cross the street; Father Egan mentioned the mortars: the major replied, 'Don't worry, I've got an umbrella.') Tatham-Warter was also injured but survived the war to run safaris in Kenya.

Jack wasn't so lucky. He was killed by fire from the tank that had forced him to withdraw his men, whom he was once again directing to safety in full view. Jack was promoted posthumously and awarded the VC. His body wasn't recovered from the Rhine until 1948. His citation reads: 'There is no doubt that, had it not been for this officer's inspiring leadership and personal bravery, the Arnhem bridge could never have been held for this time.' You must decide whether such extraordinary courage was futile, inspiring or both.

GREENWELL

When you think of Barcelona FC, Barca, you do not, unless you are hopeless at geography or an obsessive patriot, think of England; you think of Kubala, Suárez, Cruyff, of the famous maroon and blue striped jerseys moving masterfully around a packed Nou Camp, one of football's great romantic stages and shrines. Nevertheless, the English have a significant role in Barca's history: a number of

Englishmen, part of the resident expatriate business community in Barcelona, helped found the club in 1899; and its first manager was John Barrow, who was succeeded in 1917 by Jack Greenwell, the second-longest-serving Barca coach in the club's history (if not the second most successful). Jack had first visited the city to play Barcelona as a player with Crook Town, now playing in the Arngrove Northern League, Division 2, and wearing the famous Barcelona colours in Jack's memory. Those colours are, in fact, the colours of Merchant Taylor's, Crosby, the old school of one of the founding Englishmen, Arthur Whitty (who was really a rugby man, but the unturfed Catalan pitches were too hard for that). A few things to throw in there when conversation lags, I should have said, together with another famous early Jack manager in Europe, **Jack Reynolds**, coach of the almost equally great Ajax, credited with inventing their famous 'total football' style based on attack. Reynolds had one season with Grimsby before managing Ajax for twenty-five years, with an interruption while he was interned for the duration of the Second World War. When the war ended Ajax thought he was dead, but he had been repatriated to Britain, and returned for another two years. Key conversation point: a fellow internee in Upper Silesia was P.G. Wodehouse. Jack also has a stand named after him at Ajax's ground. For the other footballing **Jack Reynolds**, see under R.

GRIFFIN

The first name of the Invisible Man was not revealed in H.G. Wells's famous science-fiction novel: he became Jack Griffin in the 1933 Hollywood film of the same name, which gave a first starring role to Claude Rains, even though, obviously, he did not appear until the end. Knowledge can have its disappointments, though, don't you find? I shall never watch in quite the same way Claude's splendidly dodgy but *au fond* decent chap, Captain Louis Renault, in

Casablanca, or his foxy Prince John in *The Adventures of Robin Hood* now I have learnt that he was born in Clapham and spent his spare time farming in Pennsylvania. The film's screenplay was written by R.C. Sherriff, author of the affecting and pioneering First World War drama *Journey's End*, who embarked on his first play, I also note, to raise money to help Kingston Rowing Club buy a new boat.

Hackett

Roman Catholics, especially Roman Catholics with Irish associations, recognise Father Jack Hackett with that mixture of delight, horror and awe which so much of Roman Catholicism so often provokes. Father Jack is also an example of the sense of humour that is Roman Catholicism's saving grace. Non-Catholics imagine that Father Jack, a drunken, cursing, semi-conscious psychotic banished to a remote Irish island along with two other priests, one a complete simpleton, the other a half-simple vain rogue, is a grotesque exaggeration, an inspired imagining. Catholics just laugh. And thank God for Arthur Mathews and Graham Linehan, the writers of the *Father Ted* sitcom and acute but affectionate parodists of their remarkable clergymen. Jack has issues with hygiene: he keeps a hamper of used underwear in his bedroom, in which a visiting and preciously fastidious assistant to a bishop was once trapped. Jack is unfussy about his drink, often taking a cleaning product or two. He was sober in one episode, but that fearful experience has not been repeated. Jack, when conscious, has a limited vocabulary: 'Feck!' and 'Drink!' being particularly prominent. Jack is unpredictably violent. But he is also strangely likeable, even when responding to a polite request from Mrs Doyle, the feyly distracted housekeeper, 'What would you say to a nice cup of tea?' with 'Feck off, cup!' This could be because we admire a man who has taken such a consistent stand against hypocrisy and the impossibility of leading a flock through this vale of tears. Or it could be because he is fecking funny. My enjoyment has been greatly increased by learning that Frank Kelly, who plays Father Jack, is a greatly cultured man who likes nothing more than a bit of vigorous exercise, including sea bathing all year round. And the reported inspiration for his acting career, a cartoon of a clown on stage, sad beneath a fusillade of ire and objects from the audience, chimes pretty well with Jack's plight: 'It seemed to me like a kind of Calvary, a kind of triumph over adversity by perseverance and smiling on.' Well, not so much the smiling, obviously; more a crazed leer.

HALPERN

This Jack, though not as well known as others, yields to none for a CV simply simmering with Jackness. Jack is a lexicographer specialising in Japanese, Chinese, Korean and Arabic. He was born in Germany and has lived in Japan for 30 years. He is the founder of the Japanese Yiddish Club. His favourite language is Brazilian Portuguese and his favourite hobby is unicycling, often while playing his quena, an Andean flute. Jack is also on the advisory board of the Lifeboat Foundation, which advocates the launching of cosmic arks to protect our species from total annhilation by environmental or terrorist disasters down here. Question: on the whole, would you rather Jack brought the unicyle and flute onto the ark, or not?

HAMMER

What a great name for a porn star! Actually, his real name, Troy Dean Mainwaring, is not bad either. Sadly, or rather, fortunately, Jack is not in a position to add to his 300-film oeuvre just at present, as he is back in jail serving his sentence for armed robbery after violating parole by threatening and assaulting his then wife and frequent co-star, Sweetie Pie. But he should be out by 2013 and meanwhile is seeking pen pals.

HANNA

Jack Hanna is a former American zookeeper who favours a khaki safari suit and is well known for his television appearances and shows, often introducing the likes of David Letterman and Larry King to various exotic species. In 1995 he introduced a cougar to Newt Gingrich which bit him on the chin.

HANRAHAN

Take a look at the credits of Jack Hanrahan, comedy writer: *Rowan and Martin's Laugh-In*, *Inspector Gadget* and *Get Smart*. That last, featuring Maxwell Smart, secret agent, devised by Mel Brooks and Buck Henry, and recent recipient of a tribute movie, was a particular favourite: I trust it was Jack who wrote the sketch where Smart orders his dog to stand up and sit down again. The dog doesn't move. 'Quick, isn't he?' says Smart. 'Want to see it again?' Anyway, after living the life you would expect from a gag-writer called Jack Hanrahan (even if he did do some *Waltons*), Jack was discovered living in a Cleveland shelter for the homeless in 2007, sans teeth, sans about almost everything except his sense of humour. The *Cleveland Plain Dealer* wrote up his story, and old friends moved him into a nursing home, where he died a year later, still making with the gags, still working on his memoirs and confiding, 'I'm a lucky bum.'

HANWAY

Jonas Hanway (1712–86) was sometimes known as Jack but more often behaved in keeping with a Jonas. Merchant, philanthropist and tireless campaigner, he founded a number of charities and produced 85 published works, including *A Journal of Eight Days' Journey from Portsmouth to Kingston upon Thames*, *An Essay on Tea* and *A Comprehensive View of Sunday Schools*. Charles Wilson, the historian, called him 'one of the most indefatigable and splendid bores of English history'; Dr Johnson was no more impressed. And yet this was a man who had travelled through Russia and Persia, where he was captured by rebellious Khyars and escaped in disguise. And a man who walked through the streets of London carrying both a sword, long out of fashion, and an umbrella, previously in fashion only for the gentler sex. 'But,' as Egon Jameson puts it in his indispensable *1000 Curiosities of Britain* (1937), 'Mr Hanway simply ignored the contemptuous gestures of his shocked compatriots and strutted abroad . . . For he had learnt, during his travels in Persia, of the undeniable advantage of being able to go out in the rain without getting wet and would not have dreamt, after that, of dispensing with this blessed device.' Nor, either, the flannel underwear and several pairs of stockings he habitually wore against the cold and infection. Hanway was the first philanthropist to be commemorated in Westminster Abbey; for some time an umbrella was known as a Hanway. Nevertheless, as the *DNB* puts it, pithily if pitilessly, 'his writings were too dreary and too closely tied to issues of the day to endure'. So, please, next time you raise your brolly, think kindly on Jack.

HARGREAVES

For late twentieth-century and increasingly urban Britain, Jack Hargreaves was the link with a countryside which was becoming increasingly remote from everyday experience. Sitting in a barn dressed in tweeds, waders and wearing a fly-festooned fishing hat, he would introduce his long-running television programme, *Out of Town*, talking simply and engagingly and scriptlessly about laying hedges or baiting a hook. Being a Jack, some of this simplicity was not quite as it seemed. The barn was in a corner of a studio, and Jack was also for 12 years the deputy controller of programmes, including his own, at Southern Television. Yet further from the gently bucolic image, he had also been managing editor of that sharply edged and focused international news magazine, *Picture Post*, and editor of *Lilliput*, a literary magazine whose tastes would be most closely identified today with *The Erotic Review* and whose contributors included Ronald Searle, Bill Brandt, Nancy Mitford and Aleister Crowley. Moreover, and most Jackishly, his obituary in *The Independent* commented: 'Hargreaves, complete with pipe, battered trilby and old bodywarmers, was keen to perpetuate the story that he was from a Yorkshire farming family, although he was actually born in London. Those who worked with him had no doubt that he moved to the country and became knowledgeable about its ways, but they were never quite sure how much of his background was reality and how much myth.'

HARKAWAY

'Real *Boy's Own Paper* stuff' has long been journalistic shorthand for colourful stories involving remarkable adventures. The *Boy's Own Paper* was founded in 1879 as a moral improvement on the slightly racier boys' comics of the time, which were themselves introduced as an improvement on the Victorian Penny Dreadfuls and Penny Bloods. Jack Harkaway, who first escaped with one bound (from school) in 1871 in *The Boys of England*, continued asserting British superiority by righting wrongs around the Empire and beyond, usually by direct method. Jack was the creation of Bracebridge Hemyng, an Old Etonian barrister who required a supplement to his income in the early days of his practice. Jack was such a success that newsagents were reputed to fight over copies; Hemyng was poached by an American publisher to write Jack there, and for a time lived in some style on Staten Island. He returned to London, where he continued writing and practising law. But Jack declined in popularity and Hemyng's prowess at the Bar can be judged by the ironic fate for a Penny Dreadful writer of dying penniless. If you can take more, the first edition of one of his later efforts, *The Stockbroker's Wife and*

Other Sensational Tales of The Stock Exchange, will cost you about £500; and, in earlier life, Hemyng had helped Henry Mayhew interview London's poor and destitute.

HARKNESS

And here's twenty-first-century real *Boy's Own Paper* stuff, with Captain Jack Harkness, hunky bisexual hero of the *Doctor Who* spin-off (and anagram) *Torchwood*, featuring alien activity investigated by a team based in Cardiff (it's made by BBC Wales). Actually, Captain Jack is from the fifty-first century, 'so of course he's going to go out with men and women', as Russell T. Davies, his inventor, and re-inventor of *Doctor Who*, puts it. He has kissed the Doctor and been involved in simultaneous hanky-panky with two Cybermen (on that very twentieth-century impressionist programme *Dead Ringers*). Jack is played by John Barrowman, a gay Scot raised in Illinois, who was turned down for the leading gay role in the US sitcom *Will and Grace* because he appeared 'too straight'; the part went to Eric McCormack, who is heterosexual. John and partner have a **Jack Russell** (qv) called, as you would expect, Captain Jack. Davies named the character after Agatha Harkness, an American comic-book witch; the Jack bit allows him to be a lad as well (see **Captain Jack Sparrow**). Just to complicate matters in an entertainingly Whovian way, Jack Harkness is not the time-traveller's real name but one he borrowed from a deceased officer during his visit to the Second World War. Coincidentally or not, another – and real – Jack Harkness (1919–94) held the rank of captain during the Second World War. He was a rose-grower, writing well and wittily about them, and producing acclaimed floribundas, teas, miniatures, a shrub called Cardinal Hume and a ground cover called Fairyland.

HARRISON

A great lost Jack, a thrilling rugby player, a winger of searing speed, grace and sudden swerve, with only three seasons but ninety-one tries behind him and who knows how many ahead of him when he was cut down in an international fixture of the unsporting kind. But Jack was not a man of Twickenham or the Old Whatevers; Jack played rugby league, the northern game, the unfashionable, working-class one, for money: Jack is the only professional sportsman to win a Victoria Cross: in France, in 1917. Three years before, Jack had taken a gem of a pass from his centre, the legendary Billy Batten, to score the late try against Wakefield Trinity that won Hull the Challenge Cup final. In 1915 he volunteered for France, and was commissioned temporary Second Lieutenant in the 11th Battalion of the East Yorkshire Regiment. In March 1917 he was awarded the Military Medal for conspicuous gallantry. The next month, Jack took off on the run of his life, across no-man's-land, towards the German machine gun pinning down his men. He is reported as moving at speed, swerving between barbed wire, dodging shell holes, through enemy fire. Then Hull's Hero went down, never to be seen again, not there, or at the Boulevard, or Fartown, or Belle Vue, or Knowsley Road, or at any of the other great rugby-league grounds, flying down his wing to the roar of the crowd, not guns. But he was carrying a grenade and the gun was destroyed; it was Jack's last try. Jack was a man of imagination, a schoolteacher: who knows what thoughts, what comparisons, went through his head on that final lung-bursting swerving, sprinting run; who knows what the Germans made of this lone figure racing for their line out of the dark with the guile and balance and bravery learnt on Yorkshire mud. He was 26. The one complaint about Jack as a rugby player was that he was a touch timid. 'Before the beginning of next season,' wrote a reporter in the *Hull Daily Mail* in 1914, 'I am more than confident that the East Hull lad will be found in a more fearless mood.' Indeed. Coincidentally, or not, the next year, another Jack VC, Private **Jack Harvey** of the London Regiment, also rushed a machine gun post alone, but was luckier.

HATT

There were, Jack Hatt once grumbled to me in his old age, no real characters left in the English countryside. Then he had a thought: 'Well, I suppose, when you think about it, I'm a bit of a character myself, wouldn't you say so?' Indeed I would. He was 76 when I met him and it took a long time to describe him, starting with agricultural contractor, explosive creation of water features a speciality, 'dam and blast' his slogan, fine fisherman, crack shot, raconteur, rarely seen without fishing-fly-festooned deerstalker, copious sidewhiskers, stick with deerhorn handle which doubled as whistle for summoning his Labrador, and possessor of a voice which any Oxfordshire town crier would kill for. Jack loved life, his life, and talking about it. There was the 98lb shark, the 14½lb sea-trout, and the day in Scotland, on the Dee, when he caught five salmon to the intense disgust of his fellows, who had caught nothing for four days: 'They were spitting!' said Jack, happy at the memory. There was, too, his acclaimed feat of shooting three birds from one covey with one gun, performed most famously on the Duke of Wellington's estate: 'First with the choke barrel, second with the open barrel, then reload the choke barrel. First bird, 50 yards out, second 30 yards out, third 30 yards behind. You get about two and a half seconds to reload. It was bloody beautiful.' Jack used to tell his stories after dinners. There was the one about the old boy in 1923 who used to listen to the Greenwich Time Signal on the wireless and then put his watch forward by 20 minutes to allow for the time the signal took to get to Oxfordshire. 'Since he liked a drop of port, and could get through a bottle with his main course,' wrote Duff Hart-Davis of Jack in *The Independent*, 'his stories tended to become rather fruity – and many a time, after the first few salvoes, the vicar was seen creeping ashen-faced for the exit. But Jack Hatt's high spirits and vitality enlivened everyone who knew him.' The year after I met him, Jack lost his first wife, Gene, after 50 years of marriage. Two years after that, he married again. Jack told me a man could go on fishing until he was 90, provided he didn't fall in. And that's what Jack did and didn't, and that was the age when he died.

HAWKINS

Two Jack Hawkinses, both models for a certain type of Englishman, and a certain type of Jack. Sir John Hawkins (1532-95) was a privateer second only to Francis Drake. With great charm, and adept at the intrigue in which the Elizabethans so enthusiastically overindulged, he was also a man of adventure, undertaking several rewarding expeditions to the New World, tacking, like Drake, between peaceful trading and a rather more direct negotiating manner. His careful preparations founded the Royal Navy's success against the Armada; he ensured better ships, pay and conditions for ordinary seamen. But he also began the English part in the slave trade, shipping Africans to Hispaniola. Some seek to excuse him as a slave to prevalent mores; and his religious convictions, converted from the Catholic to the Puritan, certainly impressed his queen: 'God's death! This fool went out a soldier and has come home a divine,' exclaimed Elizabeth after reading a letter of his of 1590, five years before his death in Puerto Rico on Drake's doomed and roundly fatal expedition to capture Panama. But let us leave him with a Jack touch – he took 17 musicians with him on that last voyage. The second Hawkins is the actor (1910-73), a stalwart Jack, steady, often in uniform, what England expected in the 1950s, with a unique gravel-and-honey voice until his fatal cancer cruelly stole it away, leaving him dubbed, diminished but still more heroic.

Mention should also be made of a third Hawkins, who changed his name to Hedley to avoid confusion, but is nevertheless also an actor of the same school, besides, of course, voicing the parrot in the James Bond film *For Your Eyes Only*.

HAYS

Jack Hays (1817–83) was an early Texas Ranger. He fought large numbers of Indians and Mexicans, rushed for gold in California and helped found Oakland. Small, slim, commanding and apparently fearless, he received this tribute from Flacco, the Apache chief: 'Me and Red Wing aren't afraid to go to hell together. Captain Jack, he's too mucho bravo. He's not afraid to go to hell all by himself.'

HAYWARD

Sir Jack, born 1923 in Wolverhampton, a long ball from Molineux, home of his beloved Wanderers, the Wolves, seems more of a John Bull than a Jack, but his anglo-philanthrophy, or willingness to follow his regard for all things English with his wallet, has made the 'Union Jack Hayward' nickname irresistible. This is, after all, the man who bought Wolves to save them and insisted that only Elgar be played to telephone callers; the man whose gate bore the message 'No unauthorised or foreign vehicles', and who listed his recreations in *Who's Who* as 'keeping all things bright, beautiful and British'; and the man who, over the years, bought Lundy Island for the National Trust, saved the SS *Great Britain*, and sponsored both women's cricket and the Liberal Party. Such an arresting combination, though, suggests an element of Jackishness which he has richly borne out elsewhere, choosing to live mostly, for example, not in England, but the Bahamas, source of his property development riches. Sir Jack also has a way with words: he has described his children as 'being in the inheritance business' and himself as a 'golden tit' during his extravagant but ultimately unsuccessful ownership of Wolves. He is also responsible for one of the finest misreported remarks of recent times: 'We've got the worst team in the First Division and I've no doubt that we'll have the worst team in the Premiership.' He was, in fact, referring to the tea.

HICKATHRIFT

Jack, sometimes known as Tom, Hickathrift is a fabled figure in East Anglia, a local variation on Jack the Giant Killer, and well enough known more widely to be mentioned aside and without explanation by Laurence Sterne in his classic eighteenth-century comic work, *Tristram Shandy*. Jack is a strong and quick-witted fellow, once picking up a passing miller (that always unpopular middleman) and using him to beat the Giant of Tilney to death. Such exploits give the lie to the theory that the natives east of Cambridge lack a little in lightness and wit. This, for example, is an East Anglian joke: two men in a descending hot air balloon shout to an old Suffolk chap, 'Where are we?' The old chap replies, 'You're in a balloon.' Also, The Nutshell, in Bury St Edmunds, the smallest pub in Britain, measuring seven and a half foot by fifteen foot, has a sign on the wall which reads 'Coach Parties Welcome'. And the barman's name when I was last there was Jack.

HIGGINS

Jack Higgins (born 1929) is the best-selling thriller-writer most famous for *The Eagle Has Landed*. His real name is Harry Patterson: the *nom de plume* was taken from a Northern Irish great-uncle with a suitably gritty back-story involving Protestant extremism and a secret drawer full of handguns under his Belfast stairs. Higgins is but one of several names that he writes under, including his own. Multiple identities are essential for prolific writers whose publishers are wary of exhausting the market: Ian Rankin, author of the Rebus stories, came up with **Jack Harvey**, similarly concocted from family connections, with the added advantage of 'H' placing it in the middle of the bookshop shelves, and because 'maybe fans of Jack Higgins would be tricked into buying my titles instead of his'. Sounds like a promising start to a thriller in which one author assassinates another. Watch out for my next effort, *The Dead Beagle on the Landing in the Edinburgh Tenement*, by Rebus Huggins.

HINTON

Jack Hinton was one of those quiet, unassuming Jacks who nevertheless have a strong sense of independence and what is right. Above all, they do not like being messed about. Sergeant Hinton, serving in the New Zealand army, found himself in 1941 caught up in the desperate, doomed attempt to prevent the Germans and Italians capturing Greece. Falling back to evacuate from Kalamata, New Zealand and British forces found themselves cut off from the sea by German troops, and were ordered to pull back. Hinton, who had already had a frank exchange of views with his commanding officer, General Bernard Freyberg VC, over the effect of short rations on his men's efficiency, was not impressed. According to the official account, he shouted, 'To hell with this, who'll come with me?', and launched a frontal attack on the nearest German gun, which he destroyed with two grenades. He then 'came on with the bayonet' and 'dealt' with numbers of Germans who had fled into nearby houses. Hinton's attack merely delayed the inevitable and cost him a severe wound and capture; but it won him the VC and the admiration of his comrades then and his country ever thereafter. He was given a state funeral in 1997, when he was described in his eulogy as 'a rough diamond'. The unofficial version of what he said that day in Kalamata is 'Fuck that, who's coming with me?' I know which I prefer.

HOBBS

An unusual Jack. Not so much in the background – Jack Hobbs was the eldest of 12 children of a Cambridge slater's labourer; not so much, either, in his success in his chosen career as a gloriously gifted batsman, acknowledged as the finest England has produced, rewarded by the first knighthood awarded to an English professional sportsman. No, it's more that Jack Hobbs was too modest, equable, courtly, dignified, just too, well, nice, for a proper Jack. Jack was embarrassed by his fame, by his knighthood, by almost everything. Jack was nice to everyone, including the ones who had just got him out. Jack never forgot it was a game. This is John Arlott, the great cricket writer, commentator and poet, in his biography of Jack, on the great man's dismissal in a vital Test match, by a bad ball which had taken an eccentric turn and his wicket: 'After looking for a moment completely flabbergasted, Jack threw back his head and laughed . . . Perhaps Jack Hobbs was wrong to regard cricket as a matter of mirth. Yet, in that same summer, he had set a new record for an individual total of runs in Tests between England and Australia . . .' He also scored more first-class runs and more first-class centuries than any other cricketer, beating W.G. Grace's record for the latter on a Monday in 1926 after going to church on the Sunday and being followed around England by a growing cavalcade.

Even the plummy, pompous toffs who dominated the game in his day, the ones with the initials, the silly nicknames and the airs, liked and respected Jack, the professional to their amateur in every way. Jack had an unsilly nickname, The Master, but he preferred to be known as Jack. He made his first-class debut in 1905 against a team captained by Grace, and played his last first-class game in 1934, at the age of 51. He makes an interesting comparison with Grace, a doctor from Gloucester with, how shall we say, a pronounced competitive edge: as one bowler cried in triumph after clean bowling Grace at the end of a frustrating session which had seen W.G. refuse to budge despite several questionable incidents: 'You're surely not going, Doctor? There's a stump still standing.' The most Jackish thing I could find about Jack was that he liked practical jokes, although he did develop a weakness for champagne, but only if there were two other people to share the bottle. I'm afraid, too, that we must enter a similar saving caveat for the practical jokes. In his early days, for example, he used to love seizing the hat of the fastidious gentleman who kept the score for his county, Surrey, and then kicking it around a bit. But, being this Jack, he used to buy him a new one afterwards. But this Jack, too, still conjures lost summers, bright light and long shadows, the sharp crack of bat on ball, applause, laughter, the settled, stately and understood ritual, nature tamed, the English way: Jack on the Green, not in it.

HOGGAN

If you wanted to make a name for yourself as a painter, would you stick with Jack Hoggan? Of course you wouldn't. See **Jack Vettriano**.

HORNER

> Little Jack Horner
> Sat in the corner
> Eating a Christmas pie;
> He put in his thumb,
> And pulled out a plum,
> And said, What a good boy am I!

Endlessly fascinating things, nursery rhymes: always simple, often nonsensical, but full of arresting and, of course, memorable imagery. No wonder they attract so much speculation: see **Jack and Jill** (qv) and **Jack and the Beanstalk** (qv), for example. Jack ones seem especially mischievous, with much knavery guaranteed. Little Jack Horner has been the subject of much persuasive theorising. The most popular one is that Richard Whiting, last abbot of the great abbey at Glastonbury, sent his steward, Jack Horner, to London with a Christmas gift for Henry VIII which he hoped might spare the richest foundation in the kingdom from the worst of the Dissolution. This was a pie in which were hidden the title deeds of 12 manors owned by the monks. But Jack is supposed to have had a quick peek inside on the way up and snaffled a plum of a deed for himself. Fantastic, you say: but a Thomas Horner became lord of the manor of nearby Mells shortly after the Dissolution and his descendants live in the manor house at Mells to this day. And to this day they stoutly defend their ancestor's probity against what must be one of the most sustained and popular pieces of defamation in history. They have much on their side, too, including the price Thomas paid – £1,831 9s 1¾d – and the good word of John Leland, the noted antiquary, who in his *Itinerary* (1543) states that, 'Mr Horner hath boute [bought] the lordship of the King'. They also quite reasonably mention that their man's name was Thomas, not Jack. Against that, as those distinguished and indispensable nurseryists, Iona and Peter Opie, point out, 'Then, as now, anybody might be called Jack, particularly if he was believed to be a knave.' Rising above that gratuitous side swipe, Jackists like the Opies' further point that the rhyme could still have been aimed at Thomas Horner even if the allegation was a lie: Thomas, after all, was not only a king's man; he was also on the jury which condemned Whiting to be taken up to the Tor high above Glastonbury and there hanged. But there is no trace of the anti-Mells Horner theory until the nineteenth century; and the clincher for me is that Henry, being clever as well as greedy, would surely have thought 11 a suspicious number, and spotted the cracks in the pie crust. Besides, I live near Mells and wouldn't like any unpleasantness in the post office.

HOUSE

This is the house that Jack built, the one in which he kept malt, thus producing attendant consequences, one fatal (the rat), for a large number of species, including a cat, dog, a cow with a crumpled horn, a forlorn milk maid, a forward but ill-clothed fellow who has just got married (to the maid or someone else, possibly a shaven and shorn priest, the text is not clear), a cock and a farmer. It has been linked with a Hebrew chant, 'Chad Gadyo', first printed in Prague in 1590, which has a similarly accumulative construction, but a more impressive cast list, including the Angel of Death, as well as a cat and a dog and a kid bought for two coins. It has been interpreted as an allegory of Hebrew history; nothing convincing has been advanced for Jack's construction. Wolf Mankowitz wrote 'A Kid for Two Farthings', a numinous modern fairy tale of Jewish life in the London East End of the 1950s, which revolved around a sickly kid goat with one crumpled horn which makes magic because a small boy wants it to, until, of course, he has to grow up. Mankowitz (1924–98) was a man of perhaps too many talents who is also responsible for the Bond films, having introduced Cubby Broccoli to Harry Saltzman. At least Jack's house wasn't built by Jerry, a mysterious figure whose byword botching first appeared in Victorian times.

HOWARTH

Since we are dealing with names, has there ever been a more evocatively exact one than Albert Tatlock, Uncle Albert, late of *Coronation Street*? Albert was a veteran of war whose principal role in the soap opera appeared to be as the representative of the one in every family who complains that things are not what they used to be, even if they had included global conflict, mass murder and genocide. No matter to Uncle Albert: everything was the cue for a tart mutter. It was a part played to perfection by John Aubrey

Conroy Howarth, known as Jack, son of the comedian Bert Howarth, of Rochdale, Lancashire. Jack had a highly distinguished acting career elsewhere, which included playing Tubby Wadlow in David Lean's 1953 film of *Hobson's Choice* and Mr Maggs, the lugubrious handyman and husband of Mrs Maggs, the charlady of Mrs Dale in that early and very successful radio soap, *Mrs Dale's Diary*; but it was as Albert that he made his mark. I had the privilege of working on *Coronation Street* in a very minor capacity, and watched with appreciation the way in which Jack became Albert by the simple and only device of applying a bit of burnt cork to his top lip. There were those, too, who claimed that he was merely playing an extension of himself; and while I would never argue that he was an exuberant and bonhomous presence around the set, I do remember that after he was the subject of *This Is Your Life*, he did carry the tape of the programme around with him for what seemed like several weeks. Jack died in 1984; some prefer his successor as the Corrie Curmudgeon, Bill Waddington as Percy Sugden; but while conceding that Percy's line 'When you've made gravy under gunfire you can do anything' is a fine one, I still prefer, for its truth, this, between Albert and Minnie Caldwell, on the prospects for their engagement:

ALBERT: Have you got summat to tell me?

MINNIE: Yes, Albert, I'm afraid I have.

ALBERT: Well, if you got summat to say, spit it out instead of rabbitin' on about nothin'.

MINNIE: I am not rabbitin' on about nothin', Albert, I am definitely rabbitin' on about somethin'.

ALBERT: What?

MINNIE: Our future life together. I don't think we got one.

Two further and final points of interest: he wore the same suit for his 33 years of appearances as Albert; and he married his wife, Betty Murgatroyd, in Hull in 1927 between a matinee and an evening peformance of *Frankenstein*.

HOWE

Jack Howe is probably the most famous sheep shearer of all time, with the possible exception of that notable Tasmanian, Errol Flynn, who had a go before he was famous. (In my youth, after his death, Flynn was most famous for the alleged size of his procreative equipment. 'Have you got a match?' was a request usually met with, 'Not since Errol Flynn', which was mildly amusing the first time. Flynn tackled the subject in his delightfully entitled memoir, *My Wicked, Wicked Ways*, describing an unsuccessful amatory encounter with a euphemism far superior to the one I've just attempted, and which I still recall with admiration and awe: 'I was too big a man for the front of a sports car.') But, Jack Howe. In 1892, he set the record for a daily shear, 321 sheep, and for a weekly shear, 1,437, which still stands. The sheep didn't argue: Jack weighed 18 stone, with a 50-inch chest, 27-inch thigh, 17-inch biceps and, according to the *Australian Dictionary of Biography*, hands the size of small tennis rackets. His father had less success with llamas (they spat at him). The flannel shirt worn by shearers is still widely known as a 'Jacky Howe'.

HOXIE

Jack Hoxie (1885–1965) was a cowboy, rodeo star and wild west show and film star included here mostly because of the splendid names of his four wives: Hazel Panky, Marin Sais, Dixie Starr and Bonnie Avis Showalter.

HUBERMAN

Jack Huberman is a Canadian liberal who was never keen on George W. Bush. He has written *The Bush-Hater's Handbook: A Guide to the Most Appalling Presidency of the Past 100 Years*, and several other fusillades in a left–right direction. So far, so not that particularly unusual. But Huberman has gone a little further by changing nationalities in order to vote against Bush in 2004. That's a Jack.

HULBERT

Westminster schoolboy, Cambridge Footlight, light comedy actor, singer and dancer, long-chinned, slightly goofy, endlessly amiable, Jack Hulbert (1892–1978), perhaps even more than **Jack Buchanan** (qv), was the acme of that artful artlessness much in vogue in Britain between the wars and which sorts out the Jacks from the Johns, who tend to prefer recognition for their hard and serious work. Indeed, as Jack's obituarist in *The Times* had it: 'His Christian name was typical of the man. He was Jack – a jack tar, a bulldog jack, a jack-of-all-trades, a jack of infinite jollity and resource. The chin protruded with an amiable and jack-like resolution. He was not to be cowed or overawed. Nonplussed occasionally, it is true, and often outmanoeuvred, but never suppressed or depressed.' Jack and his wife, the equally winning Cicely Courtneidge, had a legendarily long career together, but it took them into a less sympathetic age. For a theatrical melancholy, little can improve on *Once More with Music*, the show based on their life story in which they toured the provinces in 1976, the year of their golden wedding, but which never made it to their old home, the West End.

HYLTON

Jack Hylton (1895–1965), the son of a Bolton mill worker, was a dance band leader and impresario who first brought Eric Morecambe and Ernie Wise together. Fellow nostalgics of a certain age will relish this report from *The Times* of a televised tribute to him in 1965:

> The show ranged from Miss Marlene Dietrich, dressed with stunning simplicity to sing three of her most famous songs, to the Crazy Gang doing their Piccadilly flower-sellers sketch, and from the splendours of Camelot to the charming oddity of Mr Peter O'Toole singing 'Oh, My Papa' . . . Some of the simplest contributions were among the most effective: Miss Vera Lynn singing in her own familiar manner 'Mister Wonderful', Mr Spike Milligan cheerfully improvising his way through a few unpredictable moments . . . All in all, it was a remarkable bill – not least for the final spectacle of Miss Dietrich arm in arm with Miss Sophie Tucker.

Collectors of curiosities will note the interesting assertion in the *DNB* that Sir Edward Elgar wrote an arrangement for Jack's band. More? On 4 September 1927 Jack took his band in an Imperial Airways biplane from Croydon to Blackpool, circling the tower and playing a new song ('Me and Jane in a 'Plane') while copies of its sheet music were hurled out to flutter down upon the holiday-makers below.

I'M ALL RIGHT JACK

The Boulting Brothers, Roy and John, are held to have made inferior films to those of Ealing, but that is because their output was more satirical and more of its time, a time of change and uncertainty, rather than nostalgic for a lost and often fictional Britain. *I'm All Right Jack* (1959) was perhaps their most famous and certainly their most socially influential film.

It boasted the usual Boulting repertory company of unusually skilled film actors, notably Dennis Price, Terry-Thomas, John Le Mesurier, Irene Handl, Margaret Rutherford and Peter Sellers, whose role as Fred Kite, the romantic Stalinist of a shop steward – 'Ahhh, Russia. All them corn fields and ballet in the evening' – came to define and harden popular (middle-class) attitudes towards the British trades unions from then until their decline and emasculation by Margaret Thatcher in the 1980s. It seems fashionable now to mock the plot, but I'm not really sure why when it concerns conspiring capitalist bosses ready to betray their complacent workers in pursuit of a fat Middle Eastern contract to be secured by liberal bribery.

Sellers was rarely better than as Kite, giving a sad nobility to a type popularly mocked in Britain, the self-consciously self-improving. Kite's wife was played by Irene Handl, an actress who specialised in cuddly English working-class women but was in reality the daughter of a Viennese banker and a French mother, and the acclaimed author of two charged and literary novels, *The Sioux* and *The Gold Tip Pfitzer*. It was Miss Handl who so magnificently responded to a later young director attempting to explain her motivation: 'Sorry, darling, I'm afraid you're confusing me with one of those actresses who gives a toss.' The title of the film comes from Stanley Windrush, the young, naive and Candidesque catalyst played by Ian Carmichael, commenting on the prevailing industrial and social ethos: 'Wherever you look it's a case of "Blow you, Jack, I'm all right."'

IN THE BOX

This most often refers to the toy box with the springed figure that leaps up when the lid is opened. As usual, its origins are misty. The most beguiling explanation is that it comes from Sir John Schorne, a saintly English clergyman of the thirteenth century who was reputed to have saved his Buckinghamshire parishioners from Satan by trapping the old devil in his boot. A spring discovered by Sir John near his church in North Marston was brimming with gypsum, Epsom salts and carbonic acid, very good for the rheumatics. As its efficacy and fame spread, so did the cult of Sir John, who was always depicted with the detained demon. He is also said to have had extremely knobbly knees from all his kneeling to pray. Sir John was thought to be the ideal figure to get St George's Chapel, Windsor, off to a good start, and so a fine shrine to him was the first thing built, which brought the pilgrim punters (and their cash) rolling in. He also remained popular at North Marston, despite the detection of some unholy work by one of his successors who claimed to have discovered the blessed skull, complete with three bloody wounds.

It all came to an end, of course, with the Reformation: Sir John's statue was sent to London for destruction and his chapel was made over as a tomb for Edward Clinton, the first Earl of Lincoln. This seems a bit rich for a fair-weather courtier and unremarkable soldier and sailor who had married a mistress of Henry VIII, helped lose Calais, burnt Edinburgh and had already been given one monastery and three priories, but there you go. As for Sir John and his boot/box, the first mention of the toy is not until 1702, which seems a long stride. Interestingly, one of the alternative meanings in the OED is a slighting reference to a consecrated communion host in its pyx, or container. Another theory is that the Jack is an escaped and recaptured slave from the Americas, but the name of its inventor there, in 1832, John Schorne, is too much of a coincidence even for me. The best bet seems its earlier usage for 'a thief who deceived tradesmen by substituting empty boxes for others full of money'.

The more venerable among you might remember that Clodagh Rodgers secured fourth place in the 1971 Eurovision Song Contest with an appropriately lively ditty of the same name, which we could all hum together now, if you like. Ms Rodgers went on to much success, and most lately appeared in an episode of *The Bill*, the series named after a popular sobriquet of the Metropolitan Police which no one seems entirely sure about, either.

IN THE GREEN

As I mentioned when discussing the Daddy of Jacks, Bacchus, there is much scholarly concern about recent imaginative explorations seeking to synthesise all legendary, fabled and folkloric things green into a coherent account reaching right back to where the mists of time and dense forests conceal the enjoyable magical ceremonies we practised before we had to grow up, settle down, start tilling the fields, gather together in increasingly concentrated areas so as to enjoy the economies of scale and communication, and be sensible. But rigour and caution are not the conventional characteristics of Jacks; and, in any case, call me old-fashioned, but I should have thought that, in the matter of legends, the search for facts and certainty is even more fanciful.

Besides, it seems pretty obvious that the chaps you come across today dressed fetchingly in foliage in May Day ceremonies across the land are in a line that stretches back and around through May Day, spring and fertility festivals and includes Robin Hood, the Green Knight, the Green Man, Bacchus, Adam and Eve and the apple as symbols and reminders of the attractions and threat of the untamed natural world. Experts point out there is no written evidence of Jacks in the Green, the men hidden beneath a tall basket covered in leaves, before they appeared in British towns and cities in the nineteenth century cavorting about with other chimney sweeps dressed in mock finery on May Day in the hope of a handsome gratuity. We point to the natural cycles, conservative instincts and long memories through British history that see spring festivals fading away and then being reborn in response to changes in society, whether they be the coming of the Romans, Christians, Saxons, Normans, feudalism, enclosure, Oliver Cromwell, the Restoration, the Enlightenment, increasing urbanisation or the rise of environmentalism.

And throughout it, too, Jack, the unruly, the one rarely in danger of being pronounced civilised; or dull. So here we go, then: who's for a quick hey, nonny, no and a Shepherd's Hey? Ready?

Dance at 4/3 quick-step, mark time; left hand hanging loose, until last half-bar, when it is thrown up. Right hand holds stick across the body, the stick slanting upward towards the right shoulder. Two bars from end leader calls 'All in'. All jump on last half-bar, and throw up both hands. There, that wasn't too difficult, was it? Fancy a go at the Bean-Setting Dance? Pretty apt for a Jack, and fairly straightforward, once you've got the hang of dibbing. Oy, mind that stick, my deario: you nearly had me wonglers there!

IN-THE-PULPIT

A North American wild flower that grows in moist woodlands, flood plains, thickets and swampy or boggy areas. They are also called Indian turnips or bog onions. I was confident that a Jack-in-the pulpit would have a narcotic, drowsy effect, but this does not seem to be the case, although it can be toxic if taken without adequate precautions.

JACK

Never underestimate the effect of the sound of a word. Consider, for example, why one certain Anglo-Saxon word is so universally and often applied: there's nothing quite like the 'ck' ending for forceful expression of emotions; and nothing quite like it for expelling them. Likewise, if you're looking for a short word, easy to hear, difficult to mispronounce, Jack's the lad. That's why the *OED* gives no fewer than 70 different uses and meanings for the word, and at least 80 further words which are formed in combination with Jack. Short of a quick handle? Go for Jack.

Jack can be, in the words of the *OED*, 'a generic proper name for any representative of the common people'. Jack can be 'a form of address to an unknown person'. Or he can be any 'serving-man or male attendant, a labourer, a man who does odd jobs, etc.'. Or, by extension, a jack can be any tool or piece of equipment taking the place of a servant, thus the jack for changing wheels. Jack can also imply small, as with the jack in bowls.

Actually, if we're being frank, it seems that a certain lack of imagination in the name game has resulted in anything that hasn't already got one being called Jack (see also any number of fish and trees). And you do get a certain sense of frustration with this from the lexicographers. Try this definition, for example: 'Applied to things which in some way take the place of a lad or man, or save human labour; also more vaguely to other things with which one has to do.' I do like that 'more vaguely'. Then there's their struggle to make sense of the 38th sense in which it is used: 'In names of animals (sometimes signifying male, sometimes small, half-sized).'

Somewhere in and around this, too, there is the echoing disapproval and unease of the educated and the élite for the uppity common person; a disapproval and unease which survives despite the definition now being marked obsolete: 'a lad, fellow, chap; esp. a low-bred or ill-mannered fellow, a knave'.

Time, I say, to cast aside old prejudice, abandon its scurrilous attachment to mass murderers (Ripper, 1888), those who behave imperiously in their positions (Jacks-in-Office, 1700) or feebly give up (jack it in, 1873). Time to salute this humble word, a true Jack of all Trades (1618), with the words of that grand old song (c. 1840):

> For if ever fellow took delight in swigging,
>
> gigging, kissing, drinking, fighting:
>
> Damme, I'll be bold to say that Jack's the lad!

JACKAL

You can't pin this one on Jacks: it derives from the Persian for scavenger, *shagal*. (For which information I am mostly indebted to the splendid research winningly entitled 'Jack: Wild Speculation and Dubious Etymology', posted by Ian Sanders, late of the Scottish Agricultural College, Aberdeen.)

JACKANORY

> I'll tell you a story
>
> About Jackanory
>
> And now my story's begun;
>
> I'll tell you another

of Jack and his brother
And now my story is done.

An old rhyme used to put an end to children's nagging. You might also be familiar with 'Are we there yet?', 'Please, Mum/Dad', 'What time's tea?', 'I'm thirsty'. I continue to extract revenge for that last one by replying, 'Hallo, I'm Friday', which really annoys them. A nineteenth-century Scottish version of the rhyme has a Joll McCrory shooting one Tory, then another. *Jackanory* is also the title of the long-running BBC storytelling programme, graced by such as Sir Ian McKellen, Dame Wendy Hiller, Margaret Rutherford, Alan Bennett, Kenneth Williams and Spike Milligan. Spike, an interesting man, used to have a picture of the crucifixion on his wall with a dedication in ballpoint at the bottom, 'To Spike'. His headstone bears the Gaelic inscription, '*Duirt me leat go raibh me breoite*', which translates as 'I told you I was ill'. It is curiously satisfying to learn that *Jackanory* used to share a studio at the BBC with Current Affairs.

JACKDAW

A fine creature, although seen by some, including William of Malmesbury, as a harbinger of doom. William, writing in the twelfth century, records calamity befalling a woman who heard a jackdaw's loud chattering – the 'Jack-Jack' from which its name derives. However, I think we must treat William with some caution, as his views were almost certainly clouded by the experience of an earlier monk at Malmesbury, Eilmer, who, after studying jackdaws, attempted to imitate them, launching himself with a pair of wings from the abbey tower, achieving a distance of 200 yards and then landing in the High Street, breaking both legs. Jackdaws have also been credited with the power of speech, especially by the ancient kings of Ireland. They are undoubtedly among the planet's most intelligent life forms: they will feed other jackdaws as well as their family, and will protect each other from human interference. They belong to the crow family, members of which have been variously reported tapping on windows, knocking on doors, removing windscreen wipers for nest-building purposes, imitating referee's whistles, picking up golf balls and dropping them in the hole, and using specially crafted leaves and twigs to hook out grubs. In Japan they have been seen placing walnuts on pelican crossings and returning to retrieve the crushed nuts when the lights turn red again. By way of inter-species contrast, there was also a report from North Carolina that week featuring two men who had been arrested after breaking into a police station and leaving a trail of cake crumbs. 'The Jackdaw of Rheims' is a mildly amusing offering by Richard Harris Barham (1788–1845) highlighting the liking of jackdaws for shiny things, in this case the ring of the Cardinal Lord Archbishop of that city. Jackdaws is a musical education charity run by Maureen Lehane Wishart in the villlage of Great Elm in Somerset. It is named after the setting written by her husband, Peter Wishart (1921–84), for 'The Jackdaw' by William Cowper. The poem is Cowper's translation from the Latin of his old schoolteacher Vincent Bourne (1695–1747) and contains this verse:

> He sees that this great roundabout
> The world, with all its motley rout,
> Church, army, physic, law,
> Its customs and its businesses,
> Is no concern at all of his,
> And says – what says he? – Caw.

Quite. Jackdaws, on the other hand, is well worth a donation: www. jackdaws.org.uk

JACKS

Very little of the definite kind seems to be known about the history of playing cards, which is not so surprising, given that those who knew or know would have been or will be far too busy playing cards to write anything down, an activity in any case inimical to many of them, especially the ones playing for money. So Western European and North American playing cards might have their roots in China, Korea, India or Arabia. Alternatively, we might even have come up with them ourselves, one rainy afternoon somewhere. That would have been some time in the 1300s, the century in which references to them suddenly appear, and in which they were already being used to relieve punters of large sums of money; and, of course, being banned (in Paris, for example, on weekdays).

The Jack is noted from the start, and seems to have some connection with the Nayb, or vizier, in the Arab pack. He was first known as the Knave, and was thus represented as a common soldier or servant, along with the King, the Queen and the Knight. Many variations followed, according to time and country, but eventually the Knight was universally dropped, as were, usually, the extra cards of the Tarot. The Ace was either high or low from the start, which many have taken as some sort of social commentary. French card-makers gained the ascendancy, as did, for a time, their printed attributions of historical and legendary characters to the court cards. The Kings, for example, were David (Spades), Charlemagne (Hearts), Julius Caesar (Diamonds) and Alexander the Great (Clubs). The Knaves, a little confusingly, were pretty posh. Diamonds: Hector of Troy; Clubs: Lancelot; Hearts: Etienne de Vignolles, Joan of Arc's irascible fellow commander; Spades: Ogier the Dane, legendary enemy then comrade of Charlemagne, who sleeps until the Danes are in mortal danger (presumably there was a problem with his alarm clock in 1940).

Later still, because of the easy confusion between K, for King, and Kn, for Knave, on the face of the cards, the Knaves became Jacks, for the usual reasons of synonymy, and specifically, it is said, borrowed from the game of All-Fours, where the trump knave was known as a Jack. The lack of cachet attaching to All-Fours (a simple, popular tavern game) is also said to be behind the curious social distinction applied by Estella to Pip in *Great Expectations*: 'He calls the knaves Jacks, this boy!' (But no more curious than the preference of the posh for the clumping and Latinate – lavatory, for example – over the French and flowing – toilet. Jacks laugh at this sort of thing, but tend, for reasons of solidarity, to visit neither the John nor the Jakes.) The four suits are similarly said to represent the various social estates; Spades (spearheads): the aristocracy; Hearts (and souls): the Church; Diamonds: the rich; Clubs (clover, pig fodder): the poor peasantry. Again, nothing is certain; but I suppose that's pretty apt, with cards.

The Jack of Spades, Jack of Hearts and King of Diamonds are in profile, while the rest of the court cards are shown in full face. Little use is made of this distinction, nor of the various accoutrements and weapons they are carrying. This opacity is catching, as no one seems exactly sure why *One-Eyed Jacks*, Marlon Brando's typically dense and only directorial offering, is called that, either. Tell you what, why don't we just get on with a game? First, though, some superstitions that might be helpful.

Bad luck follows a Black Jack. If a black deuce is turned, rap it with your knuckles and you will secure at least four trumps. Should you receive a hand entirely composed of black suits, don't bother with any long-term plans. Wear a hat while playing. Never play against a consumptive person. Or a cross-eyed man. The four of Clubs is the devil's four-poster: not good. I am indebted for this information to the *Encylopaedia of Superstitions, Folklore, and the Occult Sciences of the World* (1903) by Cora Linn Daniels and Charles MacClellan Stevans. Ms Daniels and Professor Stevans also confide: 'There is a superstition at Monte Carlo that immediately after a suicide, all those playing against the bank will win. There is, therefore, a perfect rush for the tables when the lugubrious news is known.' Mr and Mrs Radford, in their *Encyclopaedia of Superstitions*, published in 1948, concur with much of the above, and add that it is also lucky to bet with borrowed money, and that the barman at the International Sporting Club in Monte Carlo lends his at interest. They add:

As a humorous comment, the authors place on record that on the only occasion that they incurred serious losses at Monte Carlo, in a night of consistent bad luck, when their funds were exhausted, they borrowed 2,000 francs from the barman at the Sporting Club, returned to the table at which they had been playing roulette all evening – and promptly won back all their night's losses, and nearly 4,000 francs in addition!

Bonne chance! And, if you're in Monte, could you pop into the Sporting Club and see if the barman's still game?

JACKSON

Forerunners quite often get forgotten, particularly if their field is not renowned for its attention span or memory, especially if their efforts are passing or ethereal, and most often if their successors are slicker. So with Jack Jackson (1906–78), one of the first British radio presenters who could properly be described as a disc jockey. Jackson, who had been a trumpeter with Bert Ambrose and **Jack Payne** (qv), presented radio shows on the BBC and Radio Luxembourg for nearly 40 years, starting just after the Second World War. His gift was for filling the gaps between the records with patter playing off and against prepared effects in a way pioneered in comedy shows by Tommy Handley and the Goons and later taken up exuberantly by Kenny Everett and routinely by anyone less inspired. Neighing horses, deafening symphony orchestras, funny voices: Jack used them all first. Go to the website of the Radio Academy if you don't believe me. Jack was also responsible for the singing career of Jimmy Young (he kept playing 'Too Young') but, fortunately, has another even greater claim to fame: at 8.12 p.m. on 22 September 1955, Jack, appearing on ITV, announced: 'Here's the moment you've all been waiting for – it's time for a natural break.' There followed Britain's first ever TV advertisement, for Gibbs SR toothpaste. (For those who have often wondered, SR stood for sodium ricinoleate.) Other Jacksons who have inherited the Jack touch include the American president Andrew Jackson (for fighting 13 duels), the Confederate general Stonewall Jackson (for his attack not his defence), Gentleman Jackson, the prizefighter (for being a southpaw and teaching Lord Byron), and Glenda Jackson (not for the posh stuff or the politics, but for the Sand Dance with Morecambe & Wise in her and their epic Cleopatra sketch: Ernie/Mark Antony: 'Alone at last. Get the grapes out and let's get at it!').

JACKSTONES

A pretty pointless game where a number of small stones or similar objects are tossed up in the air and have to be caught in impossibly intricate ways. A bouncing ball has something to do with it as well, I think. Careful readers might just be able to detect that I was really bad at it. There is, I see, a theory that the jackstones are so called because the jacks were originally the heel bones of sheep: Jacob is Hebrew for heel, hence Jacks. Jackists doubt this, principally because it would admit Jacobs and Jakes into their fold, and they're not quite the same. Nevertheless, the association of human fallibility with the heel is interesting (see Achilles, Ra), especially given that **Bacchus** (qv), the urJack, is always depicted with cloven hooves.

JOHNSON

The Galveston Giant, The Big Smoke, 'the most famous and the most notorious African-American on Earth': Arthur John 'Jack' Johnson (1878–1946) was a big Jack, no mistake, although the nickname most revealing of his style was the one he gave himself: 'Li'l Arthur'. Yes, sir, this is an uppity Jack of the truly outstanding kind, not just one who didn't care, but one who didn't see why he should. This Jack was a giant killer, the son of a slave who, at that most tricky time for race relations, when the supposedly superior are starting to have doubts, came along and demonstrated their inferiority in the most blatant, elemental way: with his fists, in public. Not surprisingly, they didn't like it.

Jack became the first black heavyweight champion of the world on Boxing Day, 1908, after the holder, Tommy Burns, a Canadian memorably described as having an upper body shaped like an inverted triangle, had finally consented to fight Jack and had been humiliatingly defeated. Another **Jack**, **London** (qv), called for the return to the ring of Burns's predecessor, the retired, undefeated James Jeffries: 'The battle was between a colossus and a pygmy. Burns was a toy in his hands. Jim Jeffries must emerge from his alfalfa farm and remove the golden smile from Johnson's face. Jeff, it's up to you. The White Man must be rescued.'

Two years later, Johnson met Jeffries in Reno, Nevada, in a fight almost beside itself with tension, symbolism and hype, all further fuelled by Johnson's outrageous (for then) lifestyle. Jack was flash – the golden smile was the result of dentistry – and he loved to display all the accoutrements regarded as the preserve of white men, the clothes, the foreign capitals, cars and, crucially, white women, none of whom and which did he always treat well. Jack was no knight of the ring, either: a stylish and skilled counter-puncher, certainly, but a talker, too, always, according to taste, either taunting or joshing, but never giving the respect expected. You will be reminded, as with **Jack Dempsey** (qv), of the later black unorthodox and uncompromising champion, Ali. Johnson beat Jeffries easily, talking to ringside reporters while he was doing it, and loudly announcing, seven rounds before he finished the fight, 'I've got your measure, Mr Jeff, and can put you down whenever I want to.'

There were riots across the country. Ten states passed new laws against sexual relations between whites and blacks. A federal law was passed against taking films of fights across state borders; another forbade the taking of women across state or national borders for the purposes of prostitution, debauchery or for any other immoral purpose, which, in Jack's case, included taking a white woman. He was found guilty and left for Europe in 1913 to escape prison. But he was never quite the same again. He lost his title to the giant, and white, Jess Willard in Cuba in 1917: Jack claimed he threw the fight, but informed opinion is firmly against it, even though he was shading his eyes from the sun as he took the count lying on the canvas. He never regained the title. In 1920, he returned to the US and served a year in prison. Thereafter, it was the familiar decline, ended in 1946 by going too fast in another fast car. Jack loved opera, read widely and, an extreme rarity for a sportsman, even wrote his own autobiography. He toyed with bullfighting. Like the later Ali, he had a ready wit and was a good mimic, specialising in an English accent. But Jack was a product of his time and his past and his treatment, and so Jack was no gentleman, and his age couldn't forgive him for it. Jack could not be confused with the present **Jack Johnson**, a shy singer-songwriter from Hawaii who would rather be surfing if it weren't so competitive and if his gentle songs hadn't sold 15 million albums at the time of writing.

JONES

A few here, too. The first is the American singer, born 1938, smooth of voice, easiest of easy listening, who, despite it all, has never quite achieved unstinting acclaim. Here's Trevor Dann, former producer of *The Old Grey Whistle Test*, head of Radio 1 and mentor of Chris Morris and Chris Evans (a rare double), on one of Jack's signature numbers, the Bacharach–David song from 1963, 'Wives and Lovers': 'Let's cherish these lyrics: "Hey little girl, comb your hair, fix your make-up, soon he will open the door/Don't think because there's a ring on your finger, you needn't try any more, for wives should always be lovers too." But in the early Sixties such suggestions were quite acceptable and Jack Jones was a heart-throb for the generation that didn't understand the Beatles.'

Quite. Jack is not enough of a Jack. The same might be thought of Jones Two, the former general secretary of the Transport and General Workers' Union, a regular consumer of beer and sandwiches at Downing Street and dour if ultimately unsuccessful defender of union power and influence whatever the political persuasion of a particular government. But you should know that Jack is from Liverpool, which has a poor record of producing the unrelievedly dull, and that he went to Spain to fight with the International Brigade (and was injured at the Battle of Ebro) after hearing Paul Robeson urge the Republican cause. But what clinches his Jackness is his performance at the Labour conference in Bournemouth in 2007: at the age of 94, he was still dancing at a union bash at 12.45 a.m. and was back in the hall the following morning. Jones Three would be Lance Corporal Jack Jones of *Dad's Army*, rightly better known as Jonesy than Jack, as Jacks are sharper, and less prone to panic and ask permission to speak, sir. Lastly, there is the cockney rhyming slang: on your Jack Jones – own – which, while less colourful than some other words and phrases, at least has the virtue of clarity. Many people pondering the meaning of Hampton, for example, make the mistake of seeking a rhyme with Hampton Court, when they should, of course, be concentrating on Hampton Wick.

JUDGE

It's a long way to Tipperary,
It's a long way to go;
It's a long way to Tipperary,
To the sweetest girl I know!
Good-bye, Piccadilly!
Farewell, Leicester Square!
It's a long, long way to Tipperary,
But my heart's right there!

Tipperary: one of the great songs of the last century, a jaunty marching song that kept spirits up and then went on to summon them up, an artless cheery anthem for doomed youth that went on to serve for any occasion calling for emotion of the communal kind. How many pubs and coaches has it wavered, quavered and echoed unsteadily through? How many ironies has it attended? Who can hear it without regret?

It was written by Jack Judge, a good-hearted fellow but a gambler, a music-hall comic and singer of the lesser kind who combined his showbusiness career with a fishmongery stall. One of the ironies is that Jack seems never to have been to Tipperary. His parents fled Mayo, across the other side of Ireland, during the potato famine and settled in Oldbury in Worcestershire, in the Black Country. Jack was born in 1872; by 1912 he was making a modest name for himself in his halls with a song and a catchphrase – 'How are yer?' – that reminds you how easy it is to parody the music hall, and makes you rather wonder how good it was.

But Jack, being a Jack, was a game one. In 1910 he had secured a spot on the Moss Empires circuit by coming third in a London talent show behind Louie Gilbert's Cowboy Troupe of girl dancers from Shoreditch, and Doris Hunter, a quick-change artiste, and ahead of such others as a man who dived headfirst into a giant condensed milk can and sang through the cutaway face of a cat on the label. On 30 January, 1912, in the pub after the last house at the Grand at Stalybridge, Frank Newbury and Arthur Peel, who had a performing seal act, bet Jack five shillings that he couldn't write a replacement for 'How Are Yer?' in time for the first house next day. Unbeknownst to Frank and Arthur, Jack, unable to write music, kept a large stock of his tunes in his head, and supplemented his income with such bets. Jack had entitled one of these songs, which his mother liked, 'It's a Long Way to Connemara'. Always quick, if sometimes approximate, at the versifying, Jack changed Connemara to Tipperary (snappier) and wrote three new comic verses to accompany the soon-to-be legendary chorus. The next day he played it through at the Grand. And when even the seals began to clap in time, he knew he had a winner. And it was, is, even if the Irish jokes in the rarely heard verses would now be considered a little incorrect. On 13 August 1914, the Connaught Rangers, who had been stationed in Tipperary, marched through Boulogne on their way to the front singing Jack's song. They were witnessed by a *Daily Mail* reporter, who wrote it into history.

What is the magic of Tipperary? It's catchy, of course, but Jack's lyrics, too, catch a yearning that would become ever more poignant. In 1927, H.V. Morton, the journalist and writer, reported on the first Festival of Remembrance in the Albert Hall, which was broadcast around the world and featured the songs of 1914–18:

> How many of the millions in every corner of the earth guessed until last night how intense is the emotion stored in these strange songs; for strange they are, strange as the British temperament, full of self-satire, pungent with humour directed against our own dignity. We did not realise until last night that the songs we sang in the Army are bits of history. In them is embalmed that comic fatalism which carried us through four years of hell . . .

Jack never wrote a better song after that. Neither did the Powell brothers, Felix and George, also music-hall troupers, after their equally famous effort, 'Pack Up Your Troubles in Your Old Kit Bag'. In February 1917, Jack's son John was killed at Dahra Bend, on the advance to Baghdad. Jack continued his sterling work as an entertainer on the home front. After the war was over, the Powell brothers went to live in Peacehaven, a new settlement on the Sussex coast only fitfully fit for heroes. Jack wrote a song called 'Peaceland': 'Discontented Tommy, discontented Jack, they were promised good things when "the lads come back". Where is their employment? What good is their pay? Where is their employment? Far, far away!'

There was a continuing dispute over the authorship of Tipperary. Harry Williams, whose family owned the pub next door, could annotate music, and did so for Jack. Jack gave him a writing credit for many of his songs, including Tipperary, but it's said that was only in settlement of gambling debts. Harry's family always disputed this, but anyone reading the impressively detailed biography of Jack by Verna Hale Gibbons, *Jack Judge: The Tipperary Man*, will come down for Jack, who had an easier time disposing of claims by an American Harry Williams and by Mrs Alice Jay, of Fakima, Washington, who maintained it was a copy of 'The Fakima Booster Chorus', written by her for the ladies of the local church three years later. Jack died in 1938, still a long way from Tipperary. There's now a statue to him in Stalybridge and a bench in Oldbury. Felix Powell, of 'Pack Up Your Troubles and Smile, Smile, Smile', joined the Home Guard and in 1942 killed himself.

JUMPER

Should you find yourself on the island of Tasmania, and should you spot a large ant with yellow or, possibly, orange legs jumping up and down in a clearly agitated state, you should retreat forthwith: this is a jack jumper ant, and its sting will cause swelling, reddening and fever, followed by formation of a blister, as well as an increase in heart rate and fall in blood pressure, possibly followed by anaphylactic shock. Jack jumper ants cause more deaths in Tasmania than geckos, spiders, snakes, wasps and sharks combined. Don't think it hasn't noticed you, either, as I'm assured it has excellent eyesight. Tasmanians, made of stern stuff, treat this threat with the same sangfroid that leads them to refer to mainland Australia as 'North Island'.

KAHANE

Not particularly well known, Jack Kahane; but consider this list of the books he published: Radclyffe Hall's *The Well of Loneliness*; Frank Harris's *My Life and Loves*; Henry Miller's *Tropic of Cancer, Tropic of Capricorn* and *Black Spring*; Lawrence Durrell's *The Black Book*; Anaïs Nin's *Winter of Artifice*; Cyril Connolly's *The Rock Pool*. Classics all; classics of the kind that usually boast 'unexpurgated' on the cover. Kahane published them in Paris under the imprint of his own company, Obelisk, which he set up there in 1931. Why Paris? Because, after distinguished and injured service in the First World War, he had married a French woman. And because French obscenity laws only applied to books in French. Kahane, a dandyish, Edwardian figure, was from Salford, an area not usually associated with any sort of dandy (although it can claim to have inspired, too, *Coronation Street*, Engels, Lowry and Frank Evans, Britain's greatest bullfighter). Publishers of works such as those above often take to the high ground if they are accused of being pornographic; this was not open to Kahane, as, with that no-nonsense practicality that so distinguishes Salfordians and their Mancunian neighbours, he further exploited the advantages of Paris by publishing a series of titillating works to subsidise his classy ones. Indeed, his own first literary effort had been a racy offering entitled *Laugh and Grow Rich*, whose popularity, he had noted, was considerably increased after it was banned by libraries. His biographer, Neil Pearson, the actor, has claimed that Jack was dull; it's hard to believe, especially as he used to call the more outré side of the operation his 'DBs' (Dirty Books). He died the day before the Second World War broke out. His son, Maurice, who prudently took his mother's unJewish name, Girodias, went on to found the Olympia Press and publish Beckett, Burroughs and Nabokov. All in all, not bad for a Salford lad.

KELSEY

Goalkeepers are, of course, different. The long periods of inactivity often punctuated by cruel and isolated exposure have customarily attracted the eccentric and the thoughtful, occasionally combined. Vladimir Nabokov (see above), Albert Camus, Niels Bohr, Arthur Conan Doyle, Pope John XXIII: all minded the old onion bag in their time. Jack Kelsey (1929–92), the Welshman who quietly and unflashily and at times single-handedly kept Arsenal in the old First Division, seems at first sight, despite being called Jack, an exception. Until you discover this, at the end of one of his obituaries: 'One of his greatest joys was woodwork, for which he had shown aptitude throughout his adult life, and in retirement he fashioned doll's houses of enormous intricacy and beauty.' Excellent.

KENNEDY

John F. Kennedy (1917–63). I don't think we need bother rehearsing the essential details of the life of the world's most famous Jack. What is most interesting for our purposes are the three distinct Kennedy personas: John F., JFK and Jack. John F. is the courageous warrior, writer, thinker, serious statesman, 35th President of the United States, embodiment of his country's high and heroic purpose, the lost and slain leader of Arthurian status; JFK is the more approachable, less formal, but still respectful version of John F., also very good for headlines; Jack is the rest of him, the raffish and the rakish bit, the fun and shenanigans inherited from his often outrageous Irish forebears, the Kennedys and the Fitzgeralds. It was and is a clever, convenient and highly succesful sleight of image that still protects the proper parts of his reputation. What a pity for him that William J. Clinton didn't think to use it.

Here are some famous Kennedy quotations: can you tell which star John F., JFK and Jack? It's quite easy. 'And so, my fellow Americans, ask not what your country can do for you – ask what you can do for your country'; 'When I became President, what surprised me most was that things were just as bad as I'd been saying they were'; 'Mankind must put an end to war, or war will put an end to mankind'; 'Do you realize the responsibility I carry? I'm the only person standing between Nixon and the White House'; 'Our problems are man-made, therefore they may be solved by man. No problem of human destiny is beyond human beings.' You will get the idea. Naturally, I rather prefer Jack, who when he was asked how he became a war hero, replied, 'It was easy, they sank my boat.' Again, you might prefer your leaders proudly and unquestionably upright, and Jack, although he seems to have managed that at least once a day, often when horizontal, clearly had his peccadillos; I particularly like the way he sent his press secretary out to buy up all available supplies of his favourite Petit Upmann cigars in Washington's tobacconists (1,200 as it turns out) the day before he signed the embargo on trade with Cuba. A favourite way of distinguishing between politicians and leaders is to decide whether they are Roundheads or Cavaliers: I submit that John or Jack can be equally good. And he parked illegally at least once when he was a Congressman.

KEROUAC

This Jack precedes the Jack he follows, London, another great American writer living his words, flying high on originality and personality and energy and stimulants and then laid low by them. An original American mix, too, Jean Louis Lebris de Kerouac, the descendant of Breton Canadians who married with Mohawk and Caughnawaga Indians, brought up in Lowell, Massachusetts, educated by Jesuits. Jack read the earlier Jack when he was 18 and decided to take after him onto the road. Jack could see the beat of America, in every sense, and that is how he used it: the beat of its heart, the beat of the drum to its march, the people and the generation beaten by its simple pursuit of one idea of happiness; and the beatitude, the blessedness, what Jack called 'the pleasure in life and tenderness', the joy and sadness of existence. Jack combined all the worry of Catholicism with all the serenity of Buddhism, picked up in small-town libraries on his way. But this Jack was more of a watcher than a doer, beautiful in an American-frontier, truck-driving way, but too conscious of himself, 'a spy in somebody else's body', in the phrase of his friend and flatmate, William S. Burroughs. He needed a fellow traveller to do some of the acting for him. He found Neal Cassady, an uneducated, uninhibited version of himself, and they were off, always moving on across the expanse of America, until they broke for the border and broke out in Mexico, a place of alternative and crazy liberation that proved too much for them. Neal became Dean Moriarty, Jack became Sal Paradise, and this became his great work, *On the Road*, typed on a continous roll, scroll, of paper in three weeks in Manhattan, written up from seven years of the road and pencil-filled notebooks, edited and polished for seven thereafter. Jack said it was written with coffee and sweat-stained T-shirts. Everybody else added benzedrine. It's still a very great book, although its admirers have been much replaced by its doubters, always vocal, who accuse it of being overwritten, sentimental, embarrassing and inferior to subsequent masters like Bellow or Roth. It's written in a stream of narrative, what Jack called a symbolistic serious impressionistic novel, what Truman Capote called not writing but typing. I, being of sentimental, embarrassing mind, say to hell with that and urge anyone under 30 with some dreams left to read it now for the freedom and magic of Kerouac's words. Selected at random: 'Ah, it was a fine night, a warm night, a wine-drinking night, a moony night, and a night to hug your girl and talk and spit and be heavengoing.' It made Jack famous and he couldn't take it, or growing up and old. He married and mated but preferred living with his mother. His drinking became prodigious and proceeded towards his early death. *What Happened to Kerouac?*, an excellent documentary by Richard Lerner, shows William F. Buckley, sleek, supercilious, interviewing Jack, drunk, belligerent, a bull at last bay, almost beaten, in 1968, a year before his death at 47. Still, he'd lasted seven years longer than London. A Catholic priest, toupéed rather than tonsured, calls Jack 'a saint and a mystic' in Lerner's documentary. Gregory Corso, the beat poet, says that Jack was 'a very intelligent baby' who had the talent, exercised it and rose above the sentimental to 'hit the divine'. Elsewhere, Bill Buford has called the late Jack 'a monster' of every kind of incontinence. Last words to Jack: 'But you'll never be as happy as you are now in quiltish innocent book devouring boyhood immortal night.' Last word to you: read Jack.

KETCH

The British have long taken a lively interest in punishment of the capital kind, though with varying degrees of horror and satisfaction. That famous knack for technological innovation is evidenced by the Halifax Gibbet, which preceded the guillotine by at least a century. Even so, when Anne Boleyn was executed in 1536, the headsman of Calais had to be brought over to do the job. Further complaints about not being able to get the staff followed when the first known public executioner, Cratwell, was himself hanged in 1538 for robbing a booth at Bartholomew Fair. An axeman called Bull executed Mary, Queen of Scots in 1587, taking two strokes. Another called Derrick executed the Earl of Essex in 1601, stalwartly overcoming the embarrassment of having been pardoned by the earl only a few years before; it is his name that has been lent to the scaffold and other suspending equipment. Richard Brandon chopped off the head of Charles I with one stroke of his axe; he was paid £30, a significant figure.

Our man, Jack Ketch, was appointed in 1663 and carried out his work of chopping, hanging and flogging with such brutality and incompetence that executioners for the next 200 years were all referred to by his name ('I can see Mr Ketch at this moment,' wrote Thackeray in 1840 of a public hanging, 'with an easy air, taking the rope from his pocket.'). Ketch still features in the traditional Punch and Judy show, which seems to be taking our customary celebration of failure just a touch too far. A litany of his failings would be too much; his most famous botch was with the Duke of Monmouth, the illegitimate son of Charles II who had led an unsuccessful revolt against James II: Ketch had five attempts with the axe – interrupted by the duke rising and staggering about a bit – and finally had to separate the head from its body with a knife. And this despite a tip of six golden guinea coins from the duke, with his instructions for several more to be paid in the event of a proper job. A dispiriting chronicle continues through jeering, ogling, bungling, numbing fear and worse (the hangman was known, graphically, as the crap merchant) until 1964, relieved only by the occasional attempt at more humanity and, of course, gallows humour, as 'doing the Tyburn jig' became 'dancing in [Old] Bailey's Ballroom'.

The best joke, though, remains that of the noted Victorian poisoner, Dr William Palmer, of Rugeley, who halted in front of his scaffold and asked, 'Is it safe?' (Almost matched by Lord Palmerston, the then prime minister, who was petitioned by the great and good of Rugeley for a change of name because of the notoriety Palmer had attracted to the town. 'Certainly,' responded Palmerston, 'they can call it after me.' Some doubt this story; ignore them, they are mostly relying on a Rugeley Town Clerk, and he would, wouldn't he?)

KETCHUM

Black Jack was the nickname of Thomas Ketchum (1863–1901), a western outlaw who had his hideaway at the Hole in the Wall, Wyoming, along with the likes of Butch Cassidy and the Sundance Kid. Black Jack was shot by a train guard after making what seems the elementary mistake of trying to rob the Atchison, Topeka and Santa Fe for the second time in the same place in a matter of weeks and was hanged at Clayton, New Mexico. His last words were: 'I'll be in hell before you start breakfast, boys! Let her rip!' This turned out to be prophetic: the rope decapitated him.

KEVORKIAN

Known variously as Doctor Death or Jack the Dripper, Jack Kevorkian is a former pathologist from Michigan who has assisted at least 130 people to kill themselves. After being acquitted at a number of trials, he was sentenced to 20 years' imprisonment in 1999 for a second-degree homicide and released on parole in 2007. Kevorkian said in 2008: 'My aim in helping the patient was not to cause death. My aim was to end suffering. It's got to be decriminalised.' His son, Zachary Kevorkian, has said, 'I don't like to think of him as the "Doctor of Death", I think of him as a liberator.' In 1997, Kevorkian released a jazz album entitled A Very Still Life. He played the flute and was backed by the Morpheus Quartet.

KILBY

Bear with me, and imagine the links and connections of cyberspace as a giant bean tree, its endless branches made possible by one bean: the microchip. Invented, legendarily, by a gentle giant, Jack St Louis Kilby (1923–2005), born in Missouri, brought up in Kansas, long-time resident of Dallas, home of Texas Instruments. There are several instructive elements to Jack's tale. He won the Nobel Prize after failing the entrance exam to the Massachusetts Institute of Technology. He invented the microchip working on his own over the summer of 1958 because, as a new employee, he hadn't earned any holiday entitlement. Geoffrey Dummer, a British engineer, had come up with the idea of a monolithic integrated circuit embedded in a material like silicon in 1952, but couldn't interest any British investors. Jack didn't need a pocket calculator, which he also invented, to work out how much money he made from the chip, because it wasn't very much. He didn't complain. Nor, indeed, did he actually use a pocket calculator, continuing to prefer a slide rule.

KIPLING

A heart-rending Jack, who barely had time to be a lad, let alone a young lieutenant posted missing after his first battle. This is John Kipling, son of the far more famous Rudyard. When you read Kipling, and don't be put off by fashion or his reputation as a jingo-master, remember that young John heard a lot of them first, before he grew up a little and went to war. Like his dad, he had terrible eyesight, but that didn't stop either of them: John wanted to go, to prove himself to himself and to his dad; his dad pulled strings – there was hardly anyone more influential in the Empire than its laureate – to get him there. A most minor of ironies, and perhaps the only one obvious at the time, was that it was in an Irish regiment, the Irish Guards, and Kipling had been most disobliging about the Irish – Dublin was a city of 'dirt and slop' – and their desire for home rule.

But it is also disobliging to underestimate Kipling's subtleties and humanity. His writing is full of sympathy and understanding for the undertrodden as well as marked by that Victorianism which made everything a great game in which the worst of the other side was exaggerated just because they were the other side. Such complexities make it an insult to suggest that there wasn't much sacrifice in sending his son. They also make the poignancy of it the more unbearable.

So it should be no surprise that, although he and his wife searched unceasingly for news of John – and for John himself – Kipling hardly trusted himself to talk or write about it. He doesn't mention John's death – or that earlier of his adored daughter, Josephine, at the age of six – in his autobiography, called, tellingly, *Something of Myself*. There is only this in the wartime history of the Irish Guards, painstakingly compiled by Kipling, noting that battle at Loos and the casualties: 'of their officers, 2nd Lieutenant Pakenham-Law had died of wounds; 2nd Lieutenants Clifford and Kipling were missing'. He did write this, to a friend: 'I don't suppose there is much hope for my boy and the little that is left doesn't bear thinking of. However, I hear he finished well . . . It was a short life. I'm sorry that all the years' work ended in one afternoon, but lots of people are in our position, and it's something to have bred a man.' There is the famous poem, 'My Boy Jack', perhaps the only way Kipling could cope with the loss, controlled by metre, with its tugging repetition of 'Have you news of my boy Jack?' and 'Not with this wind, not with this tide'. And there is this, from his 'Epitaphs of the War':

> My son was killed while laughing at some jest. I would
>   I knew
> What it was, and it might serve me in a time when jests
>   are few.

But there was another account, told to Kipling's friend, Rider Haggard, of *King Solomon's Mines* fame, by one of Jack's men, of the poor man-boy weeping with the pain of a blown-away jaw. The soldier didn't go to his help because he thought John would be embarrassed to be found crying. Haggard never told Kipling, for kindness. Nor did the Kiplings ever get final news of their boy, who they hoped was lying, at best, in a grave marked with Kipling's own inspiration for the lost British dead: 'Known Unto God'. In 1992, the grave of an unknown lieutenant at Loos was identified as that of Jack, and a headstone erected; but it has since been disputed, in that untidy way the world has: not with this wind, not with this tide. The visitors' book at the cemetery has been inscribed by Christopher Hitchens, an authority on Jack and his father, with the last few lines of Wilfred Owen's 'The Parable of the Old Man and the Young', where the angel calls out to Abraham not to sacrifice his son:

> But the old man would not so,
> but slew his son,
> And half the seed of Europe, one by one.

One last glimpse, from the diary of Jack's mother, as he went to war: 'John leaves at noon. He looks very straight and smart and young, as he turn[s] at the top of the stairs to say: "Send my love to Dad-o".'

KIRBY

Boom! Jack Kirby (1917–94) created more than 400 comic-book characters, including Captain America, Hulk, The X-Men, Iron Man and the Silver Surfer. Kapow! Great pictures, but not the same without those exclamations, which have a distinguished pedigree. Orwell, you might recall, wrote rather entertainingly about them, including this gem from *The Gem*, featuring Jack Blake's schoolmate, Arthur Augustus D'Arcy, the Swell of St Jim's: 'Oh cwumbs! Oh gum! Oooogh! Urrggh! Bai Jove! This is a go, deah boy! I have been thwown into quite a fluttah! Oogh! The wottahs! The wuffians! The feahful outsidahs! Wow!' Ah, yes.

KLUGMAN

Jack Klugman is the American actor with the exasperated face who played the only coroner ever to be a TV star, Quincy. He is equally well known for his other series, *The Odd Couple*, in which he played the slobby Oscar Madison to the prissy Felix Unger of Tony Randall (they followed the fine 1968 film with Walter Matthau and **Jack Lemmon**, qv). But this Jack, born 1922, another Jacob, is included mostly for his 40-year feud with a rival actor, Norman Fell, whose career peak was playing the neighbour of the three flatmates in *Three's Company*, the American version of the British sitcom *Robin's Nest*. This is Fell on Klugman: 'What has he got that I haven't got? What did he do differently? I could have killed as Oscar. I would have been great as Quincy. I wouldn't have been so hammy. Klugman over-acted every scene. You want the show to be good, pick me. You want a chain-smoking jackass who ruins any credibility for your project, I'll give you Klugman's number.' Klugman, however, reportedly had the last word, after Norman's demise in 1998: 'Best funeral I've ever been to.' And he once shared a flat with Charles Bronson.

KRAFT

From 1961 to 1973, Jack Kraft was head coach of the Villanova Wildcats university basketball team in Philadelphia, more widely remembered for this telling response to losing a key player in the final minutes of a game: 'That was the nail that broke the coffin's back.'

KRAMER

This is a Jack of the people, a player. A player, initially, in a game having difficulty accommodating determined seekers after well-rewarded excellence and those for whom too much of that sort of thing was bad form (see **Jack Crawford**). You might see it as the old New World–Old World business. Jack, the son of a Union Pacific railway worker, found he was good at tennis and wanted to be the best and to get more than a £25 voucher redeemable at a London silversmiths for winning Wimbledon. He wanted to win Wimbledon so that he could use the cachet to turn professional and earn some decent money, which he did straight afterwards in 1947. Jack had wits and acumen to go with the first killer serve-and-volley game and he promoted the professional game to the point where an open game was the only option (even though it took until 1968). Jack was a gent as well as a player and he formed a relishable partnership in the BBC commentary box with Dan 'Oh, I say!' Maskell (excellently described by Desmond Lynam as 'coffee and cream'). But when the blazered ones sought a showdown with the infant players' union, Jack, as its chief executive, backed their Wimbledon boycott of 1973, which decisively shifted power. So Jack was cast out again for another 30 years. But if you want a final, telling Jack detail, it would be that he was the first man to win Wimbledon wearing shorts.

KYLE

The greatest rugby union fly half of all, according to most of Ireland and those who should know. There is little film for proof – his 46 caps for Ireland were won between 1946 and 1958 – but it's hardly necessary when Mr Frank Keating of the *Guardian* hits top form in contemplation of the 'pre-eminent majesty of freckled, gingery-haired Jack in his old brown boots: patient, calming, unbothered serenity, a pass here, a kick there. Till, in a sudden blur of intensity, a dip of the hip, a glinting change of pace – a trout in a pool – and the game has been snapped open and free with defenders sprawled, rooted as trees.' After he stopped playing, Jack spent nearly 35 years as a doctor in what has become Zambia, although he mocks any high motive: 'I tried to pretend to people I was the second Albert Schweitzer but I'd a golf course literally at my back door.' When Louis MacNeice, the poet, was offered one wish in life, he answered, 'That I could have played rugby like Jackie Kyle.' In an interview in 2006 with Peter O'Reilly to mark his eightieth birthday, Jack returned the compliment and then sang one the lads used to sing in the coach, a verse from a lesser hand, from 'The Charladies' Ball':

> 'At the Charladies' Ball,' said one and all,
> 'You're the belle of the ball, Mrs Mulligan.'
> We had one-steps and two-steps

And the divil knows what new steps
We swore that we never would be dull again.

But, the rugby. This is Jack, to Keating, on his one international drop goal, to beat Wales in Dublin in 1957: 'The game is almost up. I catch a clearance on their ten-yard line and way out on touch. Over the din, miraculously I hear one single little voice in the great throng behind me: "Have a wee drop, Jack." Why not indeed? So I do. And, lo and behold, we've won and all Ireland goes barmy.'

L

LALANNE

The breezy, hectoring, irritatingly and enviably lean and lissom fitness guru, you might have noticed, is not with us as often as last century. This could be because we have now learnt the wisdom of exercise and can conduct ourselves unaided to the health club, there to sweat, grunt and gaze at ourselves in the inescapable mirrors with varying satisfaction. I like to think, though, that we just got fed up with being told what to do by these tightly clad creatures who seemed mostly to want to extend their moment of celebrity at our flabby expense by flogging us DVDs or whatever to hyperventilate by. This is not a charge that can be levelled at Jack LaLanne, who has at least been doing it to Americans since 1936, when he opened what is claimed to be the first modern health club, and, now in his 90s, is still at it. But the rest of it is all there, the jump suit (Jack's baggy one was a first, too), the leaping about, and the language: 'Exercise is king. Nutrition is queen. Together, you've got a kingdom'; 'Billy Graham is for the hereafter, I'm for the here and now'; 'Life is tough. Dying is easy'; 'If man made it, avoid it!'; 'Get off your seat, on your feet!'; 'Your waistline is your lifeline'; 'Don't exceed the feed limit'. Jack's a Jack for getting in there first, but other Jacks, less slavish in their attention to their kingdom, will note that he is responsible for inventing most of today's fiendish gym equipment. And while admiring Jack for swimming around the waters of the West Coast towing behind him boats with any number of people on board (70 when he was 70, for example), they might also feel he is trying a little bit too hard for a true Jack. Nor will quite a few of them find it easy to forgive the son of French immigrants for drinking a mixture of white and red wine because 'one's too sweet and one's too sour'. I was also interested to read that his son, Jon, has worked as a pool cleaner for both Barbra Streisand and Britney Spears.

LAMBTON

John George Lambton, the first earl of Durham (1792–1840) is remembered by serious-minded students of history as 'Radical Jack', one of the principal architects of the 1832 Reform Act, which allowed a more proportionate representation for Britain's new industrial areas and extended the franchise to one in five adult males. Lambton also produced a report which led to the union of Canada, served as ambassador to Russia and famously attacked the Tory government in 1819 over the Peterloo Massacre in Manchester, where a meeting demanding reform was attacked by armed cavalry, resulting in 18 deaths. The less serious-minded will want to know that in 1812 he took 61 wickets and scored 600 runs, and in 1826 fought a duel on Bamburgh Sands with an election candidate who had accused him of lying, which was certainly a radical way of determining the outcome (if unsuccessful; neither man was hit). Nor did the radicalism extend to redistribution. The Lambtons were a wealthy landed Durham family made even wealthier by the coal beneath it; Lambton confided to the diarist, Thomas Creevey (a rash thing to do), that 'a man might jog on' with an income of £40,000 (£2.5m today). Do not suppose, though, that Radical Jack was just jogging on. He was also renowned for his bad temper, not helped by ill-health, and complained, again to Creevey, that it was 'damned hard that a man with £80,000 a year can't sleep!' Fans of *The Da Vinci Code* should also note that he favoured Freemasonry as a means of uniting classes. His descendant, Anthony Lambton, disclaimed the title to remain an MP, but resigned from Edward Heath's administration in 1973 after he was revealed to be taking inappropriate soundings from certain members of the electorate. He confided to the BBC programme *Panorama* that he 'couldn't understand what all the fuss was about – surely all men visit whores?'

LANG

Two Jack Langs, both left-wing politicians, but of rather different kidney and country. The first was Premier of New South Wales in 1925–7 and 1930–2, a farouche figure who extended suffrage, insisted on a minimum wage and was sacked in his second term by the Governor General of Australia in a row over how best to combat the economic depression then affecting Australia as badly as Europe and the United States. One of his slogans had a theme you are unlikely to encounter anywhere today, 'Lang is greater than Lenin'. The second is French, Socialist and the Minister for Culture under François Mitterrand, closely associated with that President's imposing cultural projects such as the national library, the Paris Opéra, La Grande Arche and I.M. Pei's glass pyramid at the Louvre; he also doubled the French culture budget, funded dozens of new museums, theatres, opera houses and libraries, and launched an annual national music festival. To underline what a broad church Jackism is, French Jack (his parents were anglophiles) is an ebullient theatre director and law professor, author of, *entre autre choses*, an examination for UNESCO of European cultural politics; while Aussie Jack rarely smiled, and, although he went on to found and edit his own newspaper, was one of that sensible school of editors who employ ghost writers.

LANGRISHE

The troupe of travelling players has long been a comic turn in westerns, allowing all manner of pretensions and contrasts between the effete and the fastidious and the rough and the ready. Jack Langrishe was one such, although he seemed to settle as much as travel, starting up theatres in Colorado, Missouri and Kansas before moving on to the next grateful recipients of a bit of culture in between doing what they had to do. His greatest stage was at Deadwood, where the Langrishe Theatre presented a series of productions for three years in the 1870s until it burnt down. Jack's productions seem to have been reliably middlebrow (a lot of Dion Boucicault), which is more than can be said for some of his rivals (Deadwood at that time was renowned for the number of its theatres). Al Swearengen's Gem had a particularly louche reputation; I was impressed to see that it put on 130 performances of the *Mikado* until it was pointed out that this was a 'local burlesque' production, with, presumably, its own interpretation of The Three Little Maids. It was the Gem where Banjo Dick Brown broke off from a performance to shoot dead the man who had just thrown an axe at him. The Langrishe also hosted funerals and the trial of the man who shot Wild Bill Hickok (see **Jack McCall**). Both Langrishe and Swearengen feature in the American TV series *Deadwood*. After the fire that burnt the Langrishe down, Jack was heard to say, 'Put out the Standing Room Only sign, Jimmy, there isn't a seat left in the house,' which I would like to believe is true.

LAWRENCE

The British have been condescending to the Americans since well before that incident with the tea. Lack of success or evidence has not been a deterrent. You can still hear quite well-educated ones confidently stating that the land of Twain, Mencken, Parker, Benny, any number of Allens, Larry David and Bart Simpson has no sense of irony. Part of the problem, if not the complex, is that there are too many Americans doing too many unlikely and diverse things to accommodate the pigeonholing still popular in the Old Country because it's tidier and saves thinking. This Jack, another Jacob (born in 1912), is a good example. Theatre producer and art collector, Jack has also written a large number of popular songs, including the establishing hits of The Ink Spots ('If I Didn't Care'), Frank Sinatra ('All or Nothing at All'), Dinah Shore ('Yes, My Darling Daughter'); the English translations for 'Beyond the Sea' and 'The Poor People of Paris'; and, my favourite contrast, 'Never Smile at a Crocodile' and 'Heave Ho! My Lads, Heave Ho!', the official song of the United States Merchant Marines. Otherwise, when I want to remind myself of the variety of America, I remember that Cole Porter, acme of eastern sophistication, wrote that paean to the prairie, 'Don't Fence Me In'.

LEE

Jacks rarely take second place in families: Winston Churchill's younger brother was an exception, forced away from a life in the Army into a job in the City of London in order to support his extravagant mother, Jennie, who in return devoted her time to advancing Winston's career. Jack Lee (1913–2002) was the elder, and less prominent, brother of Laurie Lee (1914–97), author of *Cider with Rosie*, an evocation of a just-disappeared English idyll, based on their indigent and poly-siblinged beginnings in Gloucestershire; its popularity is responsible for the imitations which continue to take up the time on television on British Sunday evenings. Jack's lack of success was comparative: he worked with the Crown Film Unit in the Second World War, alongside such other distinguished documentary makers as Humphrey Jennings and John Grierson; after the war, he directed a number of feature films, of which *The Wooden Horse* and *A Town Like Alice* were the best received. He had, inevitably, a long feud with Laurie and spent the latter part of his career in Australia not quite fulfilling his potential. In deference to Noël Coward's supremely stiff-lipped epic, *In Which We Serve*, Jack's wartime documentary, *Close Quarters*, about life on a submarine, was dubbed 'In Which We Submerge'.

LEMMON

Nervy, fizzy, angsty, achieving a consummate comic effect almost equalled in his more serious roles, this was not a typical Jack, as you can judge from the small number of characters he played bearing the name. But any Jack would be proud to claim kin with an actor who could make weakness attractive, whose skill was showing the struggle within, for laughs or for lessons. You will have favourite roles, from Ensign Pulver to C.C. 'Bud' Baxter to Hildy Johnson, Felix Unger, Harry Hinkle, Joe Clay, Harry Stoner and, of course, Daphne in *Some Like It Hot*. Fascinating, too, how his art imitated his life, starting with his birth, which, in a typical piece of Billy Wilder business, took place in a lift at the hospital because his mother had been reluctant to leave the bridge table. His father was general sales manager and vice president of the Doughnut Corporation of America. Jack had three mastoid and seven adenoid operations before he was 13, which accounted for that unique voice, a simmering sinus permanently on the verge of eruption. He was nervous, and he did drink (his mother liked the Ritz Bar in Boston so much that she bequeathed it her ashes). He paid his way through acting school by accompanying silent Chaplin and Keaton movies on the piano in a New York beer-hall (and how easy it is to imagine that all going wrong in best Lemmon fashion). His gravestone bears his name and a one-word inscription: 'in'. I hadn't known that Jerry Lewis had been offered Jack's part of Jerry-Daphne in *Some Like It Hot*: 'I turned down *Some Like It Hot* . . . I felt I couldn't bring anything funny to it. The outfit was funny. I don't need to compete with the wardrobe. So whenever Billy Wilder saw me, he said, "Good afternoon, schmuck, how's it going?" And, of course, Jack Lemmon sent me candy and roses every holiday, and the card always read: THANKS FOR BEING AN IDIOT.' Thanks, too, for the refusals and decisions that spared us Lucille Ball as Scarlett O'Hara, Ronald Reagan as Rick in *Casablanca*, Bing Crosby instead of Marlon Brando in *Guys and Dolls*, Ginger Rogers as Elizabeth I, and, above all, Doris Day as Mrs Robinson in *The Graduate*. And, finally, well done to you, Jack, for having the wit not to play Butch Cassidy.

LEWIS

There are some academic and literary waters into which only a Jack would have the courage to plunge fully unbriefed. I am a Charles and will confine myself to a brief outline, a few pointers, and the odd digression. First, I am not surprised that Clive Staples Lewis chose not to go through life so called, as full out it sounds like an accountant with pretensions, while Clive Lewis is either a referee or someone you avoid at the golf club. I have no objections to the initials but couldn't really see this shy academic apostle of Christian fantasy from Ulster as a Jack, his lifelong nickname. I now learn, though, that it arose at the age of four, when he insisted on being called Jacksie, after his pet dog of the same name was run over by a car, an accident of staggeringly bad luck, given that it was 1902. The loss of his mother five years later, a costive father, an English prep and public school education, and a spell in the trenches continued a life not calculated to encourage the carefree. His private life would seem to reflect this. He had a hotly disputed relationship of 30 years with the mother of a wartime comrade who did not come back, and, famously (see, or not, the movie with Anthony Hopkins and Debra Winger), married an American, Joy Gresham, to prevent her deportation, and then fell in love with her as she suffered, rallied and finally succumbed to cancer. Was he celibate? Did he smoke? Drink? If you love Narnia and all its works, turn away while I notice the unmannerly suggestion that the wardrobe is a metaphor for the most direct route back to his mother's womb. Clearly with no authority whatsoever, I wonder if he would have been happier without all the fantasy stuff.

The Inklings, the famous literary group which met in his rooms at Magdalen College, Oxford (and less formally at the Eagle and Child and the Lamb and Flag), spent much time, for example, listening to J.R.R. Tolkien muttering his way through early drafts of Middle Earth. Children, I regret to say that I echo the comment of an occasional Inkling at one such session: 'Oh, no, not another fucking elf!'

LLEWELYN DAVIES

Fairy tales, as we know, rarely survive rubbing up against reality. For the most well-rehearsed contemporary example, look to Diana, Princess of Wales. For the most vivid example of something else entirely, we should go back a century to *Peter Pan*, J.M. Barrie and the Llewelyn Davies family. The story of how Barrie came across the young George and Jack Llewelyn Davies in Kensington Gardens has been often told, but it still doesn't lose its eerie, wistful quality of some inescapable plot being worked out. Barrie was the boy from Dumfries who, quite literally, hadn't grown up, being no more than five foot tall. His childhood was spent in the shadow of the death of his bonny, vigorous, gifted elder brother at the age of 13, mourned ever after by his mother often to his exclusion. He was happiest in the company of children because he was still really one of them, mostly. He would walk in the park with his wife, even tinier, with whom he had only a childish relationship, and their giant dog, Porthos, a St Bernard bought in Switzerland on their honeymoon (you should apply your own insights as we proceed, and, if necessary, refresh your memories of *Peter Pan*). Barrie used to play all manner of games with Porthos, who, when standing on his legs as encouraged, was taller than the newly acclaimed novelist and playwright. The children brought to the park by their nursemaids were transfixed by this little adult upsetting the order, boxing his dog, wiggling his ears and eyebrows.

George Llewelyn Davies, five to Jack's four, as confident as he was striking, struck up an immediate friendship. On New Year's Eve, 1897, Barrie found himself at dinner sitting next to Jack's mother, the beautiful Mrs Sylvia Llewelyn Davies, the daughter of George Du Maurier, *Punch* cartoonist and the author of *Trilby*, the aunt of Daphne Du Maurier, author of *Rebecca*, and the wife of Arthur Llewelyn Davies, a handsome barrister, conventional in the way of his kind. Barrie and Sylvia were amazed to discover their mutual connections – this was the 'funny little man in the park' – and an intimate but unusual relationship developed, suffered by Arthur, between Barrie and Sylvia, the idealised mother-figure, and the boys he could, would, never have: George, Jack, Peter (who was in his pram when they first met), Michael and Nicholas. Out of all this grew Peter Pan, Wendy, Mr and Mrs Darling, John, Michael and Nana. Captain Hook, that most memorable, intriguing Old Etonian of a villain, was an afterthought, introduced to allow a scene-change: Peter was, in Barrie's notes, the 'demon boy (villain of story)'. His idea, too, was to have Mrs Darling and Hook played by the same actress, not the present conventional doubling up of Hook and Mr Darling.

But, reality. The handsome Arthur was robbed of his looks, then his life, by cancer of the jaw, dying in 1907, when Jack was 12. Sylvia died three years later, from a cancer close to her heart. George, a golden Old Etonian, was the first boy lost, killed in Flanders in 1915. Michael, possibly the most gifted of them all, died aged 20 in a bathing pool at Oxford entwined, either deliberately or accidentally, with his best friend, who was perhaps his lover. Peter, whose name had haunted him all his life, threw himself under an underground train at Sloane Square station in 1960. 'Peter Pan Commits Suicide', said one headline. Jack's part in this strange, overwhelming drama was more detached, and minor, as with John in the play. He seems to have been more robust than the others; unlike his brothers he didn't go to Eton, but joined the Royal Navy, serving in the First World War. His letters reveal a surprising, if encouraging, normality, along with a wariness of 'Uncle Jim' or 'The Little Bart' (Barrie was made a baronet in 1913). He married, had two children, and died the year before Peter. Barrie's obsessive attentions to the Davies family destroyed his own marriage. He nursed both the dying Arthur and Sylvia. He paid for the boys to go to Eton, became their guardian on Sylvia's death, and claimed that he and Sylvia were to marry but for it. He died in 1937, having never really recovered from the death of Michael, whom he had loved the most, 16 years before. Any conclusion should be his, and one of the notes he was always writing to himself might serve. It was written as Arthur lay dying close by, a prompt, like everything else, to thoughts for another book or play: 'There's an ironical little God smiling at us. Favours – then gives twist of string and down we fall.' So: a God who hasn't grown up, either.

LOCKETT

Jack was Australia's oldest man – 111 – at the time of his death in 2002. He was older than the Australian federation and had served with Australian forces on the Western Front in the First World War. In 2000, Jack carried the Olympic Torch, slowly, on its way to Sydney, through Bendigo, his home town in Victoria. In 1897 he celebrated Queen Victoria's diamond jubilee: 'This enormous gun went off in the park in Dunolly where we were all celebrating, and I dropped my pie, all over my only pair of shoes, which had just been polished. That's what I remember about Queen Victoria's diamond jubilee.'

LONDON

This might not, quite, be the greatest American Jack, but you surely don't need any other to personify the country's dream, and companion nightmare. This is Super Jack, the bastard child who lives life with a lust at a pace almost exactly twice normal, rising from nothing, teaching himself to become a great writer while bumming, grafting, grifting and suffering through the adventures that will provide the ore, dying burnt out by it and the drink and the drugs at the age of just 40. Hemingway as the American writer action hero? A better writer, certainly, but he was playing at the action, the manly pursuits, the hunting, fishing and the bulls; Jack London (1876–1916) was the real deal, in the Yukon, on the South Seas, in jail and factories, jute mill and cannery, pirating oysters, sealing in the Barents, on the road, farming, war corresponding in Manchuria, writing, writing, writing, 500 articles, 200 short stories, 1,500 letters and 19 novels, including *The Call of the Wild*, the fierce, primal story of a Klondyke sled dog that goes to the wolves, the book that rushed him to fame in 1903 (for an interesting Anglo-American comparison, try *The Wind in the Willows*, 1908). As E.L. Doctorow has written, 'Jack London was a quick study and leaped on the history of his times like a man to the back of a horse.' And always the energy, so elemental that it encompassed socialism, individualism (Super Jack was a big fan of Nietzsche), Kiplingesque white superiority and the dreamy embraces of Jung. Sexually, too, Jack had every inclination, including the Platonic. He had grand schemes which he pursued with the same vigour despite a consistent record of collapse: the boat he designed which wouldn't sail, the great house that burnt down, the revolutionary typesetting machine, even The Jack London Grape Juice Company. They still argue over his burnt-out death; the latest ironic effort is that it was from lupus (remember the dogs and wolves), rather than from a life that amounted to one of the longest suicide attempts in history. You might, though, prefer this from his second wife and life's love, Charmian: 'Jack chose death, or shall we say another form of rebirth. He went like a conqueror, not the vanquished. He went with the illuminated smile of one who has chosen well.'

LONGLAND

You can't keep a good Jack down. Derbyshire County Education Officer for 21 years, Sir Jack Longland (1905–93) was also chairman of the BBC panel game *My Word!* for 20 years, presiding with an easy authority over the sallies of its two stars, Frank Muir and Denis Norden, the comedy-writing epitomes of that English wordplay which probably reached its peak with their famous line 'Infamy! Infamy! They've all got it in for me!' The highlight of *My Word!* was one of their lengthy stories eventually arriving at a pun on a well-known phrase or saying. The best-remembered involves the eskimo, his boat and a lighted candle: 'You can't have your kayak and heat it'; connoisseurs prefer the multi-married American socialite whose autobiography bears an uncanny resemblance to a famous song: 'I, Wanda Hughes Kissinger Dow'. But that was by no means the end of Jack. He was also a noted mountaineer, and, on a 1933 expedition to Mount Everest, famously led eight sherpas to safety during a white-out by way of an unexplored ridge. His obituarist in *The Independent* remembered 'an uproarious afternoon sitting with Jack and his family on a sheltered ledge, halfway up a Derbyshire crag, watching the rain pour down, a few inches away'. At Oxford, Jack won a Blue for pole-vaulting: there is a photograph of him in the air on his pole, flying over a makeshift bar on Mount Everest in 1933, watched by impressed Tibetans.

LORD

Talented painter, driven producer, car salesman, fellow member of the Actors' Studio along with Newman and Brando, Felix Leiter in the first James Bond film, *Dr No*: all these things, and more: but what is Jack Lord (1930–98) remembered for? Indeed: that catchphrase, delivered with the implacable steeliness of the cell door that will surely slam: 'Book 'em, Danno – Murder One.'

Well, I suppose it's better than nothing, and Jack did play Steve McGarrett, the police chief in the televison series *Hawaii Five-O*, for 12 highly memorable years, from 1968 to 1980. This is from his obituary in *The Times*, which, forgivably, concentrated on the show:

> McGarrett was not an emotional man, nor did he ever break into laughter. There was little of the colour and light of his adoptive islands about his personality. Business-suited and carefully groomed, in marked contrast to his garish, open-neck-shirted colleagues, he seemed more likely to be at home on Capitol Hill or Wall Street than among sun-drenched Pacific atolls. Crime to McGarrett was a moral, not merely forensic, issue. His steely [that metal again] eyes narrowed at the very sound of it. As soon as a criminal act was perpetrated the awesome machinery at *Five-O*'s disposal was activated rather in the manner of avenging angel hosts. 'Chin, gimme a make on the murder weapon' and 'Kono, put out an APB (All Points Bulletin) on the car' were characteristic instructions with which McGarrett mobilised his forces and sent them into battle. Only the evil crime boss Wo Fat – Moriarty to McGarrett's Holmes – ever put up reasonable opposition to McGarrett. And even he was run down and caged at the end.

What effective aides-memoires to nostalgia such phrases are. Try these for instant teleporting, Jim: 'Don't make me angry . . . ' (*The Incredible Hulk*); 'Goodnight, John Boy' (*The Waltons*); 'Just one more thing . . . ' (*Columbo*); 'Who loves ya, baby?' (*Kojak*); 'Your mission, should you choose to accept it . . . ' (*Mission: Impossible*); 'Let's be careful out there' (*Hill Street Blues*). Further back on the trail are some fine westerns, including, 'Hey, Cisco!', 'Lonely man, Cheyenne' and 'Gil Favor, Trail Boss'. Although many used to repeat the cry of Dennis Weaver as Chester Goode, the limping deputy in *Gunsmoke* – 'Mr Dillon! Mr Dillon!' – true aficionados prefer the familiar warning from Miss Kitty, owner of the Long Branch Saloon, to Dodge City's stern protector, Marshall Matt Dillon: 'Be careful, Matt.'

I once set a newspaper competition for most overworked lines in film and television drama to accompany, 'It's a long shot, but it might just work', 'All right, I'll tell you. What harm can it do? You're going to die anyway' and 'There's still one thing I don't quite understand'. These were some of the winners: 'You'll never get away with this, you know'; 'I think I've heard just about enough'; 'Cover me and I'll circle around behind them'; '"Listen", "No, you listen"'; 'Guards!'; 'Now try and get some rest'; 'Any closer and she gets it'; 'It seems we had old Jim figured wrong all along'; '"Are you serious?" "I've never been more serious in my whole life"'; 'I must bid you good morning, gentlemen – I have a space station to run'; 'I'll see myself out'; 'Bees! Millions of bees! And they're headed this way!'

LYNCH

Jack Lynch (1917–99), twice Taoiseach of the Republic of Ireland, was a mild-mannered man much beset in office by the Troubles in Northern Ireland and those in his Fianna Fáil party caused by the ambitions of his successor, the mercurial and maverick (others have been more unkind) Charles Haughey. But Jack greatly enjoyed, in moderation, drinking Paddy, the Irish whiskey from his native Cork, and entertaining social gatherings to his rendition of 'The Banks of my Own Lovely Lee':

> 'Tis a beautiful land this dear isle of song
> Its gems shed their light to the world
> And her faithful sons bore thro' ages of wrong
> The standard St Patrick unfurled.

Fittingly, the Jack Lynch Tunnel (1999) takes the N25 Cork southern ring road under the River Lee.

LYONS

An important message here for cultural bodies that seek or accept sponsorship from wealthy business people: be very careful in your choice, and, if you name buildings after them, do ensure your signage is easily amendable. Jack Lyons (1916–2008) made a lot of money in the retail rag trade through the Alexandre and John Collier outlets. Encouraged by his wife, a professional singer, he was particularly generous in support of music, and in 1973 was knighted for it. Things went awry, however, when he became involved in the Guinness company's attempt to ensure a takeover by illegally inflating its share price, thus making itself more attractive to the target company's shareholders. Lyons, who had been an advisor to Guinness, was found guilty in 1990 and fined £3m, which corresponded to the fees he had earned. In 1991 he was stripped of his knighthood, and although subsequent appeals quashed one charge and then held that the trial had been unfair, there was no finding that he and his fellow defendants should have been acquitted. In the meantime, York University had got into a terrible flap over its Sir Jack Lyons concert hall, refusing, despite much criticism, to take the Sir bit off the sign because of expense and difficulty. At his trial, the then Sir Jack tried to put his £3m fee into perspective. 'It is a big fee,' he allowed, 'but we all forget in this country, including myself, the inflation. When you go to Italy and go into a restaurant you pay 2 million lire for your dinner.' Sir Jack had clearly been on the wrong end of a bit of dodgy business himself, as that worked out at £1,000. Still, he did manage to defray his fine by selling Monet's *Cornstack* for £9 million.

MacBride

This other man I had dreamed
A drunken, vainglorious lout.
He had done most bitter wrong
To some who are near my heart,
Yet I number him in the song;
He, too, has resigned his part
In the casual comedy;
He, too, has been changed in his turn,
Transformed utterly:
A terrible beauty is born.

(W.B. Yeats, 'Easter 1916')

'Tread softly, because you tread on my dreams.' There are no more charged and potent myths than founding ones; and no more charged and potent history than that of Irish nationalism. The unengaged and the ignorant must be especially wary that they don't become seized by that gift for image and word which is both the blessing and the curse of the Irish. But even though the case of John MacBride is clearly in point, it's still impossible not to be taken up by the sharp tragedy intertwined with what Yeats called 'the casual comedy', a besetting Irish combination. MacBride is, too, 'the drunken, vainglorious lout', the man with the temerity to wed the beautiful but batty Maud Gonne, Yeats's muse, unrequited love, obsession and despair. MacBride was one of the leading Irish nationalists who emigrated in disenchantment to South Africa at the end of the nineteenth century, and fought for the Boers against the British under the command of (that comedy again) a much removed Irish-American colonel who wore a cowboy hat and was reputed to have taken part in the capture of Geronimo. MacBride, a similarly swashbuckling figure now known as Foxy Jack, was his second-in-command, with the rank of major. They fought well, and were at Ladysmith up against, inevitably, Irish regiments, a kind of proxy civil war, and fatal with it. As a poem of the time put it:

Fitzgerald got Fitzpatrick, Brannigan found O'Rourke;
Finnigan took a man named Fay – and a couple of lads
  from Cork.

The colonel left for another unit; this one became MacBride's Brigade, until they retreated into Portuguese East Africa (Mozambique), from where MacBride eventually made his way to Paris and Maud Gonne, the Surrey girl turned Fenian, who was then part of a small group of exiles there and who saw Foxy Jack as the embodiment of Ireland. This was not a good basis for a marriage, and so it proved. There was a bitter disengagement, and MacBride, taking advantage of the eponymous approach of the new Liberal administration in Britain, returned to Ireland, steadily diminishing into humble employ and drink.

And that might have been the slow, sad end of it had he not been on his way on Easter Monday, 1916, to a wedding in the middle of Dublin, where he came across his fellow nationalists engaged in the armed overthrow of British rule. He had known nothing of it, but joined there and then. Six days later the Rising was over and hundreds, soldiers, uprisers, civilians, were dead. Eleven days later, MacBride was dead, too, shot by a firing squad, one of fifteen so despatched. Seven years, much manoeuvring, civil strife and thousands more deaths later, a viable state was established.

Arguments about the Rising's rightness and consequences have continued ever since; and about MacBride, whom legend should have a hero, but who has routinely been castigated as above and as a bonehead, layabout and drunk, and, at worst, a wife-beater and even abuser of his stepdaughter. Meanwhile, perhaps we should not be surprised that the son Maud bore him, Sean, became, among other things, chief of staff of the IRA and a founder of Amnesty International; or that the descendant of his time in South Africa, Robert, became a deadly bomber for the ANC.

MacBryan

Jack MacBryan is the only Test cricketer never to bat, bowl or get anyone out in any way. An opening batsman for Somerset, he was selected to play for England against South Africa in the Fourth Test at Old Trafford in 1924. Unfortunately, it rained for all but 165 minutes, during which South Africa batted and MacBryan played very little part, although it is believed that he touched the ball. Those who would use this to sneer at Manchester's reputation for excessive precipitation should be reminded that more open-topped cars are bought in the city each year than in the whole of Spain.

McCall

A bad Jack. This was the man who shot Wild Bill Hickok in the back of the head late on the afternoon of 2 August 1876 in Carl Mann's Saloon No. 10 in Deadwood, Dakota Territory. And that's pretty much about all we can be sure of, as the life of Hickok has become lost in the legend, was already lost in the legend well before he fell to the saloon floor, clutching or not clutching the famous Dead Man's Hand, a pair of Aces and a pair of Eights, having for once broken

JACK SHEPPARD:
the one where he
didn't get away.

MACHINE GUN JACK McGURN and The Blonde Alibi:
Reader, he married her.

JACK KETCH:
a very bad hanger.

JACK BUCHANAN:
and his mother came too.

JACK JOHNSON
giving to charity;
he received little
in return.

SIEGFRIED SASSOON:
master of Mad Jackery.

JACK LONDON taking a break from the breakneck.

SPRING-HEELED JACK: pull the other one.

JACK SPOT in stitches himself for a change.

BLACK JACK BOUVIER:
handsome man with famous daughter
before she was beautiful.

JACKIE ROBINSON:
not a bad sense of humour, either.

JACK KEROUAC:
the Jack who hit the divine.

JACK DEMPSEY:
the will to do hurt

JACK SLIPPER returning,
with faithful sidekick, without Ronnie.

TEXAS JACK, standing on the right, next to Buffalo Bill,
his fellow fine specimen of manly strength and beauty;
the ugly one on the left is the writer.

JACK TEAGARDEN with friend.

his prudent habit of sitting facing the door. As for the rest of it, you can take your choice: Hickok was an upstanding, if long-haired, upholder of the law in lawless times who played a little cards on the side, a former frontier scout and Civil War hero who had served with Custer and was about to sort out the denizens of Deadwood. Or Hickok was a cardsharp and cold killer who, according to no less than H.M. Stanley, had killed considerably more than 100 men. Or he was a drunk who was not particularly good at cards and was losing his eyesight. And then we could throw in various other features, such as the red sash he always wore and his stints in a couple of Wild West Shows, including Buffalo Bill's, and his marriage to Agnes Lake, horsewoman, tightrope walker, dancer and lion-tamer, and his marriage, or not, to Calamity Jane. All right, I'll stop now.

But those who complain about films and TV taking liberties with historical fact should be happy they were not in America in the late 1800s, when there were an awful lot of people making it up while it was actually going along. To a far eastern tenderfoot like me, the most startling thing is that both Wild Bill and Sitting Bull were killed in action after returning from stints in shows portraying it all as entertainment. But Jack: he said he had done it to avenge his brother, although he didn't have one. Some said he had done it because Hickok had embarrassed him by lending him money after beating him at cards the day before. That suggests both an unlikely sensitivity and a marked absence of gratitude. He may have been put up to it by Deadwood interests opposed to Bill cleaning up either at the tables or on the streets. My favourite is that Jack, like many another assassin, some before, most after, wanted to be famous, which he is, after a fashion. He was captured in Wyoming after boasting about shooting Bill in a fair fight, and strung up in Dakota on 1 March 1877, after a second trial; immediately after the killing a miners' court had, astoundingly, acquitted him. It must have been easy to track him down: Jack was described as having a pointy head covered by a thick crop of chestnut hair, a crooked nose and cross-eyes.

McConnell

At first sight, this one looks right for a political Jack. First Minister of Scotland (2001–7), Labour man, nickname of 'Lucky Jack', a chummy (and controversial) holidayer with glamorous Scottish media types, an appearance at a fashion show in a frilly white shirt and pinstripe kilt, even an irregular dalliance. But Jack McConnell never really quite cut it with the Scots, who, despite all that, believed him to be a touch dull and, despite some evidence to the contrary, incompetent. This, for example, is how he featured in one dictionary of Scottish vernacular: 'Numpty. Pronounced numb tea. A useless individual. As in, "See that Jack McConnell? He's a real numpty".'

It was also pointed out more often than strictly necessary that he was a former maths teacher. In vain would a friendly biographer note that Jack had been macho enough to refuse to eat his vegetables as a child on the Isle of Arran; nor was his wife's first marriage to the lead guitarist of Procol Harum any more persuasive. This was an after-dinner joke: 'Who would have believed that we would have a man on the moon and Jack McConnell would be First Minister? Pity we got it the wrong way round.' Ah, well. It rather reminds of the treatment handed out south of the border to an earlier leader, John Major, whose inescapable greyness triumphed even over a father who had been a trapeze artist (and his own extra-marital affair). Major's full name, as it happens, was John Major Ball; I have often wondered whether things might have been different if he'd called himself Jack Ball. McConnell's experience suggests not. (See also **Jack Straw**.)

McCracken

The greatest amateur basketball player of all time, Jumping Jack McCracken (1911–58) hailed from Chickasha, Oklahoma, and played for the Denver team, which, owing to changes in sponsorship, was known variously as the Denver Safeways, the Denver Ambrose

Jellymakers and, my favourite, The Denver Piggly Wigglys, after a local grocery chain.

McGurn

Another bad Jack with Caledonian connections, I'm afraid (see also **Jack 'The Hat' McVitie**). But even though his nickname is even more to the point, Jack 'Machine Gun' McGurn was not in any way a man of the kilt, seeing as he was, in fact, Vincenzo Antonio Gibaldi, born in Licata, Sicily, in 1905. So why the Jack and the Mac? Well, before he began to mow people down sub-automatically on behalf of Al Capone in Chicago, Vincenzo had been doing it one at a time as an aspiring boxer; and it seems that Scots-sounding fighters were getting better bookings. I'm sure there must have been more to it than that, but it's probably still best not to enquire too deeply. Anyway, having lost both his father and his stepfather in gangland slayings, Jack embarked upon vengeance and a flashy gangster kind of life with enthusiasm. This is, after all, the man credited with organising and carrying out the St Valentine's Day Massacre in 1929, when seven associates of Bugs Moran, Capone's rival, were lined up against a garage wall and killed. **Jack Lemmon** (qv) witnessed this fictionally with Tony Curtis in *Some Like It Hot*. The reality was less attractive. McGurn was arrested but his moll maintained he was with her at the relevant time. She was afterwards invariably referred to as The Blonde Alibi; and, reader, he married her. McGurn was also owner of The Green Mill cocktail lounge, employing equally direct methods to retain staff: when Joe E. Lewis, the comic, left for an offer he wouldn't refuse at a rival gang's club, he was severely injured in a razor attack (Frank Sinatra played him in the movie *The Joker Is Wild*, in which, for further confusion, McGurn is called Tim Coogan). McGurn was eventually and inevitably gunned down himself by two men armed with, naturally, machine guns. They also left a Valentine's card. McGurn was a talented and keen golfer (one biography mentions, without irony, his splendid hand-to-eye co-ordination). He doesn't fit the conventional profile of a golfer, but then neither do Rudyard Kipling, Patrick Hamilton, Malcolm Lowry, William Faulkner, Dwight D. Eisenhower, Peter Cook, Alice Cooper, Dennis Hopper, Harpo Marx and Dr Mohamed ElBaradei, the director general of the International Atomic Energy Agency. Still, McGurn was allowed to finish a round before police arrested him, which shows that decorum can be catching. Not though, apparently, with his boss, Al Capone, who, on the same course, once got a hole in one leg when the gun he kept in his bag next to the putter went off accidentally.

McQuesten

Leroy Napoleon McQuesten (1836–1909) was known as Yukon Jack. An immigrant from the south, New Hampshire, he set up a number of trading posts along the Yukon River, supporting and supplying the quest for Canadian gold. But not all Jacks are lucky; this one moved away from the Klondike ten years before the Gold Rush of 1897 (see **Jack London**), rushing back too late to stake a claim. Jacks can be honest, however: McQuesten was so trusted and reliable that he was dubbed 'The Father of the Yukon'. Another reward is to have had the 100-proof Canadian whisky and honey liqueur named after him. Yukon Jack, according to its label, 'is a taste born of hoary nights, when lonely men struggled to keep their fires lit and cabins warm'.

McVitie

A bad hat: Jack 'The Hat' McVitie, a small-time, inept, bald (hence the hat) dealer in drugs and violence who compounded these failings by becoming involved with the Kray Twins, and then, even more foolishly, bungling a murder on their behalf and keeping the money. Reggie Kray tried to shoot Jack, but his gun jammed, so he stabbed him repeatedly in the face, chest and stomach. This was the murder which resulted in Reggie's life imprisonment; Ronnie went down at the same time for shooting a member of a rival gang who had called him 'a fat poof'. It is often said of the Krays, in mitigation, that 'they only hurt their own'. As Neil Darbyshire, the former distinguished crime correspondent of the *Daily Telegraph*, puts it: 'They might have only hurt their own, but by God did they hurt them.'

MANIO

It is a matter of Jack that the most distinctive English voice to be heard on BBC radio during the 1960s and '70s should have been that of Jean Baptiste de Manio, the son of an Italian aviator and a Polish socialite. Jack de Manio (1914-88) was one of the first presenters of the Corporation's early morning programme, *Today*. Those who work on it today have, mostly, a background and training in the gathering of news and the analysis of current affairs, less so in the lighter entertainment arts. With Jack, it was the other way round, reflecting the difference in the times; his career had started as a clerk in a brewery and progressed to announcing at the BBC by way of assistant wine waiter at the Ritz and a Military Cross during the Second World War. Jack's greatest asset was his voice, finely timbred with the suggestion of a need for lubrication, which it regularly received (on Christmas morning, he was in the habit of taking his producer out after the programme for a champagne breakfast). But Jack's nonchalance rarely strayed into negligence; he was too old school for that, and this assurance and reassurance was what his listeners loved. And so there was the seeming inability to tell the time, or to get the hang of things, quite. Yoko Ono, for example, was referred to as 'Yoko Hama, or whatever her name is'. It couldn't last, of course, and it didn't: Jack was eased out as news gained 'an agenda', 'a harder edge', and the new seriousness arrived, promoted by young and earnest broadcasters whose degrees were definitely not from the University of Life. Jack went into the inevitable decline, had to sell the Bentley, and ended up applying for jobs as a gardener and security guard. But his much-mocked sense of timing didn't prevent him dying in the early morning and so allowing the opportunity for a handsome tribute to be prepared by his old programme. Quiz compilers might appreciate this list of unlikely *Today* presenters: Michael Aspel, Barry Norman, Melvyn Bragg and Desmond Lynam.

MAY

Appearing in soap operas guarantees regular work and a measure of fame, but there are sacrifices. Jack May (1922–97) played Nelson Gabriel in the BBC radio serial *The Archers* for more than 40 years, a role which his obituaries concentrated on to the near-exclusion not only of his life but most of his many other parts, which had ranged from all three parts of *Henry VI* to the voice of Igor, manservant to Count Duckula. Still, his Nelson was a memorable creation, contrasting with the rest of the stolid, gate-leaning cast by being fast, louche and shady; all, in fact, that one has come to expect from fictional antique dealers and wine-bar owners. His mysteriousness was pervasive. It started with an accent impossibly opposed to that of his father, Walter Gabriel, the comically relieving smallholder given to saying 'my old pal, my old beauty', richly, rustically and often. It ended in his disappearance to South America, where he died three years later, three years later than Jack, detained in soap limbo. Further intrigue was added by Jack's real-life stint as an antique dealer. But he did receive this handsome tribute from Norman Painting, who plays Phil, Patriarch of all the Archers: 'when Jack was about there was champagne in the air'. The other Jack of the Archers, is, of course, **Jack Woolley**, the self-made Birmingham businessman, held up (by the BBC's *Archers* website, at least) as a biblical lesson in the transience of earthly things, dives divested. The man who plays Jack, Arnold Peters, is also an interesting example of transience. He has been appearing in *The Archers*, off but more on, since 1953, playing no fewer than three successive characters, Len Thomas, the Reverend David Thomas, and Jack. I don't suppose this is a record.

MERCER

Ignore those looks: if you like singing out loud for no particular reason, go ahead and do it. Along with whistling, there's too little of it these days, even among milkmen. Besides, you never know where it might lead. Jack Mercer was a junior animator at the Fleischer Studios in New York at the same time – 1935 – as Billy Costello, the voice of Popeye, was proving 'difficult to work with'. One of the Fleischer brothers heard Jack singing the *Popeye* song and suddenly he was the replacement. The *Popeye* song? Some of us remember. It involved Popeye's ever-present pipe being sounded like a fog horn and went like this:

> I'm strong to the finish
> when I eats me spinach
> I'm Popeye the sailor man!
> Toot-toot! [pipe]

Jack carried on voicing the strange and pugnacious little sailor for more than 40 years, along with such other animated epics as Felix the Cat. It was Jack who ad-libbed Popeye's mutterings and tsk-tsk laugh, aimed either at his flighty girlfriend, Olive Oyl, or his dastardly black-bearded rival Bluto, who could only be overcome by large amounts of spinach, straight from the tin (those were the days). You, of course, will know that this stirring demonstration of spinach's magical qualities stemmed from a late nineteenth-century scientific paper in which a misplaced decimal point exaggerated its iron content tenfold. Bluto was often voiced by Pinto Colvig, who began his showbusiness career playing the clarinet off-key and pulling faces. Mae Questel was Jack's first Olive Oyl; when Mercer was drafted, she just buckled down and did Popeye as well until he came back.

MERRIDEW

William Golding was good on names. Consider *Lord of the Flies*, in which schoolboys stranded on a desert island play out a parable of civilisation and savagery. The strong, civilised one is named Ralph. The sacrificial, sensitive one is named Simon. The casual cruelty of boys and the fate of their clever but weak target is cleverly realised in Piggy. I'm not so sure, though, about Roger for the mindlessly savage one, even allowing for the chime with Jolly Roger. A Roger is just not a mindless savage, is he? It might be me, but I find Rogers inextricably linked with jumpers, or cardigans. And then there's Jack, Jack Merridew, for the cunning, selfish savage, the junior Stalin. This is the cleverest, most subtle choice of all. On the face of it, Jack is too light and friendly for this boy, or for what he will become. But there's also Merridew, the only surname in the book apart from that of the littl'un, Percival Wemys Madison, who incants his as a pathetic aide-memoire to home and safety. Merridew is the hint to green misrule, the gambolling in the glade free from the sensible but really dull constraints of civilisation, the happy anarchy that can turn nasty, the devil in Jack. Even so, there have been few dictators called Jack. I can think of only one: **General Yakubu 'Jack' Gowon**, the Sandhurst-educated ruler of Nigeria from 1966 to 1975, holder of the bloody, suffering line against Biafran secession, and certainly the only dictator to study political science at Warwick University after being deposed. I like to think that most Jacks have too lively a sense of humour and self-awareness to enjoy tyranny. And although it is true that Stalin enjoyed *Laurel and Hardy*, I think that was mostly for the violence. There is another island Jack, too: **Jack Shephard**, the hero of the TV series *Lost*. Jack's dead dad, the flawed Christian, is the real Jack. This Jack is not a real Jack: he cares too much. This Jack makes Action Man look rakish, edgy even. In fact, I think it was a real proper Jack who gave his son an empty box for Christmas: 'What's this, Dad?' 'Action Man Deserter, son.'

METCALF

When I was about ten, when we were learning history, I must confess that I preferred a good battle or execution to the stuff about common land, crop rotation and mills. Some of us were seized by steam and the coming of the railways and the great engineers. I expect they are quite rich by now. But Stephenson, Telford, Hargreaves, Crompton, Watt, Macadam: no. The men for me were Marlborough, Nelson and Wellington, with dash and style to their steel. I must have ignored the great Brunel as inconvenient; but I do vividly remember an illustration in my textbook of Blind Jack of Knaresborough, road builder. Blind Jack of Knaresborough, road builder! There he was in the illustration, dressed in the usual eighteenth-century attire, complete with tricornered hat, with pick raised, poised to construct another few yards of vital transport communication. I do not now remember how much I misunderstood about this, but I am certain Blind Jack was shown alone, which led me into a fixed belief, only just abandoned, that Jack had built most of the roads of Yorkshire and far beyond single-handed and sightless. The truth, or as much of it as can be disentangled from the liberal accounts, especially that of Jack's ghost writer (another of those journalists, I'm afraid), is almost as remarkable.

John Metcalf was born in 1717 in Knaresborough, not far from Harrogate, Yorks. At the age of six he became blind after an attack of smallpox. Notwithstanding, he became a highly skilled climber of trees, swimmer of rivers, rider of horses, hunter of foxes, gambler at cards and player of the fiddle. He became a big, strong man with a big, strong personality about whom, not surprisingly, stories were told. Drowning people were plucked from rivers, travellers guided through the night, and all manner of ingenious methods were used to overcome his blindness: bells, voices and that mixture of canny guile and sheer bloody-minded determination for which his county is so rightly renowned. Jack's wife at first refused him after he had fathered a child with another; he then eloped with her on the eve of her marriage to someone else, turned up at his rival's ruined wedding feast to play his fiddle, and seems to have got away with it. He travelled, to London, to Edinburgh and to Culloden, in the service of a local squire, playing his fiddle to encourage his comrades, and searching for his temporarily mislaid master, in the manner of Blondel and Richard the Lionheart, even, allegedly, into the doomed Bonnie Prince's camp. But this was no fey minstrel: Jack had a head for business. He tried selling fish, cloth and hauliering, until he found his way: roads. The time was right. The Romans in Britain had a more efficient road system than their eighteenth-century successors. Most of Jack's previous ventures had foundered on bad roads. One of his adventures, described by Samuel Smiles, the apostle of vigorous self-help, had been to walk back from London in six days, two days faster than the local colonel, who had offered him a lift on the back of his coach. This is that fine wit, the Reverend Sydney Smith, on the contemporary infrastructure (with a brief diversion):

> I have been nine hours in sailing from Dover to Calais, before the invention of steam. It took me nine hours to go from Taunton to Bath, before the invention of railroads; and I now go in six hours from Taunton to London! In going from Taunton to Bath, I suffered between 10,000 and 12,000 severe contusions, before stone-breaking Macadam was born . . . As the basket of stage-coaches in which luggage was then carried had no springs, your clothes were rubbed all to pieces; and,

> even in the best society, one-third of the gentlemen at least
> were always drunk . . . I paid 15L. in a single year for repairs of
> carriage-springs on the pavement of London . . .

The first Turnpike Act, which provided for tolls to pay for road building and upkeep, had been passed earlier in the century; in 1752 a subsidiary act provided for a road between Harrogate and Boroughbridge: Jack won the contract, and was off. He went on to build roads in Yorkshire, Lancashire, Cheshire and between them, 180 miles and numerous bridges over the next 40 years, earning him, according to Smiles, about £65,000, which would be worth £9 million today. My memory is right in one part: he did work mostly alone, surveying and quantifying amounts with the aid of what seems to have been no more than a stick and an ability to compute distance, weights and measures which he had developed to compensate for his lack of sight, and which, reports Smiles, he could not describe (canny Jack, says I). Among his many innovations was the use of heather and such as a porous base for crossing marshes and bogs, later widely used in railway construction. He retired from road building at 75 and took a smallholding near Weatherby, dying aged 93 and mourned by 4 children, 20 grandchildren and 90 great-grandchildren. Not surprisingly, certain admiring citizens of Knaresborough have a plan to erect a statue to Blind Jack. Contributions, says one of Jack's leading enthusiasts, Mr Conrad Plowman of Knaresborough, are welcome. If you seek a monument, drive along the M62, the great motorway joining Lancashire and Yorkshire high across the Pennines: Jack was there first.

MEYER

If you were to have a headmaster called Jack, this is the one he would be like. Jack Meyer (1905–91) was the founder and headmaster of Millfield School, Somerset. He was also a fine first-class cricketer, insomniac and inveterate gambler. He founded Millfield in 1935 on his return from a stint in India more noted for his cricketing performances than any success as a cotton broker. He had with him seven boys, six of them princes; they became Millfield's first pupils, to be followed by an eclectic intake that has included Gareth Edwards, the Welsh rugby player, the kings of Thailand and Saudi Arabia, the grandson of Boris Yeltsin and the children of Sean Connery, Pearce Brosnan and Elizabeth Taylor, which has always made for lively Speech Days. Teachers included the playwright Robert Bolt, and, as another former pupil, the biographer and novelist Victoria Glendinning recalled, a Colonel Barter, who taught Urdu, Arabic, Spanish and Portuguese simultaneously to different groups, 'only occasionally getting them mixed up'. In the early days, Jack also captained Somerset at cricket, eccentrically and with lumbago. He was also an enthusiastic proponent of lobbing, underarm bowling and writing letters to *The Times*. David Foot, the cricket writer, remembers, 'As a cub reporter I once wrote a slightly critical piece on Meyer, wondering whether my native county, Somerset, could afford his indulgences and permanent lumbago. I wasn't sure how he would react. "Bloody good!" he wrote.' Later on, in the 1960s, Jack was to be seen at the New Casanova casino in Mayfair, mingling with such fellow punters and friends as the bookmaker Victor Chandler, Prince Khalid Abdullah of Saudi Arabia and Tariq Aziz, Saddam Hussein's deputy prime minister. Favoured pupils and Somerset cricketers were given hot racing tips. You will now be thinking, fondly, of Alastair Sim in the St Trinian's films. 'The Boss', as he was always known, expelled Victoria Glendinning for some enthusiastic extra-curricular co-educational activity in the orchard (the boy was excused because 'It's always the woman's fault'). Meyer gave her 'a very red, very sticky, Charles of the Ritz lipstick as a leaving present'.

MONTEREY JACK

While nibbling on a piece of this cheese, it has been my practice to imagine Monterey Jack as a grizzled tuna fisherman, or a hardbitten gambler, or a venerable, if slightly tuneless, folk singer. Turns out it's named after David Jack, a grizzled, hardbitten nineteenth-century Presbyterian Scottish immigrant and land dealer with a dairy on the side, who riled his fellow southern Californians with his sharp foreclosing and other such activities. But he also donated the land to a Methodist prayer group which went on to found Pacific Grove. So, like his cheese, this Jack was semi-hard.

MUDURIAN

Don't knock those sing-songs in nursing homes. Jack Mudurian was a resident in a Boston nursing home who enjoyed taking part in them. A researcher recorded Jack singing 129 songs non-stop for 47 minutes; the recording became a novelty hit. Jack's songs included 'Chicago (That Toddling Town)', 'Step Right Up (and Help Old Uncle Sam)', 'It's Only a Paper Moon', 'Music! Music! Music! (Put Another Nickel In)', 'Any Bonds Today', 'Red River Valley', 'My Bonnie', 'Jimmy Crack Corn', 'The Wabash Cannonball', 'South of the Border (Down Mexico Way)', 'I've Been Working on the Railroad', 'Home on the Range', 'Joshua Fit the Battle of Jericho', 'Frankie and Johnnie', 'Rudolph the Red-Nosed Reindeer', 'Jingle Bells', 'Row Row Row Your Boat', 'I've Got a Lovely Bunch of Coconuts', 'Chiquita Banana', 'Your Cheatin' Heart', 'Ragtime Cowboy Joe', 'Chattanooga Choo Choo', 'The Trolley Song', 'Toot Toot Tootsie! (Goo'Bye)' and 'Take Me Out to the Ball Game' (see **Jack Norworth**).

MURPHY

This is some progression, even for a Jack: born in California in 1938, violinist with the Pittsburgh Symphony Orchestra at 15, winner of the Hurricane National Surfing contest at 25, tennis professional, movie stunt man, surfboard company owner, jewel thief (American Museum of Natural History in New York, 1964, the J.P. Morgan Collection of precious gems, including the 563-carat Star of India), prisoner, murderer (of a young Californian secretary), prisoner, born-again Christian, evangelist, prison visitor. Cocoa and an early night, anyone?

MYTTON

The maddest Jack of all the mad Jacks, who both terrorised and entertained Shropshire for the best part of 30 years, hunting anything that moved with anything that moved, often naked, and generally defying health, safety and convention in any way he could before dying in a debtor's prison of alcoholic delirium after working his way through a fortune worth millions. He was said to drink five bottles of port before lunch. He bit dogs and brought horses in to lie by the fire. Other Jack highlights in the years between 1796 and 1834 would be expulsion from both Westminster (for fighting the masters) and Harrow (after just three days); sending 2,000 bottles of port ahead to see him through his Cambridge studies, which he then decided not to take up; attending Parliament once, for 30 minutes, after spending the equivalent of £750,000 on getting himself elected; riding his pet bear into dinner and his horse up onto the mezzanine of a Leamington Spa hotel before jumping down and out through a restaurant window; and trying to cure his hiccups by setting his shirt on fire so as to give himself a shock.

Jack had two wives, several children (whom he would pelt with oranges), 700 pairs of boots, 1,000 hats and 2,000 dogs. But he could quote Sophocles, in Greek. This, perhaps, gives the best flavour of his approach to life: his biographer, C.J. Apperley, asked him not to drive their carriage quite so quickly. 'What?!' said Jack. 'Never been upset in a gig? What a damn slow fellow you must have been all your life!' He then drove it sharply up a bank to tip it over. It was Apperley who asked the pertinent question, and answered it: 'Did the late Mr Mytton really enjoy life amidst all this profusion of expenditure? No. He lacked the art of enjoyment. He was bored and unhappy. There was that about him which resembled the restlessness of the hyena. A sort of pestering spirit egged him on.' He was, writ large, the sort of person you recall rather more fondly than you experience. Shropshire had become very fed up with him, would have nothing to do with his attempt to return to the Commons, and sighed a cross-county sigh of relief when he fled from his debts to France in 1832. But, as the *DNB* has it, 'death revived public affection for him' and his funeral was handsomely attended (disappointingly, his hearse was driven at a sedate pace, although the cortège did stop at a pub on the way). And he surely would have smiled at the University of Minnesota's Jack Mytton Run, an annual streaking event.

Navy Jack

A Jack is a national flag flown on the bows of a ship. Flag etiquette, particularly at sea, seems remarkably complicated for what should be a simple form of identification and communication (see **Union Jack**). Perhaps it's all the time they have on their hands out there on the waves. The Navy Jack of the United States has 50 white stars on a blue background. The First Navy Jack of the United States has 13 alternating red and white stripes for the founding states surmounted by a rattlesnake and bearing the appropriate legend 'Don't tread on me' (the rattlesnake strikes only when provoked). The symbol dates from the War of Independence, when it appeared in a cartoon in Benjamin Franklin's *Pennsylvania Gazette*, with the rattlesnake divided into 13 parts with the motto 'Unite or die'. The First Navy Jack is flown normally only on the longest commissioned US naval vessel; since the first anniversary of 9/11 it has been flown on them all, and is intended to do so until 'The War on Terror' is won.

The Confederate Navy Jack was the last Confederate flag to be lowered in the American Civil War, in, oddly, you might think, Liverpool. This is because it was on the bows of the Confederate States Ship *Shenandoah*, which had sailed round the world from the Pacific rather than fall into Union hands. The *Shenandoah* was the successor to the *Alabama*, the armed merchantman which sank nearly 70 Union merchant ships before being sunk herself in 1864 by the USS *Kersage* off Cherbourg, in a scene painted by Manet, as spectators watched from the shore. Bought in England, then armed and converted at Madeira, the *Shenandoah*'s bold but mad mission was to force the conquering Union into negotiation by destroying its merchant fleet. A thirteen-month Flying Southerner kind of world cruise took it across the equator four times, into dock at Melbourne (where the crew were fêted at a 'Buccanneer's Ball') and on to the Arctic Circle. In all, the *Shenandoah* captured 38 Union ships, burnt 32 of them, took more than 1,000 prisoners (all paroled and released), lost only 2 sailors and inflicted $1.4 million in economic damage on the Union. The crew included Robert E. Lee's nephew and four free African-Americans. On 9 April 1865, Lee surrendered to Grant at Appomattox. The *Shenandoah* was raiding in the Pacific, oblivious. Its captain, James Waddell, a former US Navy man of 20 years' standing, headed north, in pursuit of the Northern whaling fleet. The last shot of the Civil War was a warning one, fired in the Barents Sea on 22 June 1865 after the *Shenandoah*, flying the Union flag, had come up among some unsuspecting whalers. In the next six days, the raider took some 24 whalers, destroying most of them. Fiercest resistance was offered by a 70-year-old Yankee captain, drunk and brandishing a cutlass and flintock, who was prudently abandoned by his crew. The Union ships had newspapers on board, detailing Lee's surrender: Waddell refused to believe them, and now pondered an audacious attack on San Francisco. But on 2 August, they came across an English merchantman and were finally convinced that it was indeed all over.

This grey ghost of the Lost Cause, beset, unsuprisingly, by bickering and unhappiness, set sail round the Horn for England. On 6 November, the last Confederate Jack, and the only one to circumnavigate the world, was lowered in the thick fog of the Mersey. Waddell returned to Annapolis ten years later and built a house modelled on the one where he had lived in Liverpool. The widow of one of his officers died in 1955. In 1964, the US Navy, in a handsome gesture, commissioned the USS *Waddell*, a destroyer. The *Shenandoah*'s Jack is on display at the Museum of the Confederacy in Richmond, Virginia. And the *Shenandoah* itself? It was sold to the Sultan of Zanzibar and eventually foundered and sank on a reef in the Mozambique Channel in 1879.

NEVIN

John Francis Nevin (1916–91) is the part-inspirer of this book, along with Jack Cade, Jack Ketch, Calico Jack and a few others, and inspirer of me. Lancastrian, grocer, irreverent, fun, very funny and a good friend, he had a fine line in wartime anecdotes, irrelevant verse and unusual advice often repeated, involving, respectively, the Eighth Army, pantomime verse, sitting at the back of a coach or aeroplane to get a longer ride, and a method of catching pheasants involving pepper and a hard stone. Anyone who'd like to learn more should read a fascinating book written by, as it happens, me: *Lancashire, Where Women Die of Love* (Mainstream, 2004). **Jack Cristian Diaz O'Hanlon Nevin**, born in Ilopango, El Salvador, in 1991, is, by the varied workings of fate and adoption procedures, his grandson, and already demonstrating a similarly promising eclectic and eccentric range of interests embracing choral music and gunpowder.

NEWBURY

Jack of Newbury is a fine example of the lad of the people climbing to top man's estate. A poor homeless boy in Tudor times taken in by Winchcombe Abbey in Berkshire, Jack ran away, got a job by chance with a clothier, married the clothier's widow, and by dint of wit and work, became the richest man in England, given to having King Henry and Queen Catherine over for the weekend at his fine new house. The king wanted to make him Sir Jack of Newbury, but Jack courteously and modestly declined, which made him all the more loved by all. Excellent. And not completely untrue.

Jack Newbury is in fact a conflation of a father and son in

Newbury, the Winchcombes. The second Jack can claim to have founded Britain's first factory, employing numbers under one roof to produce kersey, a cloth named after the Suffolk town where it was first produced. Kersey was often used as the material for jackets, a double diminutive ('jack' and 'et') to denote a short coat. He was also known to Edward Seymour, Edward VI's Protector, and, perhaps more pertinently, to Thomas Cromwell, Henry's mean and main man of business, prosecutor of the Dissolution of the Monasteries, who had himself risen from a family of London clothiers and publicans. Jack owes his fame to Thomas Deloney, a Norfolk weaver, who starred him in his novel *Jack of Newbury*, published in 1590. Deloney makes Jack the metaphor for the new and worthy Tudor merchant classes. This is what happens with the offer of the knighthood:

> His Majesty would have made him knight, but he meekly refused it, saying, 'I beseech your Grace let me live a poor clothier, among my people, in whose maintenance I take more felicity than in all the vain titles of gentility: for these are the labouring ants whom I seek to defend, and these the bees which I keep: who labour in this life, not for ourselves, but for the Glory of God and to do service to our dread souveraign.'

Thus the birth of the good British bourgeois values that have gone on to survive, among much else, the derision of Napoleon, the distrust of Dickens and the devotion of Margaret Thatcher. Newbury, too, remained keen on commerce long after Jack's time: in 1744 the Duke of Chandos, while staying at the Pelican inn, came across a man who was trying to sell his wife, one of the chambermaids. The duke, touched by her plight and her beauty, bought her and married her and they lived happily until her death 11 years later. And the site of Jack's fine house in Newbury now has a Marks & Spencer's on it.

NEWTON

In the 1970s there were a lot of dull professional golfers; and there was Jack Newton. Jack wore red check trousers like a bistro tablecloth, tossed his cigarette to one side when he needed to putt, and liked a beer. Jack, you will not by now be surprised to learn, was an Australian. In 1975, at Carnoustie, he went into an 18-hole play-off for The Open with Tom Watson. On the eighth, Watson produced a wild hook which was flying towards Dundee when it hit the wire on a fence and bounced back. On the final green, Newton had a putt to draw the hole and force the contest into sudden death. He missed. In 1980, he finished second to Seve Ballesteros in the Masters. In 1983, aged 33, and somewhere near his peak, he walked into a propellor blade of a light aircraft, lost an eye and an arm and suffered severe abdominal injuries. He is now a commentator. In 1999, he stood on the 18th green at Carnoustie again and had another go at the putt he missed in 1975. The ball stopped a yard short. 'That's what I did last time,' said Newton. And then he laughed.

NICHOLSON

How much of a Jack can one Jack be? This is a full-time fable; an actor, of course. And, of course, one who seems to come from nowhere, even though for years he has been working very hard, when he's not playing, to be an overnight success. He's too much of a Jack to be a straight leading man – the smile and the eyes are far too ambiguous – so he has to wait for the lucky break, the support part turned down by someone else in the movie that is both hip and a hit and right bang on the moment. That was *Easy Rider*, 1969, when the world was familiar enough with hippies for them not to be threatening. Jack says, 'It wasn't till Cannes, when I saw my character going on, and I could feel the audience's reaction, that I knew that was it, I'd made it.' Jack didn't look back: twelve Oscar nominations, three wins, the laconic New Jersey voice, always slower than the director thinks necessary, but always right; the foxy, disconcerting look, the Jack trick of being lovable and dangerous, the curled lip with the sharky smile, less always more, except when it all comes together and an axe cracks, a door shatters and, with his own ad lib, 'H-e-r-e's Johnny!' Jack's still the lad, despite claims to be slowing down, settling down; despite a lads' magazine named after him folding before he has. The fable was there from the start – his parents were really his grandparents and his big sister was his mum, even though he didn't know until he was famous and *Time* magazine told him. So don't be fooled by the smile and the dark glasses and the girls: it's not all been Easy. Jack's a lad, but lads can be perfectionists, too, and clever, and exceptionally well-read. And Jack's a director manqué, which is why he so often chooses the good parts. And Jack knows the secret of Jacks: 'If you think you're attractive, you're always attractive.'

NICKLAUS

Inside every man, there's a Jack struggling to get out. In the 1960s, Jack William Nicklaus, born in Columbus, Ohio, in 1940, was the finest golfer in the world. Trouble was, no one really warmed to him. He was a big chap with the kind of military short, creamed and quiffed blond hair that had been out of style since not long after 1940, and he wore the kind of clothes that betrayed his colour blindness. And he had taken over from Arnold Palmer, the People's Golfer, bold, fallible, a brilliant, mercurial risk-takes-all kind of performer. When Jack took on Arnold in his own backyard, at Oakmont, in the 1962 US Open, there were people in the gallery holding up signs which read, 'Miss it, Fat Gut'. But Arnold knew what he was up against: 'Everybody says there's only one favourite, and that's me. But you better watch the fat boy.' So the fat boy did for Palmer, and was further and roundly abused for it, for his grim concentration and for his failure to appreciate the enormity of what he had done. And then Jack got it, and struggled out: he lost two stones in five weeks, reduced his hips by eight inches and grew his hair. Fat Jack was now the Golden Bear, a smiling and gracious man who refused to take his golf seriously except when he was playing it. Altogether he won three Open Championships, four US Opens, five US PGA titles and six Masters, and developed a fine line in repartee: when he was asked why he teed his ball so high above the ground, for instance, he replied, 'Through years of experience, I have found that air offers less resistance than dirt.' 'Jack, you are spectacular,' he was told during an interview. 'Your name is synonymous with the game of golf. You really know your way around the course. What is your secret?' Jack replied, 'The holes are numbered.' The best, though, came at the end of his career, when he was devoting more time to designing courses than playing on them, and used to tell this joke: 'A guy goes into a bar with his dog and orders a beer. The barman switches channels on the TV and on comes the latest golf tournament. I made a birdie and the dog did a back-flip on the bar. On the next hole, I holed another putt for a birdie and the dog repeated the back-flip. "Your dog must be a real Nicklaus fan," says the barman. "What does he do when Nicklaus wins a tournament?" To which the guy replied: "I don't know, I've only had him ten years . . .".'

NORWORTH

> Take me out to the ball game
> Take me out with the crowd
> Buy me some peanuts and Cracker Jack
> I don't care if I never get back;
> Let me root, root, root for the home team.
> If they don't win, it's a shame;
> For it's one, two, three strikes
> You're out, at the old ball game.

Jack Norworth (1879–1959) was a vaudeville artist whose greatest acclaim was achieved while he was the second of the five husbands acquired by the great Nora Bayes, whose 'Over There' became the anthem of the United States Army in Europe in the First World War. Nora would appear billed as follows: 'Nora Bayes, Assisted and Admired by Jack Norworth'. Sadly, they divorced after six years when Nora discovered Jack was also assisting and admiring someone else. They had success in London, where Jack entertained audiences with tongue-twisters like 'Which Switch, Miss, is the Switch for Ipswich?' Jack and Nora also wrote 'Shine On Harvest Moon', and its not quite so successful sequel, 'Turn Out Your Light, Mr. Moon Man'. But Jack's major claim to fame is that he wrote baseball's theme tune in 1908 even though he didn't go to a game until 1940. (Another of Nora's is that she sacked George and Ira Gershwin.) Cracker Jack, featured in the song, is a favourite US snack of caramel-covered popcorn and peanut, and has played a significant and pervasive role in American culture, achieving product placement of a surely unmatched prominence and longevity: Shirley Temple held a giant pack while singing 'On the Good Ship Lollipop', a pack provided the novelty ring that was engraved by Tiffany's for Holly Golightly, and another one held the small toe, packed in ice, that had been severed from a character in *Seinfeld*. Sailor Jack and his dog Bingo have appeared on the packs since 1918. *Crackerjack!* was a highly popular and charmingly frantic British television children's programme which ran from 1955 to 1984. It featured comedy, quizzes, a deafening cry of 'Crackerjack!' from its young audience at every mention of the name, and the award to both winners and losers of the much-prized and zealously guarded *Crackerjack!* pencils. My favourite quiz was Double or Drop, devised by its winningly wooden presenter, Eamonn Andrews. Competitors had to hold on to an increasing number of prizes and cabbages, awarded for correct or incorrect answers respectively. If they dropped them, or were awarded a third cabbage, they were out. I am often reminded of it when I make the mistake of selecting a basket rather than a trolley in the supermarket.

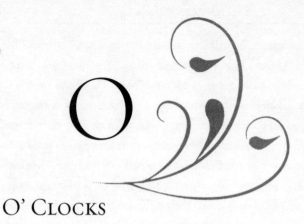

O' CLOCKS

These Jacks are carved mechanical figures which club the bells of clocks in several British churches and cathedrals and once clubbed the bells in many more. They usually mark the quarter hours and were sometimes known as quarter boys or quarter jacks. Their etymology was explored in a fascinating paper delivered to the Musical Association by Mr William Starmer on the afternoon of 6 November 1917 (it is reassuring, but not completely so, that such things proceeded as usual while the Western Front raged). Mr Starmer considered the theory that they were named after Jaquemart, the fourteenth-century clockmaker of Lille who pioneered them, but, having found evidence of Jacks at St Paul's in the thirteenth century, thought it more likely that Jack was a corruption of Jaccomarchiadus, the Latin for a man in armour, the form taken by the earliest Jacks. It was his belief that they were based on the armed sentries placed on belfries (a belfry is, strictly, a watchtower) in medieval times. Prominent Jack survivors include one at Wells, where **Jack Blandiver** sits in his sentry box in the cathedral kicking quarter bells and striking the hour with his axe. This Jack is part of one of the world's oldest surviving clocks (dating from 1390), which has knightly and jesting jacks above the face who come out to joust every quarter (good sport's note: the same one has been felled, twice, every 15 minutes for 600 years). According to Thomas Dekker, the Elizabethan playwright, there were some odd and saucy Jacks at St Paul's, lost in the Great Fire. Shakespeare has Richard II consider himself similarly enslaved. **Southwold Jack**, who stands in the town's fine St Edmund's Church, dressed as a soldier from the Wars of the Roses, has been borrowed by Adnams, the local brewers, for their labels. In Exeter Cathedral, the principal Jack is a figure of Henry VIII, which is a bit rich, given what destruction his reformation unleashed on church decoration; sensibly, Exonians re-christened him after a local miller they could set their clocks by.

ODELL

An engineer who matched attention to detail with flair and imagination, Jack Odell (1920–2007) was at one time the world's leading car manufacturer, producing a million vehicles a week. They were, though, small enough to fit into a matchbox: Matchbox Toys. Jack, a Londoner, came up with the idea in the 1950s so that his daughter would have something a little less disturbing than a spider to take into school in a matchbox. So he built her a small but perfectly formed steamroller. Today's sophisticates might raise an eyebrow without breaking off from the electronic thumb action, but back then they just loved it, and the 12,000 different models which followed. The winning gimmick of putting the toys into a mock matchbox didn't come until after Jack had sold more than a million modest models of the Queen's coronation coach. Matchbox eventually sold three billion vehicles worldwide before new times and fads overtook it. Jack was the driving force, a man who had found his way after a succession of stalled starts, including expulsion from school and the sack from film projecting after putting the reel in the wrong way round. He discovered his engineering talent in the Army during the Second World War and had his steamroller moment after joining a small diecasting business based in an old pub. He ran his company with fastidiousness and without union representation, taking his meals with his workforce, if on the other side of a partition. Some of his models had more than 100 die-cast parts, including windshield wipers and ceiling hooks; car seats, around a centimetre wide, had to give just the right appearance of padding; Jack designed a machine to spray silver paint on the tiny headlights. 'In my obituary,' said Jack, 'I want it said I was a damn good engineer.' It all makes me rather ashamed to reveal that I preferred the bigger, more expensive ones made by Dinky.

O' DIAMONDS

'Jack o' Diamonds' is a folk song that has been borrowed and covered so many times that it's not really clear what's original and where it came from. Interpretations have been made by Blind Lemon Jefferson, John Lee Hooker, Fairport Convention and Nick Cave and the Bad Seeds. There's also a pretty bad poem of it on the sleeve notes of Bob Dylan's *Another Side of Bob Dylan*. My favourite version is by Lonnie Donegan, the Cockney-Glaswegian skiffle artist; but that is not as good as his 'My Old Man's a Dustman', which has a number of fine jokes, including:

> I say, I say, I say (What, you again?)
> My dustbin's absolutely full of toadstools
> (How do you know it's full?)
> 'Cos there's not much room inside.

O'-LANTERN

The jack-o'-lantern might be the cosy candle-lit carved pumpkin which helps to make Hallowe'en so unthreatening these days (unless you haven't got any treats, in which case, snuff it out quickly and hide behind the sofa). But that's a comparatively recent coining. The original jack-o'-lanterns are those strange, flickering, somehow beckoning lights you tend to see when you are out at night alone in lonely parts and an owl has just hooted. People say that Jack is a pixie, a sprite, a goblin, intent on luring you to a disaster at which he will cackle, horribly. Although he goes by different names, from Zaltvyksle in Lithuania, Yan-gant-y-tan in Brittany, Ken Yang Ba-Shing in Taiwan to the Spooklights of Missouri and Georgia, Jack is a familiar in most cultures. Other people say he is merely burning methane, ignited by spontaneous combustion of phosphane. You go have a look.

OLPHERTS

What do you call an artillery man who charged about India and the Crimea for 35 years and never went into battle, in the words of one admiring commanding officer, without deserving the Victoria Cross? Only one name, really, for Sir William Olpherts, VC (1822–1902), and it was the one by which he was known throughout the British Army and beyond: Hell Fire Jack. Jack was never content with just lighting the touchpaper and standing back; wherever there were guns or people to be captured or rescued, there was Jack, usually in the middle of a hail of unfriendly ordnance. The VC to represent it all was won at the siege of Lucknow in 1857 during the Indian Rebellion: his commanding officer there wrote: 'My dear Heroic Olpherts, bravery is a poor and insufficient epithet to apply to a valour such as yours.' Jack's death in bed at the age of 80 was considered a marvel by all. *The Times* thought he would be remembered as a 'gallant and fiery fighter' rather than as a 'sound and scientific leader'. This was, after all, a man whose temper and soldierly quirks were legend: once, reported *The Times*, he had much impressed the soldiery at a temperance meeting with a vigorous rehearsal of the evils of drink and then rather surprised them by closing with a thump on the table and declaring 'he would not give a straw for a soldier who could not take his glass of grog like a man!'

OSBORN (1)

Jack Osborn (1899–1941) is not **Jack Osbourne** (qv). This Jack was an English Romany who travelled far, to Canada, where he joined the Winnipeg Grenadiers, and to Hong Kong, where he died. Jack was a sergeant major who played by the book and fought like a lion in the forlorn defence of the island against the Japanese, time and again rallying his inexperienced and rapidly depleting men. He recaptured Mount Butler, leading a bayonet charge against machine guns, covered the withdrawal of his men, at the end single-handedly, repeatedly exposing himself to heavy fire. When they were again surrounded, Jack picked up and hurled back several Japanese grenades; when he saw he wouldn't have time to repeat the trick, he threw himself onto one, saving his comrades and dying instantly. This is human bravery and selflessness of an order that makes you weep and almost forget the human folly that provoked it.

OSBORN (2)

Jack Osborn is not **Jack Osbourne** (qv). Jack Osborn (1929–96) was an industrial designer who worked tirelessly to promote the game of croquet in the United States. Promote, not popularise: 'Croquet,' he said, 'is a sport for the affluent class.' There are many ways of playing croquet; some felt that devising yet another – the American Rules – was not the way forward, especially as the hitting of balls through hoops somehow brings out the worst in people. Mirroring the game itself, Osborn's United States Croquet Association had rapid successes and setbacks. The cachet of keen players like Harpo Marx and Tyrone Power has never quite been regained. Darryl F. Zanuck, known among fellow players as The Terrible-Tempered Mr Bang, liked to play in his bathing suit with a cigar clamped between his teeth. Perhaps that is the way forward. Or perhaps they could get **Jack Osbourne** (qv) interested, although it might provoke too much adrenaline for him.

OSBORNE

Jack Osborne is not **Jack Osbourne** (qv). Jack Osborne is a character in the British television soap opera *Hollyoaks*. Jack, a former policeman who is the mine hoste at the The Dog in the Pond pub, has undergone many of the colourful experiences that seem to be the lot of soap-opera characters, especially those running pubs. He has troublesome children, has been married twice and had one heart attack. The Dog in the Pond has also burnt down. Plenty of adrenaline there, then, too.

OSBOURNE

Jack Osbourne is Jack Osbourne. It's a tough gig, to be the child of Ozzy and Sharon Osbourne, and Jack has had his problems, but is reputed to be a nice chap, which is another inspiring testament to human resilience. His television series, *Jack Osbourne: Adrenaline Junkie*, featured Jack training for sports like rock climbing, mountaineering, jungle trekking and motor rallying. In one episode, an elephant almost charged him. Some might judge an autobiography at the age of 21 premature, but Jack already, and not surprisingly, possesses a weary wisdom, if this view is anything to go by: 'Having a girlfriend is like Communism: on paper it sounds awesome; in reality it never really works out.'

OWEN

Jack Owen is a death-metal guitarist. A founding member of Cannibal Corpse, he left because of artistic differences and subsequently joined the Florida band Deicide, working with them on the 2006 album, *The Stench of Redemption*. Fellow band member, Glen Benton, who has an inverted crucifix branded on his forehead, has had to deny scurrilous rumours that he was married in a church, while drummer Steve Asheim has been at pains to set the record straight over allegations about biting the heads off kittens: 'I've never bitten a kitten. I have a cat and if anyone tried to hurt him I'd take a big shotgun and blow their head off. His name? I just call him My Little Buddy, you know, like from *Gilligan's Island*.'

P

PAAR

A lot to answer for, this Jack. For this is the Jack who invented the late-night chat show format of desk and sofa, and worked it so well that not much has changed nearly 50 years on. No matter how odd it seems to have the host behind a desk and the guest across and below him on a sofa, the result is that the host, protected from deference and matiness, can be cheekier, more incisive (just watch the shows when they're together on the same level if you don't believe me). But the regular stooges, the chummy house band and leader, the odd forays out of the studio, surely they are newer? Nope; all Jack. Jack was edgier, more dangerous, too: he could walk out, weep, start feuds. He lived in a less plugged age, and had guests he just wanted. True to form, he stopped at the top of his game, leaving *The Tonight Show* in 1962 after five years. His catchphrase was 'I kid you not'. A good clue to the quality that made him such good television comes from his obituary in the *Washington Post*: 'He was twice married and divorced to a pianist named Irene, whom he met early in his radio career. "The first time we were divorced, it was my fault", Mr Paar said. "The second time, it was her fault. When we felt that we were even, we quit."'

PAINTER

Jack the Painter, alias James Aitken, alias Hill, alias Hinde, and no doubt some more, was a painter (of the house variety) from

Edinburgh who took to thieving. After a failed new start in Virginia, he returned to Europe in 1775 and determined to strike a blow for American independence by setting fire to British dockyards. He received a small sum of money and a lukewarm endorsement from the American commissioner in Paris and set off for Portsmouth and succeeded in starting a small blaze at the second attempt. He had no luck at Plymouth, but rather more along the Bristol waterfront, before he was arrested at Hook in Hampshire. Jack elected to defend himself: wisely is it said that he who does so has a fool for a client: Jack was found guilty and sentenced to death.

The mizzen mast from HMS *Arethusa* was especially erected on Portsmouth Common, and there Jack was hanged from the yardarm on 10 March 1777 in front of the usual large crowd. What was Jack about? I am indebted to Neil York of Brigham Young University for his lecture and research revealing that Jack was an even earlier celebrity chaser than **Jack McCall** (qv): 'I beheld it in the light of a truly heroic enterprise, such as would never have been equalled to the end of time. I was persuaded it would entitle me to the first rank in America, and flattered myself with the ambition of becoming the admiration of the world.' Jack's body was left dangling from a gibbet for many years. His burglary tools are on display at the Portsmouth City Museum, but his mummified finger, turned into a tobacco stopper as some sort of bad eighteenth-century joke, has disappeared.

PALANCE

There appears to be a convention that an actor of bad characters will be a man of rueful charm and hidden hinterland, if his name is Jack (see also **Jack Elam**). Nor is this mere coincidence: Jack Palance (1919–2006), possessor of Hollywood's meanest ever cheekbones, deepest-set, meanest eyes and meanest, most menacing voice, was, to begin with, a Ukrainian-parented Pennsylvania coalminer called Volodymyr Palahniuk. Volodymyr, or Jack, if we may, also did a spot of boxing (hence the meanest nose) before taking to the boards and adopting the *nom de theatre* of Walter Palance. Walter! Apologies to those so called, but Walters – think Huston, or Matthau – are, when they're not wimps, too whimsical to be truly wicked. No, thankfully, Jack recognised that he was a Jack, and the world enjoyed the results, most notably the black-garbed, black-hearted Jack (yup) Wilson, the bad bad baddie up against (the come on, let's be honest, ever so slightly wet but still splendid) Shane (written, of course, by **Jack Schaefer**). That Jack earned this Jack an Oscar nomination in 1953; sending himself up in *City Slickers* got him the award itself in 1991. Jack, naturally, also enjoyed sending himself up: when he went up there to get the Oscar, he dropped to the floor and went into a series of one-handed press-ups to prove he was still fit for work at 73. Not that he was obsessive about it: in 1957 he took off to Europe and spent six years collecting antiques and mostly unimpressive roles. He was an amused critic of his work: 'I go to see maybe seven films a year at the most,' he said. 'And since I only go to see the best, it follows that I very rarely see my own.' What he made less of was his degree from Stanford University (in drama), and a stint as a journalist (wisely deciding there wasn't nearly enough money in it for the effort). He painted, and wrote poetry: 'The Forest of Love' was a blank verse effort, illustrated by him, and brave in its simplicity and openness, given his image. The image of him I like best is from his time competing on the television programme *Hollywood Squares*, when his fellow celebrities found that he had fallen asleep in his square.

PARNELL

Never underestimate the connections of a Jack. Jack Parnell has had a distinguished and aptly varied career in variety: beginning as a drummer with Ted Heath, the British big-band leader of the 1940s and 1950s, he went on to form, lead and conduct his own big-band and to become musical director of ATV, one of the first British commercial stations, as well as regularly appearing on it. No one would dispute his talent, but no one would deny, either, that it's useful if the owner of the station is a great friend of your dad, who is also a legendary impresario, responsible, among other things, for bringing the Crazy Gang together and running the London Palladium: Lew Grade and Val Parnell, respectively. Lew, later Lord, Grade, was a magnificent showman, down to the huge cigar, and one of the last links between the old, brash and flash world of variety and television before the guys with the jeans and the degrees took over. He was also author of one of the all-time great showbiz quotes, on his costly movie flop, *Raise the Titanic* (1980): 'It would have been cheaper to lower the Atlantic.'

What I didn't know, though, was that Jack's grandfather was none other than Fred Russell. Who? Fred Russell, I will have you know, was the man who invented modern ventriloquism, the whole one man, one puppet schtick which has led to the glories of Edgar Bergen and Charlie McCarthy, Arthur Prince and Jim, Peter Brough and Archie, and, his close family would argue, Keith Harris and Orville. Fascinating people, ventriloquists; I speak as someone who has witnessed an amateur Japanese ventriloquist in Las Vegas drinking a glass of milk while his doll was singing 'When You're Smiling'. Arthur Prince and Jim were buried together, with their names on the gravestone; Arthur's wife arrived later. Peter Brough was that exercising concept, a radio ventriloquist. But I digress. Fred Parnell changed his name to avoid being linked with Charles Parnell, the vivid but doomed Irish nationalist whose affair with a lady not his wife scandalised late Victorian Britain and seriously damaged his cause. Russell was the name of Fred's local MP, Charles Russell, another Irishman whose son, a solicitor, was, as it happens, selected by the Marquis of Queensberry to help fight his libel action with Oscar Wilde (the marquis chose him by the simple expedient of walking down the Strand on a Saturday and picking the first solicitor working). But I digress. One of Jack's other great claims to fame is that he conducted the *Muppet Show* orchestra; which, of course, was richly in keeping with his grandfather's tradition.

PARSONS

Medieval alchemists and Renaissance magi had no problem combining Science with Magic; for them, each was the means of achieving the other. Nor did the Enlightenment have any great objections; Newton particularly was happy to have a dabble. Now, though, it's got very dull. But Jack Parsons (1914–52) wasn't dull. Jack Parsons was the rocket man who went out with a bang. Prior to that had been pretty exciting, too. Jack had been blowing up things other than himself since he was a Pasadena schoolboy; it was an interest that, in the rather more freewheeling and freelance 1930s, saw him doing pioneering work in rocketry which led to his co-founding of Pasadena's Jet Propulsion Laboratory and beyond, if not to infinity then at least to Mars.

But Jack's interest had also been inspired by his deep adolescent and student readings in science fiction, medieval romances and ancient mysteries. Fatally, he came across the writings of the extraordinary Aleister Crowley, proclaimed by himself a great black magician, 'the Beast 666' and 'the wickedest man alive', promoter of a rich dark brew of hedonism involving lashings of sex and drugs that entranced Jack and, suitably pasteurised, many another later would-be hippie. Jack and Crowley never met, at least on this plane, but they corresponded extensively, and Jack provided the money to establish a house of believers in Pasadena after attending a 'Gnostic Mass' at the local chapter of Crowley's Ordo Templis Orientis celebrated by a High Priestess who in a former incarnation had played Mary Pickford's mother in *Rebecca of Sunnybrook Farm*.

Jack himself soon became High Priest, succeeding a clerk at the

Southern California Gas Company. Another initiate was none other than L. Ron Hubbard, founder of Scientology, who, in a typically unorthodox move, made Jack's sister-in-law (and lover) the second Mrs Hubbard before the first Mrs Hubbard divorced him. In 1946, Hubbard chanted incantations while Parsons and his new lover, Marjorie Cameron, energetically initiated the physical process which would lead to the birth of a magical moonchild on the astral plane. They were supposed to keep at it for 12 nights, but one of the rituals, involving a naked pregnant woman jumping through fire, understandably alarmed the neighbours, who called the police.

By now Jack had abandoned rocketry in favour of these less orthodox missions, fuelled by peyote, marijuana, morphine and cocaine. Even Crowley was impressed: 'I get fairly frantic when I contemplate the idiocy of these goats.' Parsons then left the Ordo Templis Orientis to follow his own path. The Lord (take your choice of which one) knows what he was up to in June 1952 when he dropped a concoction containing fulminate of mercury. The explosion was felt a mile away. Jack wasn't propelled into the heavens, but he died 45 minutes later, soon followed by his mother, who killed herself on hearing the news. The death, naturally, remains covered in mystery. Cameron went on to become a cult underground figure in the 1950s and '60s. Hubbard went on to claim that he had been working undercover for Naval Intelligence on a mission to stamp out such disgraceful practices. Jack has a crater on the moon named after him, which proves that there is still some humour left in Science: it's on the dark side.

PAYNE

As we have seen elsewhere, if not immediately above, there can be a reassuring quality about a Jack. Jack Payne (1889–1969) was one such, a very big name in Britain in the 1930s with his band, hailed and admired thus by *The Times* in his obituary:

In the early, heroic days of radio, Jack Payne's name was a household word, and with his band, the big-scale dance band of the period, he was one of the most familiar stars of the medium, which he reached before the advent of Henry Hall and his BBC Dance Band. To the dance music of the 1930s, Jack Payne and his players gave a convincing English accent. Their playing achieved cheerfulness with a certain emotional reserve. Other bands, following Transatlantic examples, sought to whip up enthusiasm by suggesting an almost hysterical abandon to the rhythm of the music they played, but Jack Payne made boisterous, cheerful or sentimentally easy-going music in a way which managed to be noisily spirited and light-hearted.

You take the point.

PEARL

Sometimes, you can have a great act, but the timing is all wrong. Jack Pearl (1894–1984) was a big star of vaudeville and early radio. In the 1930s he was getting bigger and bigger. And then his career just tailed off and away. Jack's act was his version of Baron Münchausen, and depended for its effect on his comic German accent. Shame.

PEPPER

The melancholy of the might-have-been. Edward Jackson Culpepper (1902–79) was a singer and dancer whose stage name was Jack Pepper. One of his early dancing partners was also his first wife: Ginger Rogers. They were billed as Ginger and Pepper. Forget Fred and Ginger: Ginger and Pepper could have been the one. But they were only married for two years and two of Jack's last screen appearances were as a waiter in *Perry Mason* and a banjo player in *Cat Ballou*.

PERSHING

Another famous Black Jack, more properly, John Joseph Pershing (1860–1948), leader of the American Expeditionary Force in the First World War, and General of the Armies of the United States in the Second. How did he acquire his popular nickname? It was a bowdlerisation of the one given to him by cadets when he was an unpopular instructor at West Point: Nigger Jack, after his time with one of the Buffalo Soldier regiments, soldiered by blacks, officered by whites. Charming. I'm not entirely sure, either, about the merits of having a cruise missile named after you.

PHILBY

A charged surname to Britons of certain ages. Harold 'Kim' Philby (1912–88) was the infamous Third Man in the Soviet spy ring composed of Cambridge men whose serial exposure attracted great attention while it played out for almost exactly as long as the Cold War. Harry 'Jack' Philby (1885–1960) was Kim's father and led a life at least as serpentine. The son of a tea planter, he first joined the Indian Civil Service, but the major part of his life was spent in Arabia, where he was closely and often clandestinely involved in the shifting plans, manoeuvring and machinations that have bedevilled the region for too long. He began as one of the British diplomats during the First World War charged with encouraging and directing the Arab Revolt against Turkish rule. He forged a lifelong friendship with Ibn Saud, the founder of the Saudi dynasty, urging his cause as Arab leader with characteristic independence (some said contrariness) against the British choice, Lawrence of Arabia's man, Sherif Hussein. After further, mostly disgruntled, service in Baghdad and Jerusalem, Philby resigned and went to live in Jeddah, from where, along with Mecca and Medina, Ibn Saud had just ejected Sherif Hussein.

There he began a trading company which dealt in such things as gold, oil, arms and influence. It is said that he remained in the employ of the British Secret Service; he was certainly a close, if unofficial, advisor to Ibn Saud for the next 30 years. Principal among his involvements, alleged, secret and otherwise, were plans to pay Ibn Saud to resettle Palestinians in his new kingdom and so make way for Jewish immigration; a scheme to get Saudi oil through Spain to Nazi Germany; and a long-term involvement with Aramco, the American oil conglomerate which won Saudi oil concessions and had intricate links with the CIA. More than enough, you might say, to keep a man's mind occupied. Still, he also found time to stand on an appeasement ticket for the British parliament in 1939, lose and be imprisoned briefly in Britain in 1940 for unfriendly activities. And to make a series of epic journeys through the Arabian peninsula, most notably crossing the Empty Quarter in 1932. These led to a series of books and allowed him, with some justification, to have 'Greatest of Arabian Explorers' inscribed on his tombstone. He was also much interested in birds, contributing many Arabian specimens to the British Museum and awarding them scientific names – *Otus scops pamelae*, for example – based on those of women he admired.

He converted to Islam in 1930, and was afterwards known to Saudis as Sheikh Abdullah; in 1945, according to reliable and less reliable sources, he was either given his second wife, Rozy Abdul Aziz, by Ibn Saud, or he bought her in the slave market at Taif. His first wife, Dora, mother of Kim, when she wasn't being ignored at home in Hampstead, became the first European woman to cross Arabia from sea to sea, and died in 1957. By then, Ibn Saud was dead and Philby had relocated to Lebanon. Kim was there, too, working in Beirut as a journalist and for the British intelligence services, despite having been officially discharged and ostensibly cleared of involvement in the defection of Donald Maclean and Guy Burgess, the first two men of the Cambridge ring, in 1950. You know how it is: you've read your Le Carré. Nevertheless, this was still impressive. Father, who had kept his hand in with the Arabs and Americans, and Son, who was, if anything can be believed, being paid by the British to spy on Father: all this and the Suez Crisis, too. Oh, to be a fly on the wall in the Beirut flat where the two stayed together: imagine the conversation, the revelation. But instead, one day in 1960, Jack said to Kim, 'God, I'm bored,' and died.

Three years later, Kim was in Moscow, where he stole another wife (Maclean's), kept drinking and died in 1988, also bored. The Fourth Man, meanwhile, Anthony Blunt, the Don who recruited them and went on to work for the Queen as her Surveyor of Pictures, had been finally exposed in 1979, but died peacefully at home in London in 1983, having survived a brief but fierce furore of publicity, during which I was despatched by the *Daily Telegraph* to beard him at a Sunday lunchtime Home Counties cocktail party. The host suggested I look behind the sofa; sadly, he wasn't there. The Fifth Man, John Cairncross, was next up, but by then enthusiasms had largely moved on and he died comparatively unnoticed in 1995.

PIERCE

Another Hollywood Jack responsible for nightmares (see **Jack Arnold**, **Jack Nicholson**). This one was originally Janus Piccoulas, born in Greece. But as Jack Pierce, make-up artist, he was responsible, together with the director, James Whale, for the look of Boris Karloff as Frankenstein: the square head, the enormous hatched scar and, above all, the bolt through the neck. He also worked on *Dracula*, *Bride of Frankenstein*, *The Mummy*, *The Wolf Man*, and, in a piece of bathos equal to anything Tinseltown has ever conjured, during his final, declining days, *Mister Ed*, the television talking horse. There is, as it happens, a myth that Mister Ed was actually a zebra, but not even Jack was that good, even if the programme was in black and white.

PINE

The jack pine (*Pinus banksiana*) is a small native North American species distinguished by cones which point forward along the branch and sometimes curl around it. Disappointingly, it can also be distinguished from *Pinus virginiana*, the lonesome one of which was so hauntingly sought by Laurel and Hardy. I fear, too, that it is not to be found in California, famed setting for the Hollywood film crew and their discovery of the perfect location, a high ridge marred only by a tree which was in the way of the shot. So, naturally, they chopped it down. In the nearest town, and still full of the beauty of the spot, they asked if it had a name. Yes, said the locals, Lone Pine Ridge.

PLUMB

An excellent example of the Jack revealing the Man. You might be aware of J.H. Plumb (1911–2001) from the dimly remembered spine of a history book that you never quite got round to opening. This would be a pity on a couple of counts: you would have missed the elegance and acuity of one of the great British literary historians; and you would not have been thus stimulated to find out a bit more about the author.

For while J.H. Plumb sounds like yet another of those dry dead dons, this one is far better described as Jack Plumb. The name has folklore about it, and so does his story. He was the third son of a boot-clicker in a Leicester boot and shoe factory but early discovered an academic talent. He arrived at Cambridge to take a scholarship wearing a bowler hat but, quickly realising his social solecism, hurled it from the Bridge of Sighs into the Cam. But to no avail: he was denied a place at St John's despite deserving one. Unabashed (he rarely was), Jack went to the University College of Leicester and fought his way into Cambridge as a research student to G.M.

Trevelyan. The doyen of social and narrative historians found a willing pupil in young Jack, the working-class boy who went on to succeed his patrician master with a prodigious output of books and lectures which promoted the social over the constitutional, the conclusion over the detail, and disclosed a descriptive talent and taste for the tellingly quirky which won him great popularity and financial rewards, for which he had a Jackish enjoyment.

He was, for example, much taken with fine wines, and profited much, during the Second World War, while code cracking at Bletchley (see also **Jack Cohen**), from sharing a billet with Anthony de Rothschild. Jack ended up Master of Christ's College, much fêted in America, a confidant of royalty, a backstairs bestower of patronage, and owner of an old rectory, to which, as his *Times* obituary put it, 'he would retire for the pleasure of his own company' (he never married). The Master's Lodgings during his time were known as 'Jack's Palace'. As in the best fairy tales, there were rumours about the source of his wealth (often ascribed fancifully by envious and snobbish colleagues to an interest in a Leicester lingerie factory). He had a renownedly sharp tongue, which grew ever sharper, in the manner of his Oxonian contemporary of similar provenance, A.L. Rowse, and was similarly dismissive of many of his colleagues and lately attracted by Margaret Thatcher. But he worked tirelessly for his college as well as for himself, and raised much money for it, including a lot of his own. Was he a happy Jack in this fable? Like Rowse, he was perhaps a little disappointed that his acclaim wasn't absolutely universal, but defiant, especially about his expensive tastes: 'I have no guilt,' he once declared happily. 'Having jumped on to the coat tails of the bourgeoisie, I have no intention of being shaken off again.'

POINT

The unhappy fool left unloved and distraught at the end of Gilbert and Sullivan's *The Yeomen of the Guard*, leading contender for the saddest of sad clowns. You will know the story of the Victorian gentleman who goes to his doctor complaining of depression. The doctor recommends he should go to see the great clown, Joseph Grimaldi: that will cheer him up. 'But Doctor,' says the man, 'I am Grimaldi.' Yes, I know, an unlikely story, but you get the Point. Jack Point's first interpreter was another clown inclined to stress and sadness, George Grossmith (1847–1912), a small man who, despite hating travelling, suffering from appalling stage fright and bouts of depression countered by copious amounts of morphine, nevertheless toured Britain incessantly, wrote 18 comic operas, nearly 100 musical sketches, some 600 songs and piano pieces, serious and comic pieces for newspapers and magazines and three books, including two of autobiography and, with his almost equally flightily talented brother, Weedon, that unrivalled masterpiece of affectionately cruel parody, *Diary of a Nobody*, the chronicles of Charles Pooter, The Laurels, Brickfield Terrace, Holloway. He also collaborated on a revue with Florence Marryat, the daughter of Captain Marryat, author of *The Children of the New Forest* and the adventures of the Greenwich mudlark, *Poor Jack*. I wonder what he would have achieved if he had been tall and happy. Florence Marryat, by the way, was a spirited spiritualist, comedienne, occasional D'Oyly Carte performer and dramatist who married at sixteen and raised eight children while also writing seventy books, including *At Heart a Rake*, *A Moment of Madness*, *Written in Fire* and *Love's Conflict*.

PRIESTLEY

Popular writers seldom meet with the wholehearted approval of their less popular peers; in Britain, popular writers from the provinces used to merit particular treatment, especially if they showed they resented it. And so John Priestley, or John Boynton Priestley (1894–1984), J.B.Priestley, literary biographer and essayist, novelist, playwright and Yorkshireman, was dubbed Jolly Jack. It was meant to be a sneer at the seriousness with which he seemed to take himself, but it fitted far better than was supposed. However, there was certainly a pipe and a determined accent. And there could be a gruff and a grumble about him: his great 1930s travelogue, *English Journey*, can be sapping because of it despite his justified anger with the common social conditions of the time. *The Good Companions*, his first great popular success, though, has a love of life about it all the more remarkable for one that had so far encompassed the trenches and the early death of his first wife. And although, as a good Yorkshireman, he affected disdain at the frivolities of the pleasure-seeking Lancastrians across the Pennines, you would have to be a sour southerner indeed not to be uplifted by the fun and bounce of *Sing As You Go*, the film he wrote starring Gracie Fields surviving the Depression with the help of Blackpool. The effect on morale of his radio talks during the Second World War is better remembered than their effect afterwards on Labour's landslide election victory, or his inspiration of the Campaign for Nuclear Disarmament.

He was still a Jack for all that, not least in an enthusiastic approach to romance often untrammelled by conventions, such as marriage. And in an openness to the new until the end: Barry Cryer, another witty Yorkshireman who befriended him in his later days, found him full of praise for John Cleese and *Monty Python* (but not Bruce Forsyth), and accustomed to kissing the TV screen when the glamorous news anchor of the day was on it. Cryer also has an excellent story of a dress rehearsal for the best-known of Priestley's many plays, *When We Are Married*, a comedy of northern bourgeois manners with a splendid cameo for a drunken photographer, played on this occasion by Fred Emney. At the end, the curtain failed to come down, leaving the cast standing stranded. Priestley and the director, who had an urgent meeting to attend, got up and left, followed by the loud voice of Emney: 'If he didn't like it, he shouldn't have written it.' The Jackest part of Priestley, though, was a romantic love for England that resisted fashionable metropolitan sophistications and his grumpiness. In his introduction to the *Shell Guide to England*, he wrote of the small country's magical, dense quality, the sense of so much of it being 'round the corner'; and a connection with the past so present that 'it would not surprise me if somebody decided to follow some tiny overgrown lane and then found that at the end of it Camelot was still there, with nettles thick around a dusty round table'. Exactly, Jack.

PROFUMO

This is about that great 1950s–1960s fusion, when the old generation, Establishment, conventions, discretions and mores met the enticingly liberated new ones: the evening of Saturday, 8 July 1961, Cliveden, Berkshire.

Cliveden is often described as a stately home, but it is far more a stagey one, bought by Waldorf Astor (see **Jack Astor**) in furtherance of his English ambitions for his son, Waldorf II, and his feisty wife, the whimsical force of nature, Nancy Astor, Britain's first woman MP. Nancy used it as the backdrop to her Cliveden Set, a loose, formidably well-connected but dubiously influential grouping of politicking, partying and writerly people which dabbled in rightish thinking of the unthinkable, including accommodating Hitler.

The next Astor, Bill, an occasional Tory MP, continued something of the tradition into the 1960s: on that Saturday evening, after dinner, he was strolling with a group of guests through the Cliveden gardens. It was one of those languid evenings that follow a hot English summer day, heady and luscious. Shouts and splashes from the swimming pool carried loudly through the air. Astor and a friend turned a corner and there saw a naked, laughing girl rushing from the pool to her towel. She, of course, was Christine Keeler, a 19 year old who in the former times might have been described as a showgirl, or a good-time girl, or, further back, a doxy; but in these times, all this was being redefined, adjusted, leaving her best described, with ironic apostrophes, as 'model'. He, equally of course, was John

Dennis Profumo, Secretary of State, Harrow, Oxford, Good War, a friend of royalty, a man of Establishment ease just raffish enough to be known to his friends as Jack.

That raffishness carried him into the casual dalliance with Keeler that would have clattering, echoing ramifications. Jack's bad luck was for his tumblings to be at the point of any number of coincidences, including that of a Fleet Street eager to have a good old ding-dong which would demonstrate with plenty of lurid trimmings that the times truly were a'changing, the rules of engagement were under renegotiation, and the toffs were no longer going to get away with it. And here we had a member of an old-fashioned, élitist, tired Tory government breaking its own code by lying to his fellow fellows and, worse, being found out. And, delight of delights, being found out lying about a photogenic, talkative young girl extremely well-connected to the embryonic and excitingly egalitarian and omni-liberated 'Swinging London'. It has become fashionable to claim that the Profumo Affair was and has been exaggerated in its importance and scandalousness. Come on, though: it involved not only the resignation of a government minister, but, in addition, a cast list including Stephen Ward, the son of a canon of Rochester Cathedral with a qualification as an osteopath from Missouri, who had treated Sir Winston Churchill and painted the Duke of Edinburgh when he wasn't renting a cottage at Cliveden from his friend Bill Astor or standing trial at the Old Bailey for living off the immoral earnings of Miss Keeler and her deliciously named friend, Mandy Rice-Davies. (Let's not forget, either, that Miss Rice-Davies's response in court to Bill Astor's denials of any impropriety at Cliveden has justly come to sum up the death of deference in the 1960s: 'Well, he would say that, wouldn't he?')

We will dismiss, if you like, the minor jazz-singing, trigger-happy Jamaicans caught up in an argument over Miss Keeler, and the famous actress, Valerie Hobson, married to and betrayed by Profumo, but only so as to arrive the quicker at the nonpareil of the case, the part which must have had the editors of the popular newspapers thinking they had died and gone to wherever the editors of popular newspapers would be happy – the killer fact that Miss Keeler had been granting her favours to both the Secretary of State for War and the naval attaché at the Russian Embassy, who was, as it happened, a spy.

How much more of a Crikey Factor can anyone want? Well, there was the subsequent inquiry by Lord Denning, which delightfully legitimised the frantic voyeurism, confirming, for example, disgraceful upper-class orgies featuring a man wearing only a black mask and a waitress's apron. There was, too, the undoubted and large contribution of it all to the subsequent resignation of Harold Macmillan.

Much fun was had at these foibles, but there were no happy endings. Ward killed himself, Keeler was peculiarly tainted, the Russian killed himself with drink, and Profumo spent 40 years of atonement working for a charity in London's East End. Again, this is now thought a bizarrely exaggerated penance. But although Profumo made one spectacular misjudgement, he had the cleverness to see that he had become a symbol, and that naughty Jack had to do his time for all his time in order to become honest John again.

PUDDING

Jack Pudding is a folk-tale hero and sometime stage character who has a prodigious appetite for puddings, particularly, sensible fellow, black ones. Jack has several European counterparts who, it has been observed, make for an interesting comparison of national favourite foods: Pickel-herringë in Holland, Hans Wurst in Germany, Jean Potage in France, and Macaroni in Italy. You might also care to know that a vegetarian black pudding, in which the pig's blood and ox intestines have been replaced by beetroot and caramel, is available from the Real Lancashire Black Pudding Company, based in Rossendale. It should be noted, too, that Homer writes of

Agamemnon and his fellow Greek heroes feasting on black pudding outside Troy.

PURVIS

Another lost Jack, perhaps the lostest. Impossible to pin down, Jack. Jazz trumpeter would be his lead label, but there is also aviator, chef, thief, convict, carpenter, radio-repair man and sometime proprietor of the School of Grecian Dancing for Young Ladies in Miami. Jack, the son of an estate agent from Indiana, born in 1906, white, was, by all accounts, a great trumpeter, good enough to have Coleman Hawkins and J.C. Higginbotham playing for him in his short-lived band. But Jack, for whatever reason, was so far off the wall he was round the bend. One of his best songs was 'Mental Strain at Dawn'. Scott Yanow has described his playing as 'full of fiery bursts, unrealised potential and some crazy chance-taking, just like his life was'. You bet. Jack was light-fingered, plausible and always late. When he arrived, he didn't always stay long, as he was often quickly followed by police or similar. No one seems to know how or exactly when he learnt to fly, but his trips seem to have been irregular and across the border. When he crossed the Atlantic on the SS *Île de France* with the George Carhart Band, he played for them for the one night before blagging a cabin and joining the Ted Lewis Band in First Class. When he arrived in Paris he left the hotel by the roof when a gendarme arrived (a matter of some travellers' cheques, apparently). In Louisiana, he talked himself into the New Orleans Symphony Orchestra, allegedly playing the ocarina on Paganini's 'Carnival of Venice'. In Los Angeles, where he was cheffing, he blagged himself into a job with Warner Bros, composing a little something for a 110-piece orchestra. He left Miami and his Grecian girls quickly (a matter of some morals charges) and ended up in jail in Texas on a robbery conviction in 1938. Inside, he formed a band, the Rhythmic Swingsters, Jack on piano, playing his compositions. They were broadcast on the radio regularly. Jack was released but he was enjoying the gig so much he deliberately violated his parole and went back inside with the band until 1946. It gets even hazier after that: according to John Chilton, whose Feetwarmers most famously used to accompany George Melly, a man answering Jack's description was seen sitting in a park in Honolulu in 1948 giving alternate performances of 'The Flight of the Bumblebee' on trumpet and trombone. He was supposed to have killed himself in 1962, but in 1968, in San Francisco, a man calling himself Jack Purvis approached Jim Goodwin, the cornettist, said 'I used to play one of those', and chatted about the old days. Jack hasn't been seen since, but keep your eyes open and your hand on your wallet.

PYE

Chacun à son goût; de gustibus non est disputandum; suit yourself. I have never been seized by professional wrestling; the noise, my dear, the people and, above all, the bad acting. Nevertheless I must own that there is one competition they needn't fix: wrestlers' nicknames are unbeatable. Try this small selection: Suni War Cloud, Dark Secret, The French Angel, Count Bartelli, Killer Karl Kox, Tiger Singh, Brute Bernard, Bulldog Brower, Waldo von Erich, Sky Hi Lee, Ed 'Strangler' Lewis, Kendo Nagasaki, Al 'Mr Murder' Mills, Jim 'Riot Call' Wright, Whipper Billy Watson, Chief Thunderbird, Gorgeous George, 'Crusher' Stan Stasiak, Don Leo Jonathan, Archie 'Stomper' Gouldie, Mr Hito, Dory Funk Jr, Dynamite Kid Davey, Big Daddy, Giant Haystacks, Lethal Larry Cameron, Road Warrior Animal and The Wild Samoans. Marvellous. Early among them was Dirty Jack Pye, of Lancashire and Yorkshire, who continued to cause riots of catcalling, screeching, umbrella-brandishing fury for the best part of 40 years, whether he was gouging the eyes of some undeserving opponent behind the referee's back, slamming the water bucket over his head and bashing it into an inescapable shape, or worse, or just strutting the ring, chest and jaw pushed out, stoking the fury for all his evil worth. And there is Jackness in the tale from the end of his career, when he was 60: in between taunting his young opponent when he wasn't doing fearfully violent things to him, Pye would whisper, 'Mind my back.' Those who resist the Jackie usage will find support in the contrast between Dirty Jack and the later wrestling star **Jackie Pallo**, who, despite his fame, was knocked cold by Honor Blackman in a fight in a graveyard being filmed for an episode of *The Avengers*. That would not have happened to Dirty Jack.

Quick

'Jack be nimble, Jack be quick: Jack jump over the candlestick.'
Another fairy tale, another lively Jack Everyboy. Candlestick-jumping
was allegedly a common English rustic form of entertainment: if the
candle went out, it meant bad luck. Although I am a great fan of
custom and legend, I have always been a bit sceptical about this one,
as there must have been more to do, even in the country. More lately,
the rhyme featured in Don McLean's strangely potent 'American
Pie', whose arch abstrusions have inspired endless late-night mind-
enhanced meanderings. His version reads, 'Jack be nimble, Jack be
quick, Jack Flash sat on the candlestick', which would be tricky, even
given the slight rear of Mick Jagger, generally agreed to be **Jack Flash**
(qv). Candlestick is thus Candlestick Park, San Francisco, venue for
a famous Rolling Stones concert. Another reading has **Jack Kennedy**
(qv) speedily quashing the Cuban missile (candlesticks, naturally)
crisis. What does McLean say? This: 'When people ask me what
"American Pie" means, I tell them it means I don't ever have to work
again if I don't want to.'

RABBIT

The jack rabbit is a hare. Confusing, I know, but merely the first of many mysteries and perplexments embodied by this creature. Knowing that the rabbit and the hare can be one and the same rather spoils, for example, the joke about the bald man putting two rabbits on his head so that from a distance they will look like hares. Dictionaries inform us that jack is used to denote small size, which does not apply in this case, as no less an authority than Mark Twain, *Roughing It* out west, wrote that the jack rabbit 'is just like any other rabbit except that he is from one-third to twice as large, has longer legs in proportion to his size, and has the most preposterous ears that ever were mounted on any creature but a jackass'. Indeed, Twain thought its proper name was a jackass rabbit. He then proceeded to shoot at it, questionable behaviour with an animal which has been believed magical and sacred at some time by nearly every civilisation (although the Jews consider it not kosher). No one seems quite sure why it has earned this reverence, or its reputation for wisdom and savvy (Brer Rabbit, if I have this right, is a Jack; and Bugs Bunny). Still, it ran away from Mark Twain, which argues some nous.

A lot of it seems to be connected with the Moon. Many imaginative peoples, including the Irish and the Africans, have fancied that they could discern the shape of a giant hare on the full moon, holding an egg. This, naturally, leads us to fertility (hares, unsurprisingly, go at it like rabbits), spring, Easter, bunnies and eggs. Hares famously go mad in March, sparring with each other (the female usually wins) by day and staring at the moon by night. They are considered both lucky and unlucky (and the hare's foot is hardly fortunate for the hare). Modern echoes of all this are provided by the Jack Rabbit vibrator, featured to renown on *Sex and the City*. Those who prefer folklore will rather contemplate the circular symbol of the Three Hares, which again appears throughout cultures in Asia and Europe. The hares appear to have two ears each but in fact share three. This has led to speculations about the Trinity. In European churches, too, the sign is often found with that of **Jack in the Green** (qv). See also **Jack and Jill** (qv) and the moon and then go and have a lie down.

RANCE

Jack Rance is the operatic villain in Puccini's *La Fanciulla del West*, which allows any baritone who knows his aria from his oboe repeated and determined assaults on the lovely Minnie and some of the maestro's most admired efforts. Jack is the sheriff in the gold rush mining camp in the High Sierras who tries to buy the Girl of the Golden West with the raw material. But she prefers – don't they all? – the handsome outlaw, and Jack is thwarted. Clever writers have pointed out that this is the first spaghetti western. I am also lost in admiration for the laconic *Times* headline on an unfavourable review of a 1994 production: 'Little Gold in Them There Trills'.

RANN

We spoke in the previous entry of the attraction of handsome outlaws. It is an attraction to which the English have proved particularly susceptible. Perhaps it is their usual, renowned, lengthy, admirable but less than exciting regard for the rule of law which renders the occasional outstanding example of the opposite so beguiling. Whatever, there has been a fine selection, from Robin Hood to Francis Drake (still known to large parts of the Spanish-speaking world as El Pirata Drake), Rob Roy, and **Jack Sheppard** (qv). Such, indeed, is the call and need for this that the fascination will often fix on less worthy objects: the likes, for example, of Dick Turpin, Ronnie Biggs and, heaven help us, the Krays.

But what we really like is law-breaking done with dash and panache, wit and style. The acme of this was reached with the Highwaymen, or Gentlemen of the Road. That latter was no accidental euphemism: gentlemanliness was what they aspired to, and how they were very often regarded, despite considerable evidence to the contrary. But Jack Rann, Sixteen-String Jack, stands and delivers as one of the very finest examples of the ideal. Jack lived the part, and dressed for it: the sixteen strings were the eight coloured ribbons he wore at the knees of his breeches. Jack was a dandy highwayman, a former groom who had taken to the Road to achieve the life, and most especially the style, of his masters. Jack was an early celeb, a working-class handsome sensation: when he appeared at Barnet Races wearing a satin blue waistcoat trimmed with silver, hundreds of gawpers trailed after him.

He was, of course, very much a ladies' man: one of his fancies, the fair Letitia Smith of Covent Garden, went on to be the mistress of the Duke of York and to marry Sir John Lade, the racing dandy, spendthrift rake and friend of the Prince Regent. Far from being intimidated by her ascent, Letitia refused to take the Eliza Doolittle path to acceptability. 'He swears like Letty Lade' was a common saying of the time. Jack, for his part, and true to his calling, was very clear that his status should be regarded as that of a gentleman; he was most affronted when he was not treated as one, whether by sheriff's officers arresting him or at fashionable London spots, including Vauxhall Gardens, where he paid for some acquittal celebrations by lifting two watches and three purses. Dr Johnson knew John Lade, but preferred Jack Rann: 'Yes, sir, Sixteen-String Jack towered above the common mark.' It doesn't matter that Jack wasn't a very good highwayman (he kept taking watches, for example, which provided the proof for his downfall); the important thing is that he understood exactly what was expected from one, even to the extent of announcing himself to all and sundry: 'I am Sixteen-String Jack, the famous highwayman.' Six cases were dismissed against him for lack of identification before he was damned by the watch taken from the chaplain to one of George III's daughters near Brentford. Awaiting the gallows in Newgate, Jack entertained seven lady friends to dinner. For his farewell appearance, at Tyburn, he wore a coat and waistcoat of pea-green cloth, new buckskin breeches tricked out with the famous strings, and he carried a large nosegay. After exchanging pleasantries with the hangman, he danced a little jig for his public before dancing a longer one. He was just 24. There is a theory that the verb 'hijack' derives from victims hailing Rann and his namesakes: 'Hi, Jack.' I, of course, like it, but the word only really appeared in the United States in the 1920s, probably in deference to the likes of **Jack 'Legs' Diamond** and **Jack 'Machine Gun' McGurn** (qv).

REGAN

The leading character in an important episode in the history of the British television crime series, Jack Regan was the hardbitten, hard-living, hard-everything Detective Inspector in *The Sweeney* (rhyming slang – Sweeney Todd – for the Metropolitan Police's Flying Squad). Jack was a hard, sharp contrast to London's previous most-famed television policeman, Sergeant George Dixon of Dock Green, an avuncular figure played by **Jack Warner** (qv). Jack Regan was not avuncular. Jack Regan's most usual expression was either a scowl or a snarled 'Shut it!' Jack Regan wore clothes that had been snappy before they had been lived in too long before they had just been flung on again. Jack Regan was a man whom experience had robbed of all illusions except for the triumph of good, which justified him being bad. Jack would routinely burst into the houses of suspects, discover them in bed, and announce, 'Get your trousers on, you're nicked.' He would then advise their startled and déshabille wives or wotsits to 'put them away, love'. Later in the day it would be 'We're the Sweeney, son, and we haven't had our dinner.'

Jack would engage in fierce combat with a villain and then declare, 'All right, Tinkerbell. You're nicked.' One such attempting to escape in his car was advised, 'Switch off! Or they'll collect your head in a pillow-case.' It was all jolly and heady stuff for a Britain in a 1970s which hadn't even heard of unreconstructed. And it made cult figures out of Jack's real counterparts until a series of corruption scandals came along and the country moved on into more properly sensitive times. Symbolically, John Thaw, the actor who played Regan, moved on himself to play Chief Inspector Morse, based in cerebral and cultural Oxford, an officer who loved opera and real ale and crosswords and solved his proliferate murders without recourse to crudities. And there Jack would have stayed, safely, nostalgically left behind, had not some clever people at the BBC come up with the wheeze of a coma-time-travelling politically correct copper who returns to the 1970s and encounters Jack reinvented as the sideburned, camel-hair-coated, Ford-Cortina-driving Detective Chief Inspector Gene Hunt of *Life on Mars* and *Ashes to Ashes*. This splendid conceit allowed a new generation to enjoy great gusts of taboo-breaking pleasure by mocking both the said sensitivities and the offenders. Enjoy again (or not), for example, Hunt rasping 'He's got fingers in more pies than a leper on a cookery course'; 'She's as nervous as a very small nun at a penguin shoot'; 'No, that's the drip from my fried-egg butty, love. Well done, Miss Marple, that's why we need women detectives' (Gene explaining to a female police officer why the body has a yellow substance on its ear); and 'You're surrounded by armed bastards!'

REYNOLDS

Your money on the only international footballer to score at the right end both for and against England would have to be on a Jack: Jack 'Baldy' Reynolds, of, among others, Ulster, Distillery, Blackburn

Rovers, West Bromwich Albion, Aston Villa, Celtic, England, Ireland and Willesden Town. Jack, a gifted right-half, was born in Blackburn in 1869, but joined the British Army and was posted to Ireland, for whom he made five appearances, including two against England, scoring a goal in 1890. He then joined West Bromwich Albion, where it was 'discovered' that he was English. There followed eight caps for England and three goals (but none against Ireland). Unfortunately, he possessed qualities quite often shared by Jacks, being a lad for drink and dalliance, dying unhappily young and alone in a Sheffield boarding house at the age of 48 after a later career that went down the pits, literally. Let's better remember him from the pages of Aston Villa's official journal, *The Villa News and Record*, in 1906:

> A remarkably smart half-back. For his inches a perfect wonder. Knew every 'trick of the trade', and usually showed up well in big matches. Had a happy knack of scoring at critical moments. Something of a roamer . . . Had an eye to the humorous side of football.

RIPPER

The clot on the Jack escutcheon. One of the most resonant, redolent and ghastly names in the history of crime: Jack the Ripper, perpetrator of a series of murders that took place in Whitechapel, London, in 1888, and which have continued to exercise a fell fascination ever since. Which is not surprising. The Whitechapel Murders combine almost every aspect calculated to appeal to any number of audiences, savoury and less so. Jack was the first widely publicised serial murderer. The murders were of a peculiar sexual savagery. They took place in London's East End, a desperately packed and poor place of the shifting and shiftless already invested with fear of instant violence and uprising and the unknown by those lucky enough not to live there, or to have ever been there. The East

End was the sort of thing that upright, uptight Victorians liked to frighten themselves with; but Jack gave them much more than they wanted: Jack came out from there and plunged into their own dark and secret places.

And no one could find him. There was none of the relief of what we now call closure. Techniques of detection were hardly a match for the clever, the crazed and the lucky; certainly not for all three together. Speculation, the joy of the puzzle, and the thrill of the whodunit had no confine, urged on by a press warming up its populist instincts for the tabloid times that were soon to come. And, to trump it all, that name. Jack, sharp and quick, the knave; Ripper, sharp and quick, brutal, fatal. A nickname indeed. Where did it come from? No one knows. It seems first to have appeared in a letter received at the offices of the Central News Agency on 27 September 1888:

> Dear Boss,
>
> I keep on hearing the police have caught me but they wont fix me just yet. I have laughed when they look so clever and talk about being on the right track. That joke about Leather Apron gave me real fits. I am down on whores and I shant quit ripping them till I do get buckled. Grand work the last job was. I gave the lady no time to squeal. How can they catch me now. I love my work and want to start again. You will soon hear of me with my funny little games. I saved some of the proper red stuff in a ginger beer bottle over the last job to write with but it went thick like glue and I cant use it. Red ink is fit enough I hope ha. ha. The next job I do I shall clip the ladys ears off and send to the police officers just for jolly wouldn't you. Keep this letter back till I do a bit more work, then give it out straight. My knife's so nice and sharp I want to get to work right away if I get a chance. Good Luck.

Yours truly

Jack the Ripper

Dont mind me giving the trade name

PS Wasnt good enough to post this before I got all the red
ink off my hands curse it No luck yet. They say I'm a doctor
now. ha ha

Charming, you will agree. The Central News Agency forwarded the
letter to the police on 29 September. The next day two more murders
were discovered. The day after that the Central News Agency received
a postcard in the same hand, with the same signature:

I was not codding dear old Boss when I gave you the tip,
you'll hear about Saucy Jacky's work tomorrow double event
this time number one squealed a bit couldn't finish straight
off. ha not the time to get ears for police. thanks for keeping
last letter back till I got to work again.

Jack the Ripper

Ditto. As you might imagine, these letters caused a bit of a stir, and
continue to do so. They were the first of a flurry of correspondence
allegedly from the killer; one of these, to a different recipient, and
apparently by a different hand, was famously headed 'From Hell'
and accompanied by half a kidney which could well have come from
one of the victims. That, and the letters signed Jack the Ripper, were,
not surprisingly, taken seriously by the police. The Jack the Ripper
letters were reproduced on handbills as part of the drive to find
the killer. Suspicions about them – a touch too glib, perhaps, for a
maniacal killer, a little too artfully artless – steadily grew and were
recently given some confirmation by the discovery of a letter written
in 1913 by Chief Inspector John Littlechild, one of the senior
policemen involved:

With regard to the term 'Jack the Ripper' it was generally believed at the Yard that Tom Bullen of the Central News was the originator, but it is probable Moore, who was his chief, was the inventor. It was a smart piece of journalistic work. No journalist of my time got such privileges from Scotland Yard as Bullen. Mr James Munro when Assistant Commissioner, and afterwards Commissioner, relied on his integrity. Poor Bullen occasionally took too much to drink, and I fail to see how he could help it knocking about so many hours and seeking favours from so many people to procure copy. One night when Bullen had taken a 'few too many' he got early information of the death of Prince Bismarck and instead of going to the office to report it sent a laconic telegram, 'Bloody Bismarck is dead'. On this I believe Mr Charles Moore fired him out.

Well, well. The creation of a drunken journalist. As a fellow hack, I am at once appalled, as impressed as Mr Littlechild and not surprised. Mr Bulling (misspelt by Littlechild, poetic justice for a hack) had just been covering the inquest of one of the victims, during which there had been much talk of ripping, and a suspect, **John 'Jack' Pizer**, known as Leather Apron, had been formally declared innocent by the coroner. So, a slow night, a few drinks, an idle chat and off we go. But this is Jack the Ripper, subject of more than 100 years of fevered imaginings, recently given fresh impetus by forensic enthusiasts united in their obsession by cyberspace. Nothing is certain, not even the number of victims. Timings are pored over minutely, theories promoted with head-hurting ingenuity. And, remarkably, new findings are still coming to light: in 1988, a letter signed Jack the Ripper pre-dating that of 27 September by ten days was discovered in a sealed envelope at the British Public Record Office. Too remarkable, perhaps: it has been dismissed as a hoax.

I must confess, too, that I have played my small part. In 1987, after I had written an article for the *Daily Telegraph* about the approaching centenary of the murders, the grandson of another policeman involved, Inspector Donald Swanson, contacted me to say that the inspector had named the Ripper in the margin of the memoirs of yet another policeman involved. Before you could say **Jack Robinson** (qv), I made my way into Surrey eagerly hoping for minor royalty at least, Mr Gladstone or possibly the Archbishop of Canterbury. But it turned out to be a Polish Jew of whom what little was known didn't really fit in with the inspector's claims. The *Daily Telegraph* was so impressed with my world exclusive that they didn't bother using it for a few days. This turned out to be typically shrewd news judgement, demonstrated by the story's reappearance every ten years or so, when it is invariably treated as completely new, invariably dismissed and instantly forgotten again. Journalism, eh?

Not much is known about what happened to Tom Bulling, apart from a later report of his drunkenly ringing on the doorbell of the son of the Emir of Afghanistan in a doomed attempt to obtain an interview. In *Life and Death at the Old Bailey*, published in 1935, R. Thurston Hopkins, a prolific biographer and crime writer, recalled the suspicions but didn't name the suspect:

> This poor fellow had a breakdown and became a whimsical figure in Fleet Street, only befriended by the staff of newspapers and printing works. He would creep about the dark courts waving his hands furiously in the air, would utter stentorian 'Ha, ha, ha's', and then, meeting some pal, would button-hole him and pour into his ear all the 'inner-story' of the East End murders.

Poor Tom. Mind you, there were quite a few people like that wandering about when I arrived in Fleet Street, so perhaps we shouldn't be too hasty. Meanwhile, you should note that Walter Sickert, the painter, has now been joined in the frame by Francis Thompson, the poet, and Lewis Carroll. *Alice in Wonderland* contains a confession in anagrams, apparently. Snark hunting, indeed. My own diligent researches have revealed this startlingly prescient comment from the late Reverend Dodgson cunningly concealed in 'Tweedledum and Tweedledee': 'Demented Twaddle'.

ROBINSON (I)

Another mystery involving a Jack, and almost as impenetrable. Where on earth does the phrase 'before you could/can say Jack Robinson' come from? We know that it means something done with great speed, and that its use arose in Britain in the eighteenth century, but beyond that there is only unconvincing conjecture. Determined attempts have been made to discover the identity of Mr Robinson, together with explanations as to why he might be synonymous with speed. An eccentric fellow who would leave before he could be announced has defied further identification. There has been speculation about Sir John Robinson, who was Lieutenant of the Tower of London in the seventeenth century, to do with the speed of execution; but as we have seen (see **Jack Ketch**), that could be messy rather than speedy. Its most celebrated early use was in the House of Commons in 1782, when Sheridan, the great playwright, politician, serial debtor, Irishman and wit, was challenged to name the MP he had just accused of bribing fellow members to vote for the government. This was John Robinson, secretary to the Treasury, fixer and featherer. 'Sir,' said Sheridan to the Speaker, 'I shall not name the person. It is unpleasant and invidious to do so, and therefore I shall not name him. But don't suppose, Sir, that I abstain because there is any difficulty in naming him; I could do that, Sir, as soon as you could say Jack Robinson.' Collapse of House. But the joke depends on the phrase already being in common currency, which it was, so we are no further. The palm for the most convoluted explanation involves a man-servant called Jacques, and Robinson becoming a synonym in France for an umbrella after the success of a stage production in Paris of Defoe's *Robinson Crusoe* - 'Jacques! Robinson!' The best explanation is probably that of Eric Partridge, who thought it was invented for its rolling euphony. You might compare it with 'Gordon Bennett!', which is used more for its similarly pleasing plosiveness than for any connection with any Gordon Bennett, even the rich American one who rather marred his engagement party by turning up at his fiancée's family mansion drunk and then relieving himself into the fireplace. Sheridan was routinely inspired; try this one: 'Mr Speaker, I said the honourable member was a liar it is true and I am sorry for it. The honourable member may place the punctuation where he pleases.' I am thinking of suggesting an eighteenth-century firm of bailiffs called Jack, Robin and Son. At least you get a little longer with that.

ROBINSON (2)

A great towering exception to the general Jackist dismissal of Jackies as not quite Jack enough. Jackie Robinson (1919–72) was the black baseball player who ended 80 years of professional baseball segregation by appearing for the Brooklyn Dodgers in 1947 and going on to conquer outrageous hostility through the quality of his play and force of his personality. Jack Roosevelt Robinson was the fifth son of Georgia sharecroppers. His elder brother took the silver medal behind that other great and inconveniently black champion, Jesse Owens, in the 200 metres in Berlin in 1936. Jackie also proved to be an extravagantly gifted sportsman, a schoolboy and student winner at football, basketball, tennis and athletics. Baseball was considered one of his weaker skills. These kind of attributes and successes make a man disinclined to take a backward step. Jackie was a man prepared to stand up for himself. In some ways, he is reminiscent of another great black **Jack, Johnson** (qv), but, crucially, Jackie had the discipline of a formal education. He was drafted after

Pearl Harbor, successfully fought a decision to deny him officer training, and was honourably discharged after being acquitted of insubordination charges arising from his refusal to go to the back of a segregated army bus. He might not have been the most obvious choice when Branch Rickey of the Brooklyn Dodgers was looking to break the de facto colour bar in professional baseball, but he was the right one, the tough one. His dignity and determination in the face of abuse even from his own teammates saw him swiftly become a revered figure in the most revered American game, a man who redeemed its mythic status, and led the way for all sports. Not a bad player, either. Two years later, he had won the Most Valuable Player award and 'Did You See Jackie Robinson Hit That Ball?' was in the Billboard charts. After retirement, he continued to be politically active, fund-raising for civil rights, fostering black business, and writing and speaking out for Martin Luther King and Malcolm X. Jackie himself now has mythic status, a sainted symbol rather than a second baseman. But still a Jack: as he left to play that first game for the Dodgers, he told his wife she wouldn't have any trouble recognising him: 'My number's 42.'

ROSENTHAL

An inspired marriage of the whimsy that is Lancashire with the edge of Manchester and the wit of Jewry produced Jack Rosenthal (1931–2004). Can you have three in a marriage? Ah, well, but it worked very well here, at least. In fact and life, he was married to Maureen Lipman, a rare rebuttal of Yorkshire's rather more serious approach to humour. But, Jack: after wartime evacuation to Blackpool (definitely not as much fun as it sounds) and Colne, university and a spell as 'about the only Jew' in the Royal Navy, Jack ended up writing for *Coronation Street* at Granada in Manchester. Being Jack, a master of bathos, he had already had an unsuccessful stint there in which his first task was to buy lavatory-roll holders. Jack wrote more than

250 programmes, series, episodes and plays for television, films and theatre, marked by a sympathy for the eccentric and their too-often frustrated ambitions. You need self-effacement to imagine others, and Jack appears to have been a natural. According to Jack, most of his ideas seem to have come from somebody else: 'Nothing's ever happened to me.' To be disabused, read his autobiography, written as a television play, *By Jack Rosenthal*. I recommend the incidents involving Barbra Streisand, with whom he wrote her movie, *Yentl*, and Patricia Phoenix, when she was refusing to come out of her dressing room due to a bad bout of pre-wedding nerves on behalf of her *Coronation Street* character, Elsie Tanner. And the various misunderstandings which led to his making up a film pitch on the spot to Michael Winner or sharing a bed in Hull with his prospective father-in-law. You will have your own favourites.

RUBY

The other Jack in Dallas, 1963. This is the guy that killed the guy that killed Kennedy. Or is he? Spend any time with the single most shocking act of single assassination of the twentieth century and you'll soon start doubting the evidence of anything, even of your own eyes and that stark, swift piece of film where Ruby suddenly emerges from the crush and fires into the horrified Oswald live on television. Perhaps at the same time a secret death ray was fired into the underground garage of the Dallas police headquarters by a scientist who had developed it while his beautiful daughter was being held by the KGB, or the CIA, or LBJ, or the Mafia, or the Freemasons, or the Scout Association, large extraterrestrial lizards, or all of them, plus a man stroking a large white cat in his lap. Mock if you like, but there are a lot of people out there who believe that nothing that day was as it seems. Which, if you believe a lot of other people out there, is itself a conspiracy started by the KGB, or perhaps the CIA, shortly afterwards.

Jack himself appears not so complicated. He was the fifth of eight children born to a mostly unemployed alcoholic father and a mentally ill mother. He grew up in Chicago, working when he could at any number of small-time activities united only by his failure at them. As the *American National Biography* puts it, 'He did not have the ability to be a gangster but was a hanger-on at pool halls and gymnasiums and local establishments.' That's what Jack did: hang on. Remarkably, given his business record, he was running a strip club in Dallas in 1963, employing, among others, the splendidly monikered and endowed Candy Barr and Penny Dollar. Jack had a string of minor convictions and complaints against him, including having an unconventional relationship with his dog. He often carried a gun and had such a short temper his nickname, almost prophetically, was Sparky. Despite all this, he managed to insinuate himself into a press conference at the police headquarters after Kennedy's assassination, and into the garage among the press people waiting for Oswald to be transferred to the County Jail. His trial was presided over by Judge Joe 'Necessity' Brown ('Necessity knows no law'). He was defended by Melvin Belli, a Californian lawyer to whom the word 'flamboyant' scarcely does justice: he would celebrate his victories, for example, by firing off a cannon from the roof of his office. He did not get to do this with Ruby, but he did prepare to deliver the child of the heavily pregnant Penny Dollar when she collapsed on the stand during a jail break at the courthouse.

Ruby was sentenced to death, but appealed and was due a retrial when he died in hospital in 1967 from a well-advanced but previously undetected set of cancers which have also stimulated much discussion. His hat and bullets from the gun are still put on public display. Those who criticise the ineptitude and carelessness towards documents of the Jack the Ripper investigation (see just above) should note that in 2008 the contents of an old safe at the Dallas Courthouse were made public, including what appears to be Ruby's gun holster and a document, insufficiently annotated, which might be a transcript of a meeting between Ruby and Oswald arranging to kill Kennedy on behalf of Chicago mobsters, or might be a movie transcript. Those who enjoy unlikely connections should know that the father of Larry Gelbart, the scriptwriter of *MASH* and much else, was a barber who cut Ruby's hair in Chicago before moving to Hollywood and attending to **Jack Benny** (qv), Frank Sinatra and Gregory Peck (and that Candy Barr was married to another Hollywood hairdresser, **Jack Sahakian**). It is not true, though, disappointingly, that the disc jockey John Peel was also in the garage at the time; he was merely nearby. Those who enjoy conspiracies should study this, from one of the leading authorities on the killings, Vincent Bugliosi, on the theory that Ruby was tipped off to kill Oswald: 'Ruby would have arrived at the police station too late, had Oswald not delayed his transfer to county jail by requesting a different shirt.' This, says Mr Bugliosi, would be strange, 'unless Oswald was a party to the conspiracy to murder himself'. Well worth a look, I should have said.

RUSSELL

A noble British name, embracing dukes, statesmen, composers, poets, a prime minister and the greatest logician since Aristotle (even if he was unable to provide a satisfactory answer to the London cabbie who asked him, 'So, tell me, Bertrand, what's it all about, then?'). And a name which, when combined with Jack, provides results you should be expecting by now. Jack Russell, for example, the former English wicket keeper, had a number of interesting traits, many involving diet, which majored in tea, biscuits and baked beans. In the final test of the 1989 Test series against Australia, it was estimated that he had got through 100 cups of tea, made from the same tea bag, which he kept hanging on a nail. In a Test against Australia in Perth, he dined for all five nights at the same Chinese restaurant, always ordering chicken and cashews without the chicken. He is now a painter and part-time goalkeeping coach.

His earlier namesake, a Church of England clergyman (1795-1883), is renowned as The Sporting Parson and for owning the type of terrier named after him. Parson Russell was a Devon man who hunted everything he could when he could. Hunting and the complicated attitudes for and against it are most illuminating of the English character, particularly in terms of class, envy, urban-rural tensions, and, *pace* Lord Bertrand, illogicality. The Parson, for example, prevailed on his flock to stop killing foxes with sticks and axes, requesting, as the *DNB* puts it, 'that he should be allowed to kill the foxes in a more English way'. And then he built artificial earths in which to breed and feed foxes, which when big enough were hunted and killed to order. His famous dog also has shades of the national character, being extremely noisy, almost insanely dogged (sorry) in pursuit of its aims (anything down a hole) and aggressive beyond size and sense (the writer Philip Howard, an owner, reported that an African big-game keeper had got rid of his because it kept trying to take on elephants). Only recently a Jack Russell belonging to a Conservative MP killed a polecat at the Isle of Wight Show. There have also been some difficulties between owners of the common and often mongrel Jack Russell and the taller, more refined breed known as the Parson Russell, which, in contrast, has been recognised by the Kennel Club and allowed to compete at the Cruft's dog show. 'Bred only for prettiness,' barks one side; 'Our terriers should not resemble the common little Jack Russell,' growls the other. You will be familiar enough with the idea that owners and pets resemble each other for me not to labour the point further, or to venture into those deep and twisting foxholes of controversy that are the Irish Jacks, Blue-Eyed Jacks and Mini Parsons.

The Parson himself, also a staunch promoter of Devon cream and cider, died much loved and admired by many, including the future Edward VII, who bought a portrait of Trump, the original

Jack Russell, which still hangs at Sandringham. Trump was bought by Russell from a milkman in Oxford. Later noted Jack Russells number Moose, who played Eddie in *Frasier* (his son Enzo acted as stunt double as he got older). Given some of the above, I would counsel against falling into the common error of identifying Nipper, the dog on the HMV record label, as a Jack Russell. He was, of course, part bull terrier and fox terrier, and is buried under what is now the rear car park of the Kingston-upon-Thames branch of the Trustee Savings Bank.

RYAN

With Jacks, the truth is reliably more unlikely than the fiction. Jack Ryan is the man who routinely saves the Free World on behalf of Tom Clancy. Jack is the thriller reader's thinking man; he has been both a CIA boss and President of the United States, and, if you haven't read the books, your best guide is that Harrison Ford plays him. The real Jack Ryan developed the Barbie Doll and was married, briefly, to Zsa Zsa Gabor. It had to be brief because Zsa Zsa had eight other husbands to fit in. You must remember these: 'How many husbands have I had? You mean other than my own?'; 'A man in love is incomplete until he's married. Then he's finished'; 'I'm a marvellous housekeeper. Every time I leave a man I keep his house.' Jack was number six. Number seven was the attorney who handled the divorce. Number eight was the one which was annulled because the cruise ship the captain married her on wasn't in international waters. Jack also designed Chatty Cathy, the talking doll, and toy missiles that really worked.

SAINT JACK

This is Jack Flowers, the fairly brave but shabby hero of Paul Theroux's novel of the same name. Jack, among other things, runs brothels in Singapore, one called, delightfully, Dunroamin. But Jack operates morally immorally, protecting his clients from secret societies and greedy cabbies, disease and excessive degeneracy, 'keeping those already astray happy and from harm, within caution's limits'. Jack is an ironic saint, a saint for hard times, these times, not so much making a difference as not making them any worse. Jacks seeking a slightly more orthodox patron saint might consider their near namesake, St John the Almsgiver, the seventh-century Patriarch of Alexandria, who, as his name suggests, gave away large amounts of his and the church's money and goods, including wine. Proof that moral ambiguity and complexity is not an entirely new problem comes with St John's provision of a shipload of corn to a twice-shipwrecked merchant, who sailed off to Britain, where there was a famine, and sold it at great advantage. The Jerusalem hostel which inspired both the Knights of St John and the St John's Ambulance was dedicated to John. His body, after a long spell in Constantinople which ended when it was given by a Turkish sultan to King Matthias of Hungary, now lies in St Martins in Bratislava.

SALMON

Jack Salmon is an informal North American usage covering any number of finny things, from the pike perch to the wall-eyed pike to a specific young salmon, described in a typically interesting article from the newsletter of the South Puget Sound Salmon Enhancement Group written by Richard M. Johnson:

> When I say 'jack', I'm referring to a precocious male salmon that decides to grow up in a hurry. It spends one year or less in salt water before returning to fresh water to spawn like the big boys. You may wonder why they mature so quickly and are they successful spawners? The answer to the first question is that this might be nature's way of spreading out the genetic contribution of a particular brood year over several years . . . An environmental roadblock such as flooding or poor marine survival might limit the number of spawners in a given year. Fortunately, the jacks would have returned before the problem arose (take El Niño years as an example, when adult salmon, especially coho, were hard-hit due to poor feeding conditions).

Mr Johnson goes on to provide a clue as to the essential Jackness of this young salmon:

> As to how jack salmon fare in the competitive world of reproduction – they have developed a special tactic that we know as the 'sneak attack'. While the big brutes are jousting for the right to sire the eggs of an unsuspecting female, the jack waits in the shadows and races in at just the opportune moment to add some of his own milt to the pot.

Exactly.

SASSOON

Siegfried Sassoon (1886–1967) is included here because of the nickname – Mad Jack – that he earned on the Western Front in the First World War. It was the madness of anger – as mad as hell – at the death of friends, comrades and enemies and at the madness of war. It was all the more striking for not being an unrelentingly raging fury. In 1917, he earned a bar to his Military Cross by single-handedly charging and capturing some German trenches in the Hindenburg Line, where he remained for some time, oblivious to the danger, reading a volume of poems. His own poetry and prose were justly famous for their unfussy force. He wrote not like an angel but like the soldier and country squire that he was. He had, though, a genius and a sensitivity not usually found in the latter. Still, not many of them would have been likely to have an affair with Ivor Novello, either. Nor a father from an Indian Baghdadi Jewish family who was disinherited for marrying out. Sassoon was a pacifist who went back to fight because he couldn't leave his comrades to it. And, on his return, one of them, accidentally, shot him. He was a fox hunter who hated killing animals, a cricket lover, gay, married, a Catholic convert and a highly erratic driver given to cross-country diversions at the sight of an open gate. Mad, very possibly; wonderful, certainly.

SCHMITT

There have been three spacemen called Jack. This is the Jack who walked on the moon, Harrison Hagan 'Jack' Schmitt. Jack, in fact, is one of the last two men on the moon, visiting it in December 1972. His colleage, Eugene Cernan, was the last one to leave, but Jack, a geologist, was the last one to land. He brought some rock back and is also credited with taking the Blue Marble photograph of the Earth from Apollo 17, perhaps its most famous image from space. After that, to prove his bravery was no fluke, he became a US Senator. The first Jack in Space, **Jack Swigert**, took a similar path, being elected to the House of Representatives, although, sadly, dying of cancer before he could take office. Jack Swigert would have been the first Jack on the moon, but he was a member of the unlucky Apollo 13 mission which was aborted after a technical problem in 1970. It was Swigert who first alerted Houston to that problem. It's remarkable how many famous quotations are wrong: Swigert said, 'Hey, we've got a problem here,' the Apollo commander, Jim Lovell, confirmed, 'Houston, we've had a problem.' Fittingly, the man in Houston was **Jack Lousma**, who went on to take part in Skylab and Space Shuttle missions in 1973 and 1982, and also ran for the Senate as a Republican but was defeated. Astronaut politicians split 4–2 in favour of the Republicans. The leading first name for a spaceman is Michael or Mike, with 13 so far. Next come some other dependables, William, James and, I'm proud to record, Charles.

SEWARD

Jack Seward is the asylum administrator who calls in his mentor, Professor Van Helsing, when the girl he loves, Lucy Westenra, starts acting a little strangely. She has become a victim of Dracula and fated to appear undead in the endless adaptations of Bram Stoker's 1897 novel. Perhaps Jack's finest piece of dialogue came in Francis Ford Coppola's 1992 film, in this exchange:

> VAN HELSING (ANTHONY HOPKINS): 'Jack. Come here. I know how deeply you loved her. That is why you must trust me and believe.'

> JACK (RICHARD E. GRANT): 'Believe? How can I believe?'

> VAN HELSING: 'I want you to bring me before nightfall a set of post-mortem knives.'

JACK: 'An autopsy? On Lucy?'

VAN HELSING: 'No, no. Not exactly. I just want to cut off her head and take out her heart.'

SHARKEY

Another adopted Jack, this one was originally Joseph Paul Cukoschay (sometimes given as Zukauskas), of Binghamton, New York, the son of Lithuanian immigrants. He began boxing in the Navy and changed his name on turning professional. The name came from his two heavyweight heroes, the Irishman 'Sailor' Tom Sharkey, and **Jack Dempsey** (qv). Sharkey fought Dempsey in 1927 in the Manassa Mauler's comeback fight after losing the world championship to Gene Tunney. Sharkey was 24 and mouthy, Dempsey was Dempsey, the most popular man around, but 32. Sharkey was all over him from the start. But in the seventh a desperately swinging Dempsey hit Sharkey low; Sharkey turned to the referee (another **Jack, O'Sullivan**) to complain and while he was turned away, Dempsey hit him with a haymaker which, as the *New York Times* pointed out, knocked him back into the middle of the previous morning: when he came round he told his manager he was fighting Dempsey that night. When they asked Dempsey why he had hit a man who wasn't looking, that Jack replied, 'What was I supposed to do, mail him a letter?' To cap it, when Sharkey fought the German, Max Schmeling, for the title in 1930, he was disqualifed for a low blow. But he came back to beat Schmeling in 1932, in a controversial decision which prompted Schmeling's manager, Joe Jacobs, to coin a legendary phrase into the ringside radio microphone: 'We wuz robbed!' Jacobs was Jewish; Schmeling, when he was winning, was held up by the Nazis as the embodiment of Aryan supremacy. After a victory in Germany, Jacobs found himself in the ring giving the Hitler salute along with everyone else; however, it was noted that he had a cigar between his fingers and looked as if he was hailing a cab on 23rd Street. Sharkey's last fight was against Joe Louis, who went on to beat Schmeling in 1938 in New York in a fight that was billed as the Free World against the Third Reich. Radio coverage in Germany was cut as Schmeling was counted out in the first round, large numbers of New York Jews in the audience were hugging themselves and each other, and Tallulah Bankhead jumped to her feet and shouted at the Schmeling fans behind her, 'I told you so, you sons of bitches!'

SHEPPARD

An emblematic Jack of the naughty sort, a great blast from the roaring past that was early eighteenth-century London. Unusually for a villain of the time, Jack doesn't appear to have killed anybody, which might explain his immense popularity, or not. Jack was an averagely gifted thief, but an escape artist of quite stunning brilliance, ensuring his fame by making each successive break-out more spectacular than the last. As is usual, he was young (dead at 22), fatherless, and fell away from an honest apprenticeship as a carpenter into bad company, a couple of doxies at the Black Lion in St Giles. You might judge their charms from their nicknames, Edgworth Bess and Maggott. Jack started robbing from the homes and businesses he was working in, and fencing the stuff through Bess and Maggott. Arrest came soon, and his first escape, through a roof. Although it never took long to capture Jack again, holding on to him was another matter. His next escape was from the New Prison, Clerkenwell, with Bess, sawing through an iron bar, descending 25 feet on a rope made out of a blanket, a sheet and Bess's gown and petticoat, and then scaling a 22-foot-high perimeter wall. There followed some petty highway robbery and a shabby burglary from a former employer, Mr Kneebone, who had fixed him up with the apprenticeship. His return to custody this time was accelerated by making an enemy out of Jonathan Wild, the Mr Big of London organised crime at the time. So organised, in fact, that Wild had semi-official status as a thief-taker and receiver of lost property (whose loss he had arranged in the first place). Those who refused to work for him found themselves arrested by Wild, who would then claim the reward. Jack's refusal to share his profits with Wild argues either extreme foolhardiness or supreme confidence in his powers of escapology. He was arrested by Wild, tried and sentenced to hang. Four days before his appointment at Tyburn, he escaped from Newgate disguised as a woman. London, which has always liked a Jack the Lad, was agog with it. Recaptured, he was moved and put into solitary confinement in Newgate's equivalent of a high-security block, four floors up, The Castle. Jack freed himself from his handcuffs, broke his fetters, climbed up the chimney into the room above and then cracked open six locked, bolted and barred doors on his way up onto the roof, sixty feet up. And then went all the way back again to get his blanket before returning to lower himself with it onto the house next door, climbing into the garrett window and making his way downstairs and out through the front door to freedom.

How could Jack possibly follow that? Only one way, really. The next days were spent thumbing his nose at his fate. He mingled with crowds listening to ballads about his escape, had himself driven in a carriage past Newgate, robbed a pawnbroker's, dressed finely, dined with the doxies, sent for his mother, promised he would flee the country, got more drunk, became incapable and was arrested in a brandy shop in Drury Lane. People flocked to Newgate to see him, paying the turnkeys for the privilege. His route to Tyburn was lined by weeping girls throwing posies at his open cart. He stopped, as was customary, for a final mug of ale at the Bowl Inn in St Giles, and a pint of sack (wine) in Oxford Street. There were said to be 200,000, a third of London's population, out for the hanging. At Tyburn, his autobiography was on sale, which must make the event a unique book launch. The publisher was John Applebee, who specialised in (almost) true crime; the writer, though it is doubted, is said to have been Daniel Defoe, reformer, spy, pamphleteer and writer of *Robinson Crusoe*, and, more to this purpose, *Moll Flanders*. Even greater doubt and mixed accounts attend a supposed plot, also said to have involved Applebee and Defoe, for the body to be whisked away for revival. This was foiled, according to one version, by the crowd rushing forward to pull down on Jack's legs to hasten his end: he was a small, slight man and death by hanging was then a matter of slow strangulation rather than the later device of a sharp neck-breaking drop. Other reports say the crowd came forward after Jack's death to prevent the plotted removal, believing it to be for the purposes of dissection.

Whatever, Jack's legend was unaffected: ballads and books and theatre productions followed and flowed, most notably *The Beggar's Opera*, by John Gay, which draws lightly on Jack for Captain Macheath, but heavily on Jonathan Wild as the villain, Peachum. Wild finally arrived at Tyburn the year after Jack; he had tried to take his life the night before and was stoned by the crowds on his way. He was not allowed to rest. His body was snatched from its grave; what was said to be his skeleton turned up in Victorian times and was donated to The Royal College of Surgeons. By then, too, he was playing the villain in the great revival of Jack's fame, which followed the publication in 1839 of *Jack Sheppard: A Romance*, written by W. Harrison Ainsworth, the Tom Clancy of his day. Such a fame that successive Lord Chancellors refused to license plays with Jack's name in the title, for fears that it would encourage *les autres*. Which it did: Jesse James, for example, used the alias Jack Sheppard in his writing to newspapers. James provides part of the answer for Sheppard's great popularity, and for that of other criminals like Sixteen-String Jack (see **Jack Rann**): outlaws who could outwit the law at times when it was struggling to cope with injustices created by great social change and often corrupt enforcers. But there has, too, to be charm and style, which can be augmented and polished in the telling. It seems that Jack, despite a stutter, was an engaging fellow, and no doubt he would have agreed with the sentiment attributed to him at Newgate, when he was said to have told a visiting clergyman that one file was worth all the bibles in the world. And if you still remain uneasy with the morality of all this, take as your example the clergyman of the time who was said to have exhorted his flock to follow the example of this alternative Shepherd and 'open the locks of your hearts with the nail of repentance, burst asunder the fetters of your beloved lusts, and mount the chimney of hope to the roof leads of divine meditation'.

SHORT

A bad Jack of the shadowy kind, one of the many shadows surrounding the mighty Sir William Wallace, or Braveheart as he has been familiarly known since Mel Gibson restored him to his fabled fame. The facts, for those whom they concern, are fewer, including exactly where Wallace came from, and where he gained the remarkable military skill which allowed him to defy the hammering of Edward I. We know how he came to his end, on the scaffold in Smithfield in 1305, mocked, hanged, drawn and quartered by the English as an outlaw but still refusing to acknowledge an allegiance he did not owe. We are not exactly sure of the manner of his capture, but the contemporary English chronicle of the Augustinian canon, Peter Langtoft, stated that it had come about through the treacherous information of Jack Short, his servant, who received 40 marks (worth about £10,000 today) for his trouble. My opinion, for what it's worth, is that we should resist this particular slur on the good name of Jack. The relevant part of the chronicle was not written by Father Langtoft, who was dead by this time, but by an unknown hand, probably that of an English courtier, and is eager to foster the idea of native Scots treachery. And choosing the common name for a servant and then such a descriptive surname smacks to me of slack reportage. We say, bringing in the verdict allowed by the still proudly independent Scottish legal system: not proven!

SIEG

It's one of those freezing, marrow-bothering days outside, but that doesn't seem to matter one jot to your heartless games teacher. He (it's always a he) is warm and tracksuited and on the side; you're in the water. And, for some reason, he doesn't rate your modified, alternate-limbed propulsion freestyle adaptation. Doggy-paddle, indeed! No, he doesn't want you to give him your breast stroke, your back stroke, or even those six elegant water-slicing strokes of the crawl that you can accomplish before swallowing half the county's chlorine supply. No: he wants you to do the butterfly, that torturing, muscle-contorting, more-swallowing lunge and lurch through the water that bears as much resemblance to the delicate fluttering of its inspiration as a dyspraxic elephant with a drink problem. The man you have to thank is Jack Sieg, who developed the stroke with his coach, David Armbruster, at the University of Iowa in 1935. No wonder he seems to have kept a profile as low as his stroke thereafter.

SIM

Jacks, as you will have noticed, have the cheek to go where others fear. Our first Jack Sim is the president of the Restroom Association of Singapore and the founder of the World Toilet Organization. Jack is on a mission to improve and provide facilities, for reasons of health and civilisation, and doesn't even seem to care that he might be offending those who insist on calling them lavatories or loos or restrooms or powder rooms. The Romans called them necessaria, which still seems the most elegant euphemism (we have already noted our natural opposition to John and Jakes). Mr Sim, who is a Singapore businessman, also doesn't mind posing for any number of photographs with the relevant porcelain or enduring any number of references to being flushed with success. He has also founded the World Toilet College and instituted World Toilet Day (19 November, also the date the British National Lottery was launched in 1994). Our second Jack Sim won the George Medal in 1940 for defusing unexploded German bombs near Montrose, went on to study philosophy under Karl Popper and, after retirement from the RAF, became senior lecturer in mathematics, logic and the philosophy of science at St Mary's College of Education, London.

SIMMONS

A stalwart Jack, a dependable Jack, a cricketer now Chairman of Cricket for the England and Wales Cricket Board, no less.

Jack arrived in the Lancashire county side late, aged 27, after a solid but unspectacular career in local league cricket and continued in the same way for the next 20 years. He was a tidy spin bowler with a trajectory that earned him his nickname of Flat Jack, and a reliable, unflashy lower-order batsman who helped Lancashire to the county's great one-day successes in the 1970s and also found time to pop Down Under during the winter for six seasons to lead and inspire Tasmania to full first-class status in Australia. He was a shrewd businessman who, among other things, operated an agency for bringing overseas players to England. Jack's legendary status, though, is based not principally on any of this, but instead on another solid, dependable and unflashy ancillary activity: his eating. To give you some indication, consider the Simmo Special, available at the Blackburn fish-and-chip shop he has long patronised: it's a combination of steak-and-kidney pudding, chips and peas topped with a fried fish. His friend and captain, David Lloyd, once drove Jack home in the early evening after a day's play. When they were nearly there, Jack asked him to stop at a chippie, where he bought a considerable portion of fish and chips which he then ate sitting on a wall outside the shop. Lloyd asked him why he didn't take the food home. Jack explained that if he did that, his wife wouldn't make him any supper. Rapid ingestion of two large apple pies was justified thus: 'They said I was to eat a lot of fruit.' Bon appetit, Jack, who is unlikely to be confused with either the noted transport historian or the gay porn star.

SISSON

Jack Sisson was one of 40 volunteers who took part in a daring raid during the American War of Independence to kidnap the commander of the British garrison at Newport, Rhode Island. He was also probably the only black one. Sisson steered one of the whaleboats which made their way to Newport with muffled oars and landed undetected. They overpowered the sentry outside Brigadier General Richard Prescott's lodgings, but, once inside, found the door to his bedroom locked. Sisson, described as short and powerful, then headbutted the door twice, breaking a panel open. The raiding party then got away with the half-clothed brigadier general across Narragansett Bay to Warwick and safety. The daring exploit was roundly celebrated by the Americans, for whom the war had been going badly; Sisson's direct approach to breaking and entering was particularly celebrated, even in verse. But I can do no better than quote the *American National Biography*: 'It is unclear to what extent the emphasis on Sisson's use of his skull as a battering ram partook of a longstanding penchant among many white Americans for making lame jests about the imagined hardness of black people's heads.' I am reminded of the former England cricket captain Tony Greig, born in South Africa, who, commentating on a West Indies game when one of the fielders was struck by a ball, asked his West Indian colleague at the microphone whether he and his fellow countrymen bruised the same way as white people.

The brigadier was then exchanged for the captured American general, Charles Lee, a colourful figure who had previously seen service in the British Army in America, and was briefly a colonel in the Portuguese Army fighting against the Spanish, a major general of Russian forces fighting the Turkish, and an officer on the staff of King Augustus Stanislaus of Poland. He also lost two fingers in a duel, married the daughter of White Thunder, a chief of the Seneca Indians, and had been seized by the British after spending the night in a tavern. He was, as you might gather, a gifted but mercurial character and caused more harm than good after Jack's heroics. He quarrelled with Washington and was court martialled, dying shortly afterwards and being buried in the graveyard of Christ Church, Philadelphia, despite a request in his will not to buried in consecrated ground. Jack died in 1821, aged 'about 78', reportedly and familiarly disappointed at being celebrated in the terms of others.

SKELLINGTON

So you've got The Pumpkin King of Hallowe'en Town and he's a skeleton, but you want to show that he's not just scary, he's a fun guy, too? Tim Burton, in his *The Nightmare Before Christmas*, cleverly called him Jack, Jack Skellington, and now he's cuddly enough to feature on duvet covers as well as frighten.

SLIPPER

'There is nothing more stimulating,' remarked Sherlock Holmes in *The Hound of the Baskervilles*, 'than a case where everything goes against you.' By the standards of the Great Detective, Jack Slipper had a stimulating time indeed in Brazil in 1974. Until his trip to Rio de Janeiro that year, Detective Chief Superintendent Slipper, or Slipper of the Yard, as he was known to Britain's newspaper readers, was the acme of the successful Scotland Yard policeman: six foot four inches tall, smart, moustachioed, in command of that posh, stilted Cockney way of speaking known to filmgoers and television watchers everywhere. He had successfully tackled a number of high-profile crimes, including The Great Train Robbery of 1963, a daring snatch of £2.6 million from the Glasgow to London night mail train that had much excited that abiding British liking for a bit of cheeky outlawry (see also **Jack Rann** and **Jack Sheppard**). Among those he had brought to justice was Ronald Biggs, a bit-part player who achieved celebrity status with a dramatic escape from Wandsworth Prison in 1965. Biggs made his way to Australia, where he was spotted, and then to Brazil, where the *Daily Express* found him. All Slipper had to do was get him. But where a Fleet Street exclusive is involved, there is more secrecy, shiftiness, drama and duplicity than even the most experienced police officer or criminal can handle. Biggs was sold up and down the river, and things went similarly and sadly awry for Slipper after his moment of triumph in Room 909 of the Hotel Trocadero, whither a slow and faulty lift had brought him, along with his deputy, Inspector Jones, the British consul, the British vice-consul and two Brazilian policemen. Slipper knew what he was going to say. 'Hello, Ronnie,' he said. 'Long time, no see.' Biggs said, 'Fuck me! How did *you* get here?' Thereafter, Slipper became mired in a series of complications and twists which made it inevitable that he would return without Biggs. There was, for example, the lack of an extradition treaty with Brazil. There was Slipper's lack of Portuguese. There was the mutual encouragment of secrecy by the *Express* and the Yard, which led to a lack of preparation and notification of the proper authorities. And then there was Biggs's fortuitous and fortunate discovery, given the current condition of his Brazilian girlfriend, that the father of a Brazilian child could not be extradited. In the full glare of a Fleet Street pack desperate to catch up, Slipper flew home alone except for the faithful Jones, who would perform the crowning cruel but completely unconscious betrayal: as Slipper slept on the plane, Jones went off to the lavatory, leaving the *Daily Mail* photographer sitting nearby with the picture he was waiting for: Slipper asleep next to an empty seat. The legend of Slip-Up of the Yard was born. His reputation never really recovered, although he successfully sued the BBC to protect it. But Biggs fared worse: he did another deal with another newspaper, the *Sun*, and came home at last in

2001 because he wanted to 'walk into a Margate pub as an Englishman and buy a pint of bitter'. Instead, he got MRSA in HMP Belmarsh and is still in prison. Should you ever wish to warn your children of the dangers of unhealthy eating, point out that Biggs was caught in the first place because he left fingerprints on a tomato sauce bottle in the Train Robbers' hideout. Should you need further confirmation – or warning – of the dedication, ingenuity and professionalism of Fleet Street, I will add that the *Sun* also got a picture of the empty seat on the plane when Inspector Jones went off again and the *Daily Mail* photographer was asleep. Or you could read Anthony Delano's excellent account of the affair, *Slip-Up*.

SLIPPERY JACK

A slimy, reddish-brown cap mushroom, available all over the northern hemisphere, remove the pores before eating, can cause allergic reaction, glutinous coating an acquired swallow, could be a toadstool: that's *Suillus luteus*, the Slippery Jack mushroom. Yum.

SMITH (I)

There were crooners, but, first, there was Whispering Jack Smith, so named because of his way with a song and the infant microphone. Jack makes that new fellow, Bing Crosby, sound as soft as Celine Dion, as subtle as Dame Shirley Bassey and as soothing as Meatloaf. He sang that way, allegedly, because he had been gassed while in the trenches in the First World War and was thus incapable of anything louder or more driven; whatever the cause, inspiration or necessity, listen to Jack giving his elegantly understated and unmatchably enunciated all to, for example, 'Miss Annabelle Lee', and wonder. A New Yorker, he died, under-appreciated, in 1950, and remains so, lying in an unmarked grave and fairly forgotten. Next time you are on public transport next to someone with leaking headphones, think of Jack and sigh, softly.

SMITH (2)

The novelty song has a curious fascination for listeners and lovers of British pop music. You might attribute this to a lack of taste. I prefer to see it as a tellingly critical and cleverly anarchic judgement on the excess of seriousness with which popular culture tends to take itself. Aficionados also cherish the fixed smiles and general embarrassment that used to accompany their performances on BBC's *Top of the Pops*. Even so, 'I Was Kaiser Bill's Batman' by Whistling Jack Smith, which figured in both the British and US charts in 1967, is not one of my favourites, ranking a little way above 'The Smurf Song' by Father Abraham and the Smurfs, 'My Boomerang Won't Come Back' by Charlie Drake and 'The Streak' by Ray Stevens, but some way below 'Gilly Gilly Ossenfeffer Katzenellen Bogen by the Sea' by Max Bygraves, 'The Deck of Cards' by Wink Martindale ('I know, I was that soldier'), 'You're the One That I Want' by Arthur Mullard and Hylda Baker, 'They're Coming to Take Me Away' by Napoleon XIV, and, of course, 'Grocer Jack (Excerpt from a Teenage Opera)' by Keith West (see under Xavier).

Sources are divided on exactly who it was whistling on the song, which was originally entitled 'Too Much Bird Seed', and was written by Roger Cook and Peter Greenaway, also responsible between them for the Coca-Cola song, 'I'd Like to Teach the World to Sing' (originally 'True Love and Apple Pie'), 'Gimme Dat Ding' by the Pipkins, and advertising jingles for Allied Carpets, Asda and British Gas. Some say it was the record's producer, Noel Walker. Others say it was a session whistler (indeed), the revered John O'Neill, of Essex, who was also responsible for the haunting lipwork on Sergio Leone's *The Good, The Bad and The Ugly* (although in the clearly contentious world of whistling, this is sometimes disputed).

All agree, though, that the chap who appeared as Whistling Jack Smith – the name was a spectacularly inapt tribute to Whispering **Jack Smith** (qv) – merely mimed. He was Billy Moeller, the brother of Tommy Moeller of Unit 4 Plus 2, who co-wrote that band's one hit, 'Concrete and Clay', in 1965. All agree, too, that WJS's follow-up album, *Around the World with Whistling Jack Smith*, has a truly remarkable selection of whistles: 'Tom Hark', 'Battle Hymn of the Republic', 'Rose, Rose, I Love You', 'Union Jack', 'Waltzing Matilda', 'Song of the Steppes', 'Scotland the Brave', 'Frère Jacques', 'Hava Nagila', 'Happy Wanderer' and 'Early One Morning'. Cognoscenti point out that on the single of 'I Was' etc., the one word spoken is 'Hey', while on the album it is 'Oy'. The lyrics of 'Concrete and Clay', by the way – 'The concrete and the clay beneath our feet begin to crumble, but love will never die. Because we'll see the mountains tumble, before we say goodbye' – is a clear tribute to the Gershwins' sublime 'Our Love Is Here to Stay' – 'In time the Rockies may crumble, Gibraltar may tumble. They're only made of clay. But our love is here to stay.' Which also shows that Ira was a great songwriter but a lousy geologist.

SNIPE

The smallest of the Snipes, but with other Jack traits, too, being secretive, but flashy with it. The courtship aerial display is especially over the top: bobbing, hovering, climbing 150 feet, steep dives, roll-overs with half-folded wings, and then pulling out at the last second before climbing again. The Jack's call has been likened to the sound of a horse galloping in the distance. The Jack Snipe is also a nippy sailing dinghy, and a flower (narcissus, naturally).

SPARROW

That old Hollywood magic is still there. And never more than when it is re-inventing itself and history with all the self-obsession, hang-the-expense ingenuity and painstaking determination which makes you wonder what would happen if it were applied to the real problems of the world. The *Pirates of the Caribbean* series is a brilliant mining of the old pirate movies of the sort that Errol Flynn, Gene Kelly and Burt Lancaster used to make, full of acutely judged parody and fun. All the savvy and wiles of the new technologies are winningly applied, but the chief adornment is Johnny Depp's Captain Jack Sparrow, a new age Errol, Gene and Burt, all swagger and stagger, mascara and slur, ambiguous in every way, the best and worst pirate anybody has ever seen. The eyeliner is a particular inspiration: pirate movies have always featured plenty of rolling eyes (in this one some are detachable) but never has mugging been so archly accomplished as by Captain Jack. The combined creation of four screenwriters, the director and Depp, Captain Jack's chief influence would seem to be Keith Richards: Depp, by his own account, saw shrewdly that the pirates of the Caribbean were the rock idols of their day, rebellious, daring and, above all, free. 'It's all about childhood dreams,' Stuart Beattie, one of the screenwriters, has said. 'To sail the seas and be free – that's what Jack Sparrow represents.' Those among you equally philosophical will mull over the distance between then and now, dreams and reality, represented by Keith Richards' fall from a coconut tree and subsequent cranial surgery in 2006.

But there's more to Jack. He was written as a talkative trickster whose daffiness is there to deceive. Jack, the writers say – and you can see it now they've said it – is Groucho Marx and Bugs Bunny with a touch for good measure of Pepe Le Pew, the vainglorious but still malodorous cartoon skunk. And then there's the name. Sparrow was chosen for the freedom, and the frailty; Jack because it's a fine name for a pirate, and because another of the writers, Terry Rossio, has divined an essential truth about Jacks: 'He's a guy who feels, no matter how bad things are, somehow the universe will come round to his point of view if he just hangs in long enough.'

Here are two defining passages:

ELIZABETH SWANN (HEROINE AND GOVERNOR'S DAUGHTER):
'There will come a moment when you will have a chance to show it. To do the right thing.'

JACK SPARROW: 'I love those moments. I like to wave at them as they pass by.'

JACK SPARROW: 'Put it away, son. It's not worth you getting beat again.'

WILL TURNER: 'You didn't beat me. You ignored the rules of engagement. In a fair fight, I'd kill you.'

JACK SPARROW: 'That's not much incentive for me to fight fair, then, is it?'

Excellent. They called the monkey Jack, too.

SPRAT

Jack Sprat could eat no fat,
His wife could eat no lean,
And so, between them both you see,
They licked the platter clean.

Jack ate all the lean,
Joan ate all the fat.
The bone they picked clean,
Then gave it to the cat.

Another nursery rhyme subjected to interesting interpretations beyond that of a recipe for marital harmony, if not pet welfare. Some think Jack Sprat, sixteenth- and seventeenth-century slang for a dwarf, refers to Charles I (who was around five foot tall) and his wife, Henrietta Maria, illegally taxing their realm to the state of a clean plate or a picked bone. Others say it's King John and his first wife, Isabel of Gloucester, who is alleged to have been greedy besides being known by a remarkable number of alternative names, including Hadwisa, Hawise, Joan, Eleanor, Avise and Avisa. One other version of the rhyme has Jack as Prat, slang for a buttock, which is very much in the same area as I would file these theories, under 'a load of old'.

I am surprised, though, that King John wasn't more often called Jack Lackland rather than the usual John Lackland, a reference to his having no estates, unlike his flashy older brother, Richard the Lionheart. For John is very much the Jack of the Kings of England, despite the biased and over-simple version of him handed down by popular history. He was exceptionally well-read, for one thing, which provided him with a sophistication evidenced by his cynical and mischievous sense of humour and scorn for the orthodoxies of medieval Europe. This is the man who responded to his papal excommunication by raiding the homes of the English clergy and taking away their 'housekeepers' (as they were euphemistially known) for ransom. The man, too, who sent emissaries to the Emir of Morocco to explore the advantages of converting England to Islam. The man, too, who laughed at the prophecy for the end of his reign from the crazed hermit, Peter of Pontefract, and held a great feast on the appointed day to mock him (being John, of course, he then hanged Peter, and, for good measure, his son, too). And surely it was a joke when he offered to pay the ransom for his Lionhearted brother, provided they agreed to keep him. His enemies accused him of inexcusable indolence while the French were recapturing France from him; and it is true that he spent an unusual amount of time in bed; but, there again, he did have at least 17 children, mostly bastards.

Detective Inspector Jack Spratt is also the hero of a series of whodunits by Jasper Fforde featuring the deaths in suspicious circumstances of the likes of Humpty Stuyvesant Van Dumpty III. Jack has a fat-free diet and unresolved issues with giants. If you don't know Jack Schitt, another of Fforde's characters, give him a try.

SPRING-HEELED JACK

Nowadays, thanks to living in a global village connected through any number of mediums of communication, there are an enormous number of things to panic and worry about, from genocide, global warming and unceasing disasters to the credit crunch, bird flu, obesity and Paris Hilton. In nineteenth-century Britain, the choice was more limited, and local problems, like surviving, were often more pressing. And there was also Spring-heeled Jack, a demonic figure with red eyes and clawed hands who breathed fire and leapt out of the shadows to attack the unwary before escaping with prodigious leaps over walls and even roofs. Jack's attacks were sporadic but continued for most of the century, sending the more excitable parts of the populace, particularly in London and the surrounding countryside, into repeated fits of thrilled panic. With this Jack, I am in some difficulty. While yielding to no one in a liking for mystery and intrigue, I am also compelled to concede that recent exemplary examinations of Jack, notably by Mr Mike Dash of the *Fortean Times*, have revealed the whole thing to be – and here I go slightly further than Mr Dash – tosh.

It seems very clear that there was some initial pranking by persons unknown, probably some bored young toffs of the type who terrorised London for several centuries until their supposed inferiors took over and now make a much better fist of it. This was then copied well and badly in various parts of the country at regular intervals, setting off further copycat incidents. There is no proof for the giant leaps (experiments with springs and boots by the Wehrmacht last century produced not much more than a lot of broken ankles), and the fire-breathing stopped pretty pronto when the would-be imitators of circus artists discovered that setting fire to inflammable liquid as you breathe it out can be very dodgy in a bit of a breeze. Why Jack provoked such panics and convictions of the existence of a maverick and malevolent supernatural figure is more interesting. To those who would point to less sophisticated times, I say: UFOs, crop circles, conspiracy theories and the large audiences today for old-fashioned mediums whose communications are alleged to come from well beyond cyberspace. And while it's true that the limited technologies of detection and information available then made Jack's sway much easier, that doesn't quite explain why so many people today are so eager to believe in him. Indeed, the educated classes then sneered at the believers, and would be amazed at his survival. I put it down, once again, to the potency of the name: as with the far graver Whitechapel Murders, Jack was, and is, the link to magic and mischief, the signal to shiver, the threat from the forest, the Green Man, the Wild Man, Bigfoot, never stronger than when times and certainties are changing. Wait a minute, though, what was that, over there? Time, perhaps, for the world's shortest ghost story: a man is sleeping in a haunted room, suddenly awakes, fumbles to light the candle, and the matches are put into his hand.

STABBER JACK

See **Jack Beasley**.

STEINBERGER

Jack Steinberger grew up in Chicago, working in the family delicatessen. So when you learn that Jack is big in neutrinos, you can be forgiven for thinking they are some sort of artificial sweeteners, rather than atomic particles. Jack, who fled pre-war Germany with his family, won the Nobel Prize for Physics in 1988, is regarded as one of the finest experimental physicists in the world, but is not flashy with it. He says: 'You imagine that we, the old and a little bit successful, might have a message for the young people. One thing which is very sure is that older people are not as clever as younger people, and I think that these younger people will probably be able to figure out what is good for them far better than I can tell them.' Indeed: his son John is the designer of a highly regarded bass guitar.

STRACHEY

An English composer, born in Brighton in 1894, Jack Strachey, or, more properly, Jack Strachey Parsons, was responsible for two of the most instantly evocative tunes of two differing decades of the last century. The first, in the 1930s, was 'These Foolish Things (Remind Me of You)', rarely bettered for conjuring up what comes after the end of an affair. The words were by Eric Maschwitz, who deserves to be better remembered for:

> and still those little things remain
> that bring me happiness or pain

and

> the scent of smoking leaves,
> the wail of steamers,
> two lovers on the street
> who walk like dreamers.

I once knew a similarly plaintive version, 'The tattered remnants of a late-night final, the sound of laughter from the men's urinal', but can remember no more. 'These Foolish Things' has been much covered; Robert Cushman in the entertaining *Lives of the Great Songs* makes the point that Sinatra's version sounds suprisingly like the late Sid James. Strachey also wrote 'In Party Mood', the jaunty theme of *Housewives' Choice* on the BBC Light Programme, which is still used as an instant time-travel device to the 1950s. Eric Maschwitz, who went on to become head of BBC television light entertainment, wrote the lyrics to that other 1930s hymn to Mayfair, 'A Nightingale Sang in Berkeley Square', with the incomparable line, 'There were angels dining at the Ritz.' Maschwitz had a lively marriage with Hermione

Gingold; in her autobiography, *How to Grow Old Disgracefully*, she describes dashing from a performance to catch the final curtain at the first night of one of Eric's musicals, *Balalaika*. Eric was at the back of the stalls, shouting, 'Author! Author!' before rushing up to take a bow.

STRAUS

In his book about poker, *The Biggest Game in Town*, Al Alvarez quotes Walter Matthau: 'the game exemplifies the worst aspects of capitalism that have made our country so great'. This reminds me of something I should have mentioned when we were on Jack Lemmon: the time when Matthau hurt himself in a fall on set and Lemmon took off his jacket, put it gently under Matthau's head and said, 'Walter, are you comfortable?' 'I make a living,' replied Matthau. Jack Straus, one of the star's of Alvarez's book, made his out of poker, most famously in the World Hold'em Championship in Las Vegas in 1982, when he was cleaned out on the first day, but found one last chip under a napkin on the table and went on to win the title, and $500,000. Or perhaps it was in 1970, when he was down to his last $40 and set off on a series of gambles at blackjack and poker, each time betting all he had, and ending with $20,000 after a bet on the Super Bowl. Jack was aptly named, as the general usage of Jackpot is derived from draw-poker, where the pot accumulates until someone can open with a pair of Jacks or better. Those wishing to emulate or avoid Jack's path should know that his father, a Texan packing-factory manager, worked and saved hard all his life so as to enjoy his retirement and then died when he was 58. 'If they'd wanted you to hold on to money, they'd have made it with handles on,' said Jack. Not that Jack didn't take his poker seriously: he once played against a painter and decorator in El Paso, winning the man's monthly pay cheque and taking an IOU for $100, which he drove him home to collect. The man's wife didn't take the news well, and from the next room Jack could hear her weeping with worry about how she was going to feed their six children. Jack noticed her purse lying open, with a $10 bill and a $1 bill inside. What did he do? 'I just took the $10 bill and let him slide for the rest.' As it happens, Jack also died when he was 58. What are the odds on that?

STRAW

Very little, as we have seen, is known about Jack Cade, the leader of the Kentish rebellion of 1450. Even less is known about the leaders of the Peasants' Revolt of 80 years earlier, and, in particular, Jack Straw, whose severed head was said to have been placed next to those of John Ball and Wat Tyler on London Bridge after the latter had been struck down at the great meeting of peasants and their boy king, Richard II, at Smithfield in 1381. Indeed, many have argued, contrary to the chronicles, that Jack Straw was merely a symbolic name given to Wat Tyler. Certainly, there is no provenance for Jack, and the verdict of dictionary definitions seems clear: a Jack Straw was a harvest festival effigy and by extension a worthless man; and so a Man of Straw is a counterfeit or a sham, an imaginary adversary, an argument that is invented so that it can be triumphantly defeated. More support comes from the names of other rebels, equally suspicious sounding: **Jack Carter**, **Jack Trewman**, and Erl of the Plo. In the Lollard uprising of 1431, William Perkins, the leader, assumed the name of **Jack Sharpe**, while the peasant protagonist of an anti-clerical tract of the time is **Jack Upland**. It's not surprising, then, with all these Jacks, that connections have been made with the old tensions between settlement and wander, order and freedom, forest and field, town and country; tensions given regular release in the festivals of mumming and misrule and Jacks and Green and Wild Men, less regularly in those periodic uprisings which have continued right up to today's Bank Holiday Britain.

But whoever they were, the language of the rebels still has the power to move across the centuries. This is the stirring start to a letter said to be from John Ball, the third man of the peasant troika, the rebel priest: 'Jon Balle gretyth yow wele alle and doth yowe to understande, he hath rungen youre belle . . . ' Rungen youre belle! Another continues: 'Now regnith pride in pris, and covetys is hold wys, and leecherye withouten shame and glotonye withouten blame.' Another, from Jack Trewman, declares, 'falsnes and gyle havith regned to long, and trewthe hat bene sette under a lokke, and falsnes regneth in everylk flokke'. Ball's most famous declaration was, 'When Adam delved and Eve span, Who was then the gentleman?'

Like Jack Cade, the rebels of 1381 were long after fiercely condemned for seeking to overthrow order with anarchy, but the truth seems to lie more in their invocation of the spirit of Piers Plowman, hero of Langland's great contemporary poem, with his echoing plea that the goodness in men's hearts should prevail over the temptations of privilege and provide fairness for all. Still a work in progress, then. By one of those happy conjunctions of history, two of the leading British politicians of recent years have been the former Conservative prime minister John Major, full name, John Major Ball, and Jack Straw, the Labour MP who has held several high offices of state. Both, too, appear at first sight to share a certain ungraspable anonymity, a greyness or lack of colour; but in both cases further investigation reveals a spark and a willingness to risk the unconventional. Major, for example, although the son of a circus performer and garden gnome manufacturer, chose to become a banker. Straw, at the age of 11, growing up in Loughton, Essex, told off the local ice-cream man for sounding his chimes after 7 p.m., as it was illegal. These are traits which many clearly find attractive. Major's charms are too well-rehearsed to need repetition here; and I can reveal that in March 1999, in Blackburn, where he is the MP, a framed photograph of Jack Straw was stolen from the wall of a community centre.

Tar

A very large amount of British myth and sentiment is embodied in Jack Tar, the common term for a sailor, especially a sailor in the Royal Navy, who, along with his comrade on land, Tommy Atkins, is an often grumbling, occasionally feckless and invariably put-upon common man who nevertheless, when the chips are down, the drums begin to roll, the metal's flying and the munitions are low, has a heart of oak, is as firm as a square and will willingly give up his life for his country and comrades. In large, this is a belief that has survived, despite some striking instances to the contrary, because it is true.

The derivation of 'Tommy Atkins' is variously cited, most legendarily from a man of that name whom the Duke of Wellington witnessed dying bravely, but it is probably earlier. 'Jack Tar' seems to come from the tar with which sailors waterproofed their clothing and dressed their pigtails to prevent them from being caught in the rigging. Jack's history is that of the Royal Navy and the wider seas, too broad a canvas even for my impudent summaries. But there are some points which might be of interest. The most famous impudent summary is that of Winston Churchill: 'The only traditions of the Royal Navy are rum, sodomy and the lash.' Naturally enough, there is no record of his ever making it, although an aide later asserted that he wished he had done.

Even so, there is little evidence of Jack's alleged second characteristic: recent research of some fifty logbooks from naval ships of the early nineteenth century revealed only one incident of buggery, and one of bestiality (let us but mention the practice of keeping livestock on board and then tack tactfully away). The other two practices, though, were undeniably prevalent. Flogging wasn't abolished until the late nineteenth century. Admiral Sir Charles Napier became a Liberal MP and fierce campaigner for more humane treatment of sailors, despite an earlier enthusiasm for 'scratching a man's back' up to three times more than the dozen lashes officially sanctioned. It says something for Jack Tar, although I'm not quite sure what, that HMS *Powerful*, his command at the time (the 1840s), is described as 'not an unhappy ship' by contemporary standards.

But then this is Dr Johnson, a little earlier, on Jack's lot: 'No man will be a sailor who has the contrivance to get himself into jail; for being in a ship is being in a jail with a chance of being drowned. A man in jail has more room, better food, and commonly better company.'

You can see what the good doctor meant: a typical man-of-war of around his time measured roughly 165 foot by 45 foot and would have a crew of some 600 men berthed on a single deck. The space allocated to each man's hammock was 14 inches in width, although in practice, because of the rotational watch system, Jack had a full 28 inches to spread himself out in. And he did have his rum. Captain James Pack's magisterial work, *Nelson's Blood: The Story of Naval Rum*, is most instructive on the drinking, which was truly heroic. Up to a gallon of beer a day was supplemented by brandy and wine. But after Cromwell's Commonwealth Navy captured Jamaica in the 1660s, rum became the tot of choice. Admiral Vernon (named Old Grogram, after the material of his waterproof coat) ordered the daily ration to be watered, and lime added for the avoidance of scurvy, in 1740. The twice-daily ration of what now became known as grog was half a pint until 1824, when it was halved and restricted to once a day, and then halved again in 1850. It was finally abolished on 31 July 1970, known as Black Tot day, when black armbands were worn and barrels consigned to the waters in solemn ceremonies all over what was left of the British Empire. The complete history of the influence of alcohol on world events has yet to be written. Churchill himself is an instructive example: first whisky and soda soon after breakfast, followed by more steadily through the day, champagne at dinner, several brandies and more whisky and sodas as the night wore on. One does think, however, of what our leaders now achieve sober.

Nelson's Blood, the Navy nickname for rum, is said to have originated after Trafalgar, when the admiral's body was immersed in a barrel for reasons of preservation. But it is also said that the barrel was of brandy (which was still being bought by the Navy from French merchants during the Napoleonic Wars). There is an accompanying legend, too, that Jack Tars drank from the barrel, either in an attempt to imbibe some of Nelson's spirit, or because they fancied a drink. When I mentioned this to the naval officer conducting our tour round HMS *Victory* in Portsmouth, I was rewarded with a look that amply demonstrated the ineffable hauteur with which the Royal Navy upholds its rank as the Senior Service.

TAYLOR

Jacks have made a select and typically exuberant contribution to the Summer Game. Jack Taylor (1873-1900) was a great pitcher, mostly for the Philadelphia Phillies. But he was renowned for arguing with the umpires, he died young and his nickname gives a clue to another foible: Brewery Jack. **Jack Glasscock** was the top short stop of his era, the 1880s and 1890s. He was known as Pebbly Jack after his prudent habit of removing stones from the infield. But he was also, it seems, less than a gentleman: 'I have heard him use language during the progress of a game that would put the meanest tough in the country to shame,' as one commentator put it. Jack argued with umpires, too, and upset lady fans. **Jack Chesbro** (1874-1931) was another fabled pitcher with the Pittsburgh Pirates and the New York Highlanders. His nickname, Happy Jack, is more encouraging. Jack was one of the great spitball pitchers, applying his oracular lubrications to great effect: his 1904 record for games won still stands. Jack won 41 games; it would have been 42, and Jack would have been even happier, but for the spitball that his catcher missed, giving the Boston Pilgrims the game. The miss was blamed on Jack's wild throw: long after his death, his widow was still trying, in vain, to get the blame shifted officially to the catcher. Spitballing was outlawed in the 1920s; **Jack Quinn**, who was allowed to continue with the practice, was the last spitballer (it would be a Jack), retiring in 1933 after a remarkable 24 years in the top flight. **Jack Warhop**, another great pitcher (you will be discerning a pattern), is fated to be remembered as the man who provided the ball which gave Babe Ruth his first home run. **Jack Morris** is a suitably controversial figure who played for five Major League teams in a career that lasted from the 1970s to the 1990s. Jack was a devastating but high-risk pitcher with other quirks, such as wearing a T-shirt bearing the American flag and the legend 'Let the hippies try and burn THIS one'. He also refused to give a woman sports reporter a post-match interview because 'I don't talk to women when I'm naked, unless they're on top of me or I'm on top of them'. **Cactus Jack Billingham** (born 1943) could pitch a bit, too.

TEAGARDEN

Jack Teagarden (1905–64) proved that white guys can play the trombone and sing the blues. He also proved that playing the trombone and singing the blues doesn't necessarily equip you to run a band. And that too much whisky will kill you. Jack was born in Vernon, Texas. His father played in a brass band and his mother was a piano teacher. Jack was playing the trombone by the age of ten, and within five years was playing professionally in San Antonio. He went on to play with the variously doomed Bix Beiderbecke and Glenn

Miller (with whom he wrote the verse of 'Basin Street Blues' that everyone remembers, about New Orleans being the land of dreams). But his most famous collaboration was the black and white one with Louis Armstrong. Funny how things work: when Louis and his All Stars played the South, the guy segregated was Jack, who, as the only white member, had to stay on his own elsewhere. Jack's style was cool, calm and understated, which was not that surprising, given his regular and prodigious intake of alcohol. But it rarely had any effect on his playing, although quite a lot on his private and business life, which was uneven. Into this mix should be added Jack's lifelong liking for model trains. When he invited girls up to his room after the show to see his trains, it wasn't a euphemism. 'Those poor chicks would just sit on the bed waiting for something to happen, while Jack laid out on the floor blowing the whistles and making the engines work,' recalled his fellow All Star, Barney Bigard, the clarinet player. Barney also paid this tribute: 'He never bothered anyone. He was just a quiet man. A real wonderful guy to be around, but when he played his horn, he really played it, believe me.'

TRACY

The memory of Phyllis Dixey is revived every so often, mostly to evoke the imagined innocence of former times. Phyllis was Britain's first modern striptease dancer of acclaim; she was neither exotic nor erotic, but rather prim, whether unclothed on stage or clothed off it, constrained by her own inclinations, watch committees and the Lord Chamberlain, the royal courtier charged with protecting the moral fibre of British theatregoers until 1968. Phyllis's talents as a singer and actress were similarly modest, which led her to her calling. Jack 'Snuffy' Tracy was her husband, agent, and sometime accompanist. They met in Australia in 1935 in a show promoted by Wallace Parnell, her former lover and brother of **Jack** (qv). This Jack was a shade over five foot, an orphaned Irish boy who had emigrated to the US at a young age and had arrived by way of supporting W.C. Fields at a double act which featured gags, songs, music and a statuesque showgirl whose embonpoint he would become stuck in. Jack, like the previous entry, also played trombone, but not quite so well. He was, however, adept at making rude noises with it, which proved surprisingly popular over the years. Snuffy was a wiseguy character he developed after he partnered up in every sense, including marriage, with Phyllis. Their great years were the war years, once Jack had worked out that stripping was what Phyllis would do best.

It began with a routine entitled 'Confessions of a Fan Dancer' at the Tivoli, Hull, and moved to the Whitehall Theatre, London, which Jack and Phyllis hired for most of the war, and which rivalled the Windmill Theatre as the venue of choice for troops on leave. *The One and Only Phyllis Dixey*, by Philip Purser and Jenny Wilkes, reveals one of those familiar and sad declines thereafter, occasionally halted but most often helped by Jack's infectious enthusiasms, almost pathological optimism, love of golf and eye for other ladies now younger than his wife. It ended with a week's engagement at The Palace, Burnley, in 1958. After that, Phyllis took a job as a cook at what would now be called a hotel and conference centre, catering for, among others, those Young Socialists Shirley Williams, Denis Healey and Tony Benn. Jack tried his hand as a handyman and milkman (Phyllis would come and help him reach the higher crates). But he was not cut out for that sort of thing and was far happier when Phyllis's uncle by marriage, a Parsee who had turned to spiritualism, found him a job as a Surrey golf club steward. Phyllis, in that familiarly cruel way, contracted cancer, but found consolation first in her uncle's spiritualism and then in the Roman Catholic Church, dying in 1964. Jack was last heard of in Surbiton, married to a retired bank clerk, playing a spot of golf and studying French.

TRIPP

December or January, afternoon, getting dark outside. Inside the theatre, popcorn all over the floor before it starts, school parties and granny parties, deliciously hot and noisy and sticky with anticipation. And then Abanazar leering, thundering and hissed, Widow Twankey fluttering, encamped, much ado with boobs, Aladdin spirited, splendidly thighed, Wishy Washy racing around, awful puns and delighted shrieks. Or it could be *The Babes in the Wood*, or *Cinderella*, or *Dick Whittington*, or *Robinson Crusoe*; but it wouldn't matter, or make that much difference: this is pantomime, panto, the great and uniquely British popular art form. Jack Tripp (1922–2005) was the master and mistress of it. Jack was a pantomime dame, the great panto comic turn, the arch and cross-dressed foil, all pursed lips, frequent and violently hitched frontage, astonishment that anyone could possibly interpret what s/he was saying in that way, and an affronted dignity that could survive an outfit of outrageous chic involving a hat designed as a frying pan with bacon and eggs, or a dress resembling a green baize snooker table with carefully positioned pockets. Jack specialised; daming was what he did. He had no time for the here-today, gone-later-today soap opera or reality TV figures who arrived as the instant draw for the quick buck with neither the respect for the tradition, nor, excuse me, the right equipment. 'How bloody dare they?' he would say. 'I could play at Lord's if somebody asked me but it wouldn't do the cricket much good.' Unsurprisingly, Jack was more than equal to descriptions of him as 'The John Gielgud of Pantomime', or, earlier in his career, 'The Fred Astaire of Plymouth', from where he came. He lived, naturally enough, in Brighton, and was wise enough to retire in time and resist a return: 'I think not. I prefer my memories. I don't think it's worth blowing up my boobs any more.'

TURNBULL

Another lost Jack. Lieutenant Colonel Jack Turnbull was leading a bombing mission on Germany back to Britain in October 1944, when his B-24, The Flying Ginny, crashed, killing all its crew. He was 34. Jack had been a sportsman of rare gifts, rated the finest attacker American lacrosse has produced, captaining the Olympic demonstration team which beat Canada in the 1932 Los Angeles games. Lacrosse was not selected as a sport for the notorious Berlin Olympics in 1936, so Jack swapped to hockey, another talent of his, along with football, basketball and ice hockey. His citation in the Lacrosse Hall of Fame recalls a man of very few words. According to a wartime comrade, James J. Mahoney, he used some of them 'over our warm beer in a cold Nissen hut' in East Anglia, remembering that in 1936 he had been invited into Hitler's box: 'I could have reached over and strangled the son of a bitch then, and we wouldn't be here now!' That's a Jack.

UNION JACK

The ancient-established British practice of avoiding problems by not mentioning them or writing anything down often causes troubles of its own. To go back some way, for example, much of the unpleasantness that followed Harold Godwin's trip to Normandy might not have ensued if everyone had been a little clearer about whether he had promised the English throne to Duke William, or not. More recently, there was that meeting in a then fashionable Islington restaurant which left quite distinct impressions in the minds of Mr Tony Blair and Mr Gordon Brown about much the same thing that was bothering Harold and William. Overall, too, there is the British constitution, which seems to attract equal measures of praise and obloquy for being unwritten, and certainly any amount of discussion which would not otherwise take place. Some see the national flag as a symbol of all this, which is not unreasonable when you consider that, after 400 years, agreement has still not been reached on what to call it.

The popular name for it is 'The Union Jack'. There are those, however – and here the disagreement is whether they are purists or pedants – who insist that the Jack is its name only when it is flown at sea (the term comes from the use of Jack as a diminutive, the flag being smaller than an ensign). Otherwise, they say, it should be called the Union Flag. I would point them to an Admiralty Circular of 1902, and a statement by way of reply in parliament in 1908 (which was, of course, spoken), both of which sanction the use of Jack. The flaggists receive their strongest support from the *Daily Telegraph*, which insists on their usage in its style book. This, though, is also the newspaper that restricts the use of 'amok' to Malays since it is a Malayan word, and 'berserk' to Icelanders (actually, Norwegians, Swedes and Danes are also entitled to go it, as the wild Berserker warriors were more of a general kind of Norse thing).

The flag itself is a fine example of yet another proudly proclaimed British virtue, that of compromise. When James I of England and VI of Scotland united the two kingdoms in 1603, the question of how to unite the two flags, the English Cross of St George and the Scottish Saltire, required sensitive heralding. The heraldry of the day favoured placing the two flags side by side in a larger flag. But this would inevitably lend precedence to the one on the left. Someone (it seems not to have been written down) came up with a solution from earlier practice, and placed the English flag over the Scottish one. This might have the effect of imposing the English on the Scottish, but it also gave the Scottish top ranking in the vital upper left quadrant. Excellent, except that many Scottish versions had the Saltire imposed upon the Cross up until Victorian times. In 1801, following the Act of Union with Ireland, the Cross of St Patrick, a red saltire on a white background, was added to achieve the flag as it is today. Again, there was a sensitive nicety: to place the Irish cross exactly over the Scottish cross would give the impression of obliteration by the newcomer. So it was narrowed and set slightly lower, which also achieved the happy and subsidiary effect of making it asymmetrical and thus allowing the pedants to complain when it was flown upside down (which became the signal for distress, and not just theirs).

So, if you were being positive and benign, and no one was going to write it down, you might well think that the Union Jack, with its clever accommodations, is a characteristic symbol worthy of island pride. Even if, of course, you had to ignore its late imperial impedimenta, the less subtle activities which led to some less willing subjects referring to it, by way of its predominant red, as 'the butcher's apron'. But, in truth, the days of serious flag-waving were not many, and, in many ways, the current post-modern ironic usage, on dresses and wellington boots and such, suits the British better. It certainly explains an almost instinctive wariness of plans by the current British prime minister, the aforesaid Mr Brown, to make more of it.

To help, I reproduce the words of a fine old song, words, Lord Tennyson, music, Sir Arthur Sullivan: 'One with Britain, heart and soul! One life, one flag, one fleet, one Throne! Britons, hold your own!'

It's also worth mentioning the origins of the constituent flags, especially since in his fascinating book, *The Union Jack*, Nick Groom explores links between St George of England and our old friend, The Green Man. The cult of St George in his town, Lydda (now Lod, in Israel), became mixed up, in the way of these things, with that of al-Khidr, The Evergreen, ancient Arab discoverer of the Fountain of Youth and symbol of regeneration. To suggest, though, that naming our flag Jack betrays a similar mystical message would be pushing it a bit, even for me. The Saltire has just as splendid a provenance, appearing as a silver cross in a blue sky to the Christian king of the Picts, Angus, on the eve of victory over the Vikings in the eighth century. It is the symbol of St Andrew, the Apostle of the North, martyred, allegedly, on a cross so shaped; a tooth, an arm bone, a kneecap and some fingers of the saint were said to have been brought by St Rule from his tomb in the Greek city of Patras and used to found St Andrews. (They disappeared during the Reformation; most of the rest of his body is now in Amalfi, although a part of his shoulder blade was given by the Archbishop of Amalfi to help re-establish Catholicism in Scotland in 1879. The saint's head, after some travels, was handed back to the Greek Orthodox church by Pope Paul VI in 1966.)

St Patrick is not thought to have much to do with his cross (and neither, as a non-martyrish kind of saint, is he really entitled to one). You will be wondering about the Welsh input: as a principality, rather than a kingdom – none. (Mr Groom mentions the *Encyclopaedia Britannica*'s entry of 1895: 'Wales. For Wales, see England.') Oh, and since the southern part of the island of Ireland became a full republic, the part that remains in the United Kingdom cannot be considered a kingdom, and so St Patrick's Cross should have been removed from the Union Jack in 1937. Thank you.

VAHEY

Private John Vahey, or Fahey, of the 17th Lancers, took part in the Charge of the Light Brigade and was awarded the Distinguished Conduct Medal. But John was a Jack and so his part in that unreal, extraordinary event is even more unreal and extraordinary. Vahey had a fantastic story to tell, which he did, to to the great war correspondent Archibald Forbes. This was the thing: Jack liked a drink. If Jack had liked a drink less, he would have been more than a private after 14 years in the Army. Jack liked a drink so much that he always volunteered to do the company butchering, as rum came with it; hence his nickname, Butcher Jack. The day before the Charge, Jack had been butchering and drinking, and drinking, until, royally beboozled and still in his bloody apron, he was carried off to the guard-tent along with another butcher of similar inclination, Private Paddy Heffernan.

Jack and Paddy had a few more from Paddy's secret supply and then slept it off until the next morning, when 'we were wakened by the loud thundering of a tremendous cannonade close by, making the very tent poles quiver'. Although 'still deucedly muzzy', they deduced what was up and why the guard-tent was now unguarded and the camp deserted. Returning to their tent, Jack and Paddy had, naturally, some more rum while they pondered 'in a boozy sort of way' what to do. After a few more tots, Jack said to Paddy, 'Why the devil should we be out of the fun?', and they were off down into the

Valley of Death to join the Charge, Paddy armed with a sword, Jack with a butcher's axe. Down there, Jack, having mounted a blood-soaked horse lately vacated by its late Russian officer, 'galloped up to the Heavy Brigade and formed up coolly on the left flank of the old Royals'. This gallantry was not well received:

> They laughed at me as if I had been a clown in a pantomime; and I had not been in position a couple of minutes when up came Johnny Lee, their adjutant, on his old bay mare, at a tearing gallop, and roared to me, 'Go to Hell out of that.' There's no mistake, I was not much of a credit to them. I was bare-headed, and my hair was like a birch-broom in a fit. I was minus a coat, with my shirt sleeves turned up to the shoulder, and my shirt, face and bare hairy arms were all splashed and darkened with blood, which I had picked up at my butchering the day before, and had never wiped off. A pair of long, greasy jack boots came up to the thigh, and instead of a sword I had the axe over my shoulder at the slope as regimental as you please. The Russian must have ridden very short, for my knees were up to my nose in his stirrups, and so you may imagine that, taking me all in all, I was a hot-looking member, especially if you remember I was fully half-seas over.

Nothing daunted, Jack spotted the Light Brigade ahead, just beginning the trot that would lead to the Charge, with his own 17th Lancers on the right of the front rank:

> Ramming my spurless heels into the ribs of the little Russian horse, I started off in pursuit of the Light Brigade as fast as I could make him go, with shouts of laughter from the Heavies ringing behind me, and chased, unsuccessfully, by a couple of officers of the Greys, who tried to stop me for decency's sake . . . Just as I came up in line with the flank sergeant of the

front rank, who looked sideways at me as if he had seen a ghost, Cardigan turned round to say a word to the field trumpeter riding at his heels, and then with a wave of his sword went off at a score to the front. In another second, all the trumpets of the Brigade sounded the Charge, and sitting down on our saddles and setting our teeth hard, off we went pellmell across the valley as hard as ever horse could lay foot to ground . . .

What with the drink in me, and the wild excitement of the headlong charge, I went stark mad, and sent the plucky Russian horse ahead at a pace which kept me in line with the very foremost. Nearer and nearer we came to the dreadful battery, which kept vomiting death on us like a volcano, till I seemed to feel on my cheek the hot air from the cannon's mouth. At last we were on it. Half a dozen of us leaped in among the guns at once, and I with one blow of my axe brained a Russian gunner just as he was clapping the linstock to the touch-hole of his piece. With another I split open the head of an officer who was trying to rally the artillery detachment in the rear; and then what of us were left went smack through the stragglers, cutting and slashing like fiends, right straight at the column of cavalry drawn up behind the battery.

What happened then, say you? I can't tell you much more than this, that they were round us like a stream of bees, and we, not more seemingly than a couple of dozen of us to the fore, were hacking and hewing away our hardest, each individual man the centre of a separate mêlée. I know I never troubled about guards myself, but kept whirling the axe about me, every now and then bringing it down to some purpose . . . I'm hanged if I don't think I should have been there till now, had I not chanced to hear above the din a trumpet from somewhere far in the rear sound . . .

Jack joined the retreat, 'knocking over an artilleryman or two as I passed', and made it back to the Heavies, but not before leaping down from his horse to pluck up a young fallen Hussar, sling him across his saddle, and then remount and gallop off just ahead of the 'damnable Cossacks' pursuing them 'like so many wolves': 'As the lad's busby rolled off when his head touched the ground, he gave a look up at me which went to my heart, rough as I was. God pity him, he was only a boy, and I had a mother myself once.'

This being the British Army, Jack was, of course, immediately arrested and put on a charge of leaving the guard-tent 'when confined thereto'. The next day he was taken before Lord Lucan, commander of the cavalry, who said the charge would not be pursued 'in consideration of the use I had made of the liberty I had taken . . . And that's how, sir, I came by this little medal, which is Britain's reward for distinguished conduct in the field.'

Well. Was it? By now, you should know that any Jack is likely to be engaged with fable, and often temperamentally disinclined to let the facts get in the way of a good story. But it seems certain, at least, that Jack charged with the Light Brigade. There is, though, no independent confirmation of either axe or heroic rescue, and another account has Jack going missing for three days until he heard he was to be pardoned. Whatever, as a scribbler and conductor of many interviews, I must salute Mr Forbes, who did such a fine job with Jack. A certain amount of what we call, occasionally euphemistically, 'tidying up' has clearly gone on; but the voice of a Lancer comes through wonderfully well. Terry Brighton, whose *Hell Riders: The Truth About the Charge of the Light Brigade*, reprints the account, must be spot on when he says it reads like it was conducted in an ale house, particularly as his last words in the interview are, 'Thank you, sir, I'll be sure to drink your health.' Jack died in 1860, six years after his great Charge, in India, still a Lancer, of cholera. He had taken to grave digging for more grog; he was buried in one he had dug himself. No more seems to have been heard of Paddy.

VERMILLION

It's hardly suprising that there have been several claimants to the title Texas Jack. The two most famous offer a pleasing contrast, one quite bad, one quite good. Texas Jack Vermillion was born in 1842 in Virginia, and ended up in Kansas after service during the Civil War under the command of Colonel J.E.B. Stuart. He acted in a minor capacity for the Earp brothers during their lively period of law, order and vendetta, killing several people, including a fellow card player believed to be cheating (never more of a high-risk enterprise than west of the Pecos in the late nineteenth century). This incident earned him a new nickname, Shoot Your Eye Out Vermillion, which must have made it very difficult to warn people in time that he was coming. Perhaps they had to rely on his sense of humour: when people used to ask him why he was called Texas Jack, Jack would reply, 'Because I'm from Virginia.' After his time with the Earps, Jack went on to act as a bouncer and bodyguard for the egregious Jefferson, or Soapy, Smith, one of the most accomplished and organised confidence tricksters in history. Soapy's scams, carried out mostly in Colorado and Alaska, still excite awe wherever such artists gather, whether it be the telegraph office without any wires, the stock exchange which didn't exist, his raids on his own gambling dens, or his trademark trick, in which, with a flourish, he folded dollar bills round some of his soap bars before wrapping them and selling them to his associates in the crowd. (The manager of the great bullfighter El Cordobès worked something similar to promote his protégé's early career, fluttering down peseta notes on excited gatherings featuring his own men, who would briskly gather them back in.) Vermillion died in his bed back in Virginia in 1911.

The second Texas Jack was also from Virginia, and also served under Colonel Stuart, which must have made for confusion. **Texas Jack Omohundro** wasn't a gunfighter, but he did play a major part in the mythification of the west promoted by the remarkable Ned Buntline, who, when he wasn't lecturing on temperance (despite being a heavy drinker), starred Buffalo Bill and Texas Jack in the dime novels and plays that proved such a hit back east. This was the *Boston Journal* on his first play, *Scouts of the Prairie*: 'Two finer specimens of manly strength and beauty were never seen on the stage or off the stage.' And this the *Rochester Democrat and Chronicle*, when Jack announced his engagement to another co-star, Josephine Morlacchi, reputedly America's first can-can dancer: 'The man of her choice is a magnificent specimen of physical manhood. He is about six feet in height and of the finest proportions. A native of Virginia, born in 1846, the blood of Powhatan flows in his veins, and the aquiline nose, jet black hair, erect form, and piercing eye of that famed warrior are reproduced in the gallant "Texas Jack".' It's somehow especially poignant that in the middle of this heady conflation of art and life the magnificent Jack should have been struck down by something far more mundane than a bullet but equally deadly: pneumonia, at the age of 33. Nearly 30 years later, Buffalo Bill replaced Jack's humble marker in the cemetery at Leadville with a fine headstone, a splendid gesture, even if his name as benefactor is at least as big as Jack's.

VETTRIANO

It's only right that 'The People's Painter' should be called Jack. He was, in his earlier days, as I mentioned earlier, called Jack Hoggan, the son of a miner from Fife. But I was also a little unfair in suggesting that the name change had been merely cosmetic and calculated. Vettriano is his mother's maiden name, and he adopted it to differentiate his later and better work from the works he had produced when he was learning his craft by copying his betters. Since, as you might have noticed, I work mostly in generalities, I fancy I see much Italian in his work, from the naive lust in some of his paintings to the gangsterish quality of others to a hint of Caravaggio. This would enrage art critics if they were to take me any more seriously than Vettriano, who seems to arouse a scorn in them disproportionate even to the 750,000 smackers gladly shelled out at auction for his most famous painting, *The Singing Butler*. This is perhaps because although in technique and subject it should be easy to condemn, impossible to defend, there is something almost perversely and deeply attractive about it, the attraction of the simple and untutored for those of us similarly disposed, defined by Cicero and Coward, quoted by Gombrich and also exhibited by Rousseau, Lowry and the great Tretchikoff. Jack, being a Jack, stubbornly goes his own way, while being hurt by this refusal of the current arterati, whom he would like to admire, to come with him. Being a Jack, too, his paintings are either very dark or very bright, beach or bordello. He talks of the fallen angel that lies within us, and, unusually, doesn't reveal much of a sense of humour. But he is an admirer of Leonard Cohen, which must surely count in his favour.

WALKER

A pair of Jacks here, both Lancastrian. The first (1929–2000), although real enough, had a life which reads like fiction. He rose from dealing in scrap iron on a barrow round the streets of Blackburn to dealing in steel on the world markets, becoming one of the richest men in Britain, and, most improbably of all, managing to buy success in football and remain popular. Like **Jack Hayward** (qv), Jack pumped vast amounts of cash into the team he had followed as a boy; but this Jack got luckier. He was clever as well, though, pulling off the difficult task of splashing out shrewdly, making two signings in particular which demonstrated great intent and produced great effect: those of Alan Shearer, a splendid, match-winning centre forward, and of Kenny Dalglish, a formidable but unorthodox manager. (I once asked Dalglish for his forecast for an FA Cup final involving his then team, Liverpool. 'It'll be sunny,' he said; and it was.) Walker and Dalglish took Blackburn Rovers into the Premier League in 1992 and, with the aid of Shearer, to the championship within three years. That was the best it got, but Blackburn loved him for it, and called him Uncle Jack. He died in 2000. Outwardly a touch shy for a Jack, his style was nevertheless revealed by the sign in his office which read 'Rule One, I am always right. Rule Two, when I am wrong, read Rule One'.

The second Jack was a work of fiction, but true to life, the long-suffering husband of Annie Walker, the magnificent, monstrous landlady of the Rover's Return, Coronation Street. Jack's ambition had always been to run a pub; with the Rover's he had achieved it, no matter that it was in a northern back street inhabited by some pretty rum characters. Not so, Annie: there was a great deal of Margaret Thatcher about Annie. Indeed, some thought Lady Thatcher might unconsciously have drawn inspiration from Annie: the determination to triumph over a humble start, the dignity, the certainty, the careful diction, the froideur that could freeze, instantly, at almost any range. But not even the baroness could compete with the exquisite stare into the middle distance above pursed lips with which Annie greeted yet another piece of coarse badinage from the appallingly ignorant clientèle foisted upon her by a cruel fate when she really should have been running a tearoom in the tantalisingly nearby and leafy lost home county that is Cheshire. But good old Jack was always there to smooth feathers and feelings with oft-repeated sighs of understanding and commiseration at the shortcomings of the world, joined with just the gentlest, subtlest reproach: 'Eee, Annie, love', or 'Now, lass, easy on'. He died before her, of course – heart attack. But Annie sailed on alone indomitably for many years, the rock of reproof around which her fallible fellows revolved. Our thanks should go to two fine actors, Arthur Leslie, the first of the *Street* company to die, in 1970, and the wonderful Doris Speed, as kindly and charming as Annie was not. I am indebted to an internet forum for the information that Jack is the most common name among leading male soap characters. Here are some of them, along with their key Jack characteristic:

Jack Abbott, *The Young and the Restless*: ageing lad
Jack Branning, *EastEnders*: handsome
Jack Dalton, *EastEnders*: villain
Jack Deveraux, *Days of Our Lives*: charming, selfish, kindhearted: typically mixed Jack

Jack Duckworth, *Coronation Street*: see his entry

Jack Edwards, *EastEnders*: lives on a narrowboat

Jack Evans, *EastEnders*: very young but omens not good

Jack Gates, *Family Affairs*: wrong 'un

Jack Holden, *Home and Away*: things happen to Jack

Jack Marone, *The Bold and the Beautiful*: dodgy parentage

Jack Osborne, *Hollyoaks*: see his entry

Jack Scully, *Neighbours*: sporty

Jack Snyder, *As the World Turns*: everything happens to Jack

Jack Sugden, *Emmerdale*: ageing lad

Jack Walker, *Coronation Street*: see above

Jack Wilson, *Home and Away*: reformed lad

WARD

Another pirate, my hearties, but closer to home waters than the Caribbean. Jack Ward was a fisherman from Kent who had served as a petty officer on the Royal Navy's splendidly named *Lion's Whelp*, but found working for the Bey of Tunis far more rewarding, particularly as James I had closed down other lucrative privateering pursuits by making peace with Spain. Jack seized a French square rigger which, in a not entirely convincing piece of PR aimed at associating himself with an outlaw of nobler intent, he renamed *The Little John*. After picking up a Cornish crew, Jack plundered his way into the Mediterranean. There he made his base in Tunis, one of the main ports of the Barbary Corsairs, whose attacks on European shipping and coasts ranged as far as England's West Country. Much treasure was gathered in, and many prisoners, who were either ransomed or sold into slavery in North Africa. The Corsairs, not too fancifully, have been called the al-Qaeda of the seventeenth century. Jack became one of their most feared captains, commanding at his peak some 20 ships. But not a dashing pirate: a contemporary account describes him as 'very short, with little hair, and that quite white, bald in front; swarthy face and beard'. There were, though, some traditional touches. He 'raps out oaths like pellets out of a piece', was 'drunk from morn to night' and 'sleeps a great deal'. Jack had a palace of alabaster in Tunis, they said, where no 'Peer in England . . . beares up his port in more dignitie, nor hath his attendants more obsequious unto him'. Not a man, either, to be troubled by qualms about attacking his countrymen or co-religionists, or by anything much at all. According to the Venetians, his most popular prey, he converted to Islam, or 'turned Turk' as it was known then, taking the name of Issouf Reis. He also abandoned one of his foundering captures, leaving its crew of 400 Muslims and Christians to a watery fate. Jack's behaviour contrasted with that of the famous Captain Mainwaring, Sir Henry (1587–1663), whose brief but successful corsair career was conducted with the courtesy you would expect from a man with a BA from Oxford. Sir Henry, however, went straight and died practically penniless, while Jack departed this life from his palace, a very wealthy man.

WARNER

A studio head, a movie mogul; is there any other calling which so well blurs the facts and the legend? He has to be a monster, of course, and there seems no lack of willing witnesses in the case of Jack L. Warner (1892–1978), including large parts of his own family. Another of the famous brothers, Harry, apparently tried to kill him with a large plank. His son said: 'If his brothers hadn't hired him, he'd have been out of work.' And more: 'He existed behind a self-made wall. Besides, a lot of him wasn't that nice to know. At times he gloried in being a no-good sonofabitch.' There had been, you gather, falling-outs. Indeed, when Albert Einstein visited the Warner Bros studio in Hollywood, Jack told him: 'I have a theory of relativity, too. Don't hire them.' But I think we can acknowledge that someone who had come from nothing to the top and stayed there for 40 years is unlikely to please all of the people all of the time. And David Niven, Bette Davies and Errol Flynn seemed to like him, some of the time. If not Simone Signoret: 'He bore no grudge against those he had wronged.' There were 12 Warner brothers (and sisters) in all, the children of a Polish cobbler whose original name became lost along the way. Jack was born in London, Ontario, and is one of those Jacks who started out as Jacob, with not much else. He was a frustrated performer, with his singing and dancing used by his already hard-nosed elder brother to clear audiences at the end of their infant cinema showings. But the urge never left him; to be introduced to him was to have a quick softshoe shuffle followed by a lot of bad jokes (including one to Madame Chiang Kai-Shek, wife of the Taiwanese leader, about laundry). He affected less learning than the little he had, but his was a shrewd taste. When one of his lowly writers compared an upcoming Errol Flynn vehicle to a piece of Venetian glass, Jack was clear, too: 'The hell with that! This is Flynn. He's either going to be fighting or fucking. Get some guts into the thing.' But Warner Bros produced some fine movies with a liberal bias, notably its James Cagney and Paul Muni gangster films of the 1930s, and Edward G. Robinson's *Confessions of a Nazi Spy*, which didn't go down at all well in the private cinema at Berchtesgaden. And they pioneered sound (after paying Caruso to appear in a silent one), even if Al Jolson, star of *The Jazz Singer*, said later, 'I can't see what J.W. can do with an Oscar. It can't say yes.' Jack carried on, kept it up, in traditional Hollywood fashion, privately and publicly, right into the 1970s, falling in and out of style and with his family, especially after they all agreed to sell the company and then Jack bought his shares back in a side deal. He was hot against pinkos and commies, too, naming names (of writers he'd clashed with) to The House Committee on Un-American Activities, although he later withdrew his accusations. His funeral was, as they say, sparsely attended. But we'll always have *Casablanca*.

WATERS

Originally Horace Waters, this Jack changed his name to Jack Warner, to avoid a clash and confusion with his older sisters, Elsie and Doris Waters, who, when he was starting out, were very big indeed, playing a much loved and broader version of themselves, the Cockney housewives, Gert and Daisy, mistresses of the artful commonplace conversation of a sort that would later be adopted and adapted by double acts such as Peter Cook and Dudley Moore, The Two Ronnies, Smith and Jones, Les Dawson and Roy Barraclough, and French and Saunders. Their success was achieved by a heroic resistance to the double entendre beloved by the music hall but frowned on by wider audiences in the 1930s. Their brother purveyed a similarly genial kind of comedy: his was the confiding monologue, most famously during the Second World War, when he would arrive on stage on a bicycle and utter a catchphrase now almost utterly forgotten but which had them rolling in the aisles then: 'Mind my bike.' Is there anything so dead, or liable to lampoon, than a catchphrase that has lost its time and story? Warner went on to develop another one, still remembered, but probably not for much longer: 'Evenin', all.' It was with this that he introduced the television series *Dixon of Dock Green*. Warner was (until a late promotion) PC George Dixon, the calm, friendly, solid, sensible London copper who had seen it all before, sighed as he saw it once more, but knew his duty was to stop it all over again. In his first appearance, in the 1950 film *The Blue Lamp*, he had also stopped a bullet, from a dangerous young Dirk Bogarde who had ignored his calm and friendly advice to 'hand it over, son'. *The Blue Lamp*, about as edgy as Ealing Studios got, is cited, a little unconvincingly, as a major influence on **Jack Webb**'s (qv) *Dragnet*. But it impressed British audiences so much that George was brought back from the dead and given the TV series. Warner played George for 21 years, until he was nearly 80. Meanwhile, crime elsewhere on television was being fought by the likes of **Jack Regan** (qv), and crime on film was being carried out by the likes of **Jack Carter** (qv). But that's the thing: this Jack, as admirable as the values he represented, was always really a Horace.

WATSON

Even the most stolid-seeming Jack can have a hidden fascination. Jack Watson (1915–99) was a craggy-featured, reliable supporting actor in the tough but expendable and usually non-commissioned roles in action films such as *The Wild Geese*, *Tobruk*, *The McKenzie Break* and *The Hill*. He made 70 films and appeared on British television even more frequently. But before that, he had been a comedy impressionist, appearing on such revered radio programmes as *Take It From Here* and such less revered radio programmes as *The Clitheroe Kid*. And before that, he had been Hubert Hubert, the straight man, or boy, to Nosmo King, the music-hall impressionist who took his name from a No Smoking sign and was Jack's dad. His real name was Vernon Watson; Jack's really was Hubert. My favourite detail, though, is that, for a long time during his career, Nosmo was an enthusiastic partaker of cigars.

WEATHERILL

A persuasive example of the man becoming the name. Bruce Bernard Weatherill was born in 1920, the twin son of Bernard Weatherill, a tailor. His twin was a girl; they became known as Jack and Jill. Jack went to Marlborough and spent the Second World War serving in the Indian Army, later becoming a Conservative MP. So far, so conventional. But Weatherill Senior was a Fabian socialist, and had founded the successful family firm after an earlier history as a strike leader. When Jack returned to the family firm after the war, his father insisted he complete his apprenticeship sitting cross-legged in the workroom working on a pair of breeches for the king, George VI. These pleasingly fairy-tale Jack touches continued when he entered parliament: he always carried a silver thimble in his pocket as an aide-memoire to his origins and against any *folie de grandeur*. Not that it was necessary: in the lavatory on his first day, he overheard a Tory grandee complain, 'Don't know what the place is coming to. Even me tailor's got in now.' Jack, unabashed but understated, persevered diligently until he was elected by his fellows Speaker of the House of Commons. The appointment was opposed by Margaret Thatcher, the then prime minister and leader of Jack's party, because she, as right as usual, feared his independence. Jack became a defender and promoter of the ordinary MP, regardless of party, against a government less keen on the scrutiny this entailed. Jack was for the right of the people to watch parliament on TV, too. An officer and a vegetarian after witnessing famine in India, Jack spoke Urdu fluently and English poshly, practised meditation and occasionally used soft but terse Anglo-Saxon asides if tested too far in the House of Commons. A People's Jack.

WEBB

The man who brought us *Dragnet*, the first television cop series, and played its hero, Sergeant Joe Friday, as straight as Philip Marlowe but not as soft. *Dragnet* is still instantly evocable, to those old enough to remember, through this: 'The story you are about to see is true. Only the names have been changed to protect the innocent'; and this: 'Just the facts, ma'am', both of which were routinely pronounced in 1950s Britain with accents as execrable in their way as the one Dick Van Dyke produced in *Mary Poppins*. Jack did all right thereafter but never really repeated the success of *Dragnet*. And he never actually said 'Just the facts, ma'am' (see also **Jack Swigert**, under Schmitt), but, possibly controversially, I don't care.

WELCH

Let us have a strategy meeting, re-evaluate our goals and consider whether our fables and fairy tales are delivering value or need an element of rationalisation and re-evaluation to meet their targets. If Jack were starting out today, would his best route to CEO status still involve swapping that cow for magic beans, without options or security? Jack Welch (born 1935) took a slightly different approach. Jack is the son of a railway conductor from Massachusetts. The company that Jack built, General Electric, became the largest industrial conglomerate the world has ever seen. Jack did it by expending a lot of energy and a lot of people. Jack's magic number is not 5 but 20-70-10: the best 20 per cent of his workers got bonuses and love; the next 70 per cent got told to do better; the bottom 10 per cent got told where to go. Now, moving from fables to parables, you might argue that this is how Jesus's CEO operated in the story of the employees given those talents to invest. Jack, however, got dubbed Neutron Jack, after the bomb, for the way he removed the workers but left the businesses standing. Did he live happily ever after? Well, when he retired, the company gave him the use of its jets and helicopters, a New York apartment on Central Park West, chauffeured limousines, meals at fine restaurants, flowers, wine, computer equipment, top tickets to sports events and the opera, and security, on top of a reported $9 million annual pension and a fortune in GE stock estimated at $900 million. But, being Jack, with all that energy, he didn't just sit back. Among other things, he wrote books telling people how to do what he had done, with titles like *Straight From the Gut*, pulling, as you might imagine, no punches. But then an odd thing happened. Jack gave an interview about one of the books to a journalist. She was called Suzy, and Jack fell in love with her, there and then, on the spot, even though Jack was very old (69) and Suzy was quite young (45). Which was very romantic. But, unfortunately, Jack was already married to Jane. So Jack and Jane divorced. And here was another odd thing: Jack, who told everybody else how to do things, screwed up. The prenuptial agreement had expired, and Jack had to pay Jane an amount believed to involve no fewer than eight zeros, which was a lot, even for Jack. But Jack married Suzy and, as I write, they are living happily ever so far, and Jack gives away large quantities to charity. The moral of all this? You work it out, kids, it's far too complicated for me.

WHITE

There have been an impressive number of Jack Whites. Our first two are voluntary, and musical: Jack White is a German record producer whose real name is Horst Nussbaum. He has worked with Audrey Landers (Afton from *Dallas*) and Pia Zadora, whose performance is the most often quoted in the apocryphal story of the theatre production of *The Diary of Anne Frank*, where the arrival of Nazi soldiers is interrupted by a cry from the audience, 'She's in the attic!' Jack's style is Eurodisco, or Schlager, which, I learn, is the one adopted by most Eurovision entries. Such is the style of the other Jack White that I'm surprised he hasn't collaborated with the first Jack White. This Jack is the main, indeed, only man of The White Stripes, the Detroit guitar garage band he forms with his ex-wife, Meg, who drums and pretends to be his sister. Jack's interests and influences would be constrained if they were described as eclectic. Some of them are Led Zeppelin, Paul Simon, Hank Williams, Bob Dylan, Frank Sinatra, the late Pope John Paul II and Marimba music. He has also paid public tribute to Lonnie Donegan. This would be less interesting if Jack weren't actually very good, in interviews, The White Stripes, movies (*Cold Mountain*) and The Raconteurs. Jack was formerly Jack Gillis; when they married, he took his wife's name, and has kept it even though they have now parted. His father and mother worked for the Cardinal Archbishop of Detroit; Jack was hugged by the late pope on his visit to Detroit in 1987 (John Paul also met Clint Eastwood; nuns were handing out T-shirts with the legend, 'Thou hast made my day'). Jack had intended to join the priesthood, but decided against it because he had doubts about whether he would be allowed to bring his amplifier along. He worked as a furniture upholsterer. His second wife is Karen Elson, a model from Oldham, in Lancashire. This almost explains why the million-selling White Stripes album *Icky Thump* is so called: 'Ecky Thump' is an exclamation of surprise attributed to Lancastrians by people who are not Lancastrians. Jack and Karen married in 2005 on a canoe in the Amazon. The service was conducted by a shaman and the wedding later blessed by a Catholic priest. Jack did not become Jack Elson.

Another Jack White won the Open golf championship in 1904. Another won the Victoria Cross in 1917 after he had dived into a river near Baghdad and towed a pontoon to safety under heavy Turkish fire, saving several lives. A third was one of those restless rebels which the British officer class often throws up, and out. This Jack was the son of Field Marshal Sir George White (1835–1912), hero of the siege of Ladysmith in the Boer War. Jack was educated at Winchester, trained at Sandhurst and also served, under his father, in South Africa, where he won a DSO. But by 1908 he had resigned his commission and undertaken his restlessness, beginning a political journey which began in Tolstoyan socialism and moved to the revolutionary variety and to joining the Anarchists in the Spanish Civil War. Jack's family home was in Ireland, and he became one of the most prominent Protestants involved in the movement pressing for Home Rule, his socialist ardour inflamed by the grim plight of the Irish working classes. His most practical achievement was his formation, with James Larkin, of the Irish Citizen Army during the large-scale strike over the recognition of Larkin's transport and general union in 1913. Initially the ICA was a self-defence body, trained by White; but administration was never really his forte, and he resigned in 1914. He served briefly with an Australian ambulance unit in Flanders, and then, as the *DNB* puts it, 'drifted off to Paris'. The ICA took part in the Easter Rising of 1916, but went on to play a minor role in subsequent Irish republican history, as, increasingly, did White, after he was jailed for trying to bring the South Wales miners out on strike against the executions of the Easter rebels. He died in 1946 after a series of minor imprisonments for agitation, his Spanish interlude, many a pamphlet and a couple of abortive attempts at getting elected. He described himself as 'an ineffective crank' but 'not necessarily a fool'. A better epitaph comes from Sean O'Casey, the playwright, who had his dealings with Jack in the ICA days: 'Captain White was a noble fellow, but a nuisance.'

WIGGINS

Tap dancing has claims to be the most impressive accomplishment of the cultural integrations of the twentieth century. Mind you, the competition is not inspiring: the Eurovision Song Contest, the baseball cap, Paul Simon's *Graceland*, Paul McCartney and Stevie Wonder doing 'Ebony and Ivory', 'Melting Pot' by Blue Mink, the hamburger and two world wars. But when you watch tap, as you admire the controlled, precise effort and timing producing a contrasting and carefree exhilaration, you are watching elements, elegantly fused, of, among much else, Celtic folk dance, Spanish flamenco, South African gum boot, African shuffle and Lancashire clog dancing, taken from the timing of the looms of the cotton mills. One of the great integrators was Jack Wiggins, a black New Yorker, who took the influences of the great immigrations on the great city and shaped them into a distinctive dance. Jack was among the first to wear the formal wear and patent leather dress shoes graced by Astaire; but he also pioneered the sudden swoops of energy, the splits, developed by the Nicholas Brothers and adapted and blended with ballet by the more muscular Gene Kelly, the truck driver's dancer, and none the worse for that. Why haven't you heard of Jack

Wiggins? Because the great integrator was mostly confined to the black vaudeville theatre circuit. And some people claim that irony isn't multicultural.

WILD

Jack Wild (1952–2006) made a very appealing Jack Dawkins, better known as the Artful Dodger, in both the highly successful stage and cinema productions of Lionel Bart's *Oliver!*. Dickens based the Dodger partly on **Jack Sheppard** (qv). None of these Jacks ended well, sadly. Sheppard was hanged, Dawkins was transported, and Wild, familiarly, fell foul of drink, never again approaching his early success. Better to relish Dickens's genius in his first description of the Dodger:

> He was a snub-nosed, flat-browed, common-faced boy enough; and as dirty a juvenile as one would wish to see; but he had about him all the airs and manners of a man. He was short of his age: with rather bow-legs, and little, sharp, ugly eyes. His hat was stuck on the top of his head so lightly, that it threatened to fall off every moment – and would have done so, very often, if the wearer had not had a knack of every now and then giving his head a sudden twitch, which brought it back to its old place again.

The very Jack!

WILKES

Considerations of the richly remarkable life of the great John Wilkes (1725–97) often struggle to reconcile the outrageous and feckless wit and rake with the noble, principled, suffering upholder of freedoms. The answer, I submit, is in the distinction I outlined earlier in the case of John F. Kennedy: there was Jack Wilkes and there was John Wilkes. Jack was almost all the young Wilkes, the rake, the man who loved only one thing more than talking wittily about wine and women and worse, which you can guess. Jack was so dissolute that he even shocked James Boswell, no mean man at it himself, with whom Wilkes shared a riotous time in Italy, when Jack was in exile and Jim was supposed to be on The Grand Tour. 'You too like the thing almost as well as I do,' Wilkes told Boswell, 'but you dislike the talk and laugh about it, of which I am perhaps too fond.'

Talking the talk was something Wilkes was famously good at, the thrust of repartee, the fine art of blandishing. Perhaps his most renowned remark is about the squint, the crooked jaw and flat nose he had been born with: 'Give me half an hour and I can talk my face away.' The second was addressed to his enemy and former companion, the equally dissolute Earl of Sandwich, who wondered whether Wilkes would die on the gallows or of the pox: 'That depends on whether I embrace your lordship's principles or your mistress.' But has anybody ever thought more quickly and more wittily than this, to a vacuous Hooray who asked him, 'Isn't it strange that I was born on the first of January?' Wilkes: 'Not strange at all. You could only have been conceived on the first of April.'

Jack was born in Clerkenwell, London, the son of a malt distiller and a tanner's daughter. But he was indulged and educated, attending the University of Leiden in the Netherlands, where he began to indulge himself. On his return to England, he found that his father had arranged a marriage for him with the heiress to the manor of Aylesbury, ten years older than he, unattractive and, worse, without any discernible sense of humour. Wilkes was to say later, after the marriage was over, that he had stumbled on the threshold of the temple of Hymen, although the union did produce his much-loved daughter, companion and Lady Mayoress of London, Polly. For some time he was squire and magistrate John in Aylesbury and Jack in town and elsewhere, such as Medmenham Abbey in Buckinghamshire, where Sir Francis Dashwood and his friends relaxed from the rigours of being Enlightened by playing at being pagans and enthusiastically engaging in any amount of drinking, feasting, devil-bothering, rumpy-pumpy and general roistering.

You can get a feel for the times from this, in a letter to Jack from Thomas Potter, a younger son of the Archbishop of Canterbury, no less, urging a visit to Bath, should he 'prefer young women and whores to old women and wives, if you prefer toying away hours with little Sattin Back to the evening conferences of your Mother-in-Law but above all if the Heavenly inspired passion called Lust have deserted you'. Another member of Dashwood's Medmenham Hellfire Club was Jack's great friend, Charles Churchill, a vicar.

But it was Potter who also introduced Jack into politics, and to a career that would encompass bribing 300 of the 500 voters of Aylesbury £5 each to elect him as their MP in 1761 and introducing the first ever motion to reform parliament and remove the rotten boroughs, in 1776. In between came his great libertarian causes, most notably resistance to the general right of arrest and search which the government sought to employ against his fiercely critical weekly, *The North Briton*, accompanied by imprisonment, riot, expulsion from the House of Commons, two duels, exile in Europe, numbers of disputed elections, the Lord Mayoralty of London and who knows how many late-night sessions of how many kinds.

How much was Jack and how much was John? Well, some of *The North Briton* was Jack, writing to please himself, his patrons and allies, and infuriate his enemies with his wicked wit. Peter Quennell, in his study, thinks it chance that a fundamental principle of liberty became caught up in Jack's fun. But he is equally clear that John had the vision, the courage, the obstinacy and the principles to employ Jack's natural bravado, sense of drama and love of risk (cards and games of chance are about the only things he didn't gamble on – 'I have no small vices'). You might say that he stumbled across the threshold of the Temple of Liberty.

It's John, though, who tempers Jack's radical tendencies. Jack supported America in its resistance to taxation without representation; John stopped short at independence. John, too, was horrified by the French Revolution. Jack's time as Lord Mayor of London, achieved after the usual politicking and opposition, was lavish and fun. John's time as Lord Mayor was marked by a campaign against prostitution. Jack wanted the plum role of City Chamberlain to help with his debts, always a problem. John took the job very seriously. The people rioted for Jack over *The North Briton*; John defended the Bank of England from the Gordon rioters in 1780. But if you want the finest example of John and Jack together, it would be his prosecution and imprisonment for publishing not just *The North Briton* but also the *Essay on Woman*, a bawdy parody of Pope's *Essay on Man*.

But which one amassed the splendid library, charmed his old enemy Dr Johnson, or enjoyed his stays with Voltaire and in the King's Bench Prison, where Freedom's Martyr enjoyed the company of his female admirers and such gifts as game, ham, salmon, a butt of ale, and, from America, live turtles and 45 hogsheads of tobacco?

Lewis Kronenberger finds Wilkes guilty, too, of an irresponsible belief that the world owed such a man as he a living, together with insincerity and untruthfulness. I like Peter Quennell on the later Wilkes better:

> No touch of public humbug clouded his private utterance. He preserved always his equanimity and air of ironic pose; yet his cynicism was not untempered by the addition of Christian virtues, in particular the twin virtues of Hope and Charity. He was unacquainted with Faith, he once remarked to his daughter, 'but the other two good girls are my favourites . . .'; and during the course of a long life he had certainly needed their assistance.

But to expect consistency and tidiness is to expect too much of a Jack, especially one of the most rollicking men of a most rollicking century. Nor should we forget the Wilkes sense of humour and of irony. And so, when, for some reason or other, a London mob smashed his windows in 1790, Wilkes refused to prosecute, saying, 'they are only some of my pupils, now set up for themselves'. And so, when at about the same time, an old woman hailed him on the street with the old cry, 'Wilkes and Liberty!', John, or was it Jack, shouted back, 'Be quiet, you old fool, that was all over long ago!'

WILSON

History repeats itself, and there is no more popular plot than the emergence of someone with an enticing message at times of change and consequent hurt for the oppressed. Rarely do too many of the oppressed profit from it. (We can argue about the effects of Christianity, Jewry and Islam on each other and everybody else. And about whether the large number of Jacks among the messengers is entirely a coincidence; the clincher, I feel, would have been Jack the Baptist.) Jack Wilson (c. 1856–1932) is another American shaman (see **Jack Fiddler**). His Paiute Indian name was Wovoka, and he was the Prophet of the 1890 Ghost Dance, that sad, strange episode which can now be seen as the last moves of Native American resistance to the white tide coming over their lands. We know who tends to write the history of unsuccessful popular movements, and, as usual, the details do not always agree. Wovoka was the son of a shaman; his Anglo name came from the Wilson family of Mason Valley, Nevada, for whom he worked. Wovoka's father had been involved in the Ghost Dance of 1870, when another prophet, Wodziwob, had preached the end of the world and the birth of a better one. The latter would not have been difficult for the Native Americans. White settlers were making ever more incursions and had brought with them a typhoid epidemic in 1867. Wodziwob's invocation to use the traditional round dance to usher in the new age was followed by many tribes, but the movement, as they do, dwindled when the prophecy failed to materialise. But when Wovoka emerged with a similar prophecy, granted to him in a vision during an eclipse of the sun in 1889, the dancing began again and spread further. The tribespeople would dance for hours in sun or snow, chanting in that eerie and primal way familiar to anyone who has ever watched a western, entranced in another world. The new settlers were greatly unsettled by this outbreak of mysticism, although it is clearly fanciful to attribute guilt to their unease. Representatives of many tribes came to Wovoka, and took away his teachings.

Most seem agreed that the message was non-violent: it is less clear whether he was foretelling peaceful co-existence, or the destruction of the white race in 'a great shaking of the earth'. That latter was certainly the view of Charles Eastman, himself a contemporary Native American and defender of their rights. Eastman also pointed out that the message became even more potent because of its blending of traditional belief and custom with messianic Christianity, to which the Native Americans, and Jack Wilson himself, had become increasingly exposed (the Wilson family were evangelical Protestants, and Jack talked of Jesus in his prophecies). As usual, too, the message was reinterpreted to suit local tastes and conditions: the Lakota Sioux, who, led by the great Sitting Bull, had wiped out Custer and a battalion of the US Seventh Cavalry at Little Big Horn 14 years before, and were still skirmishing, took a more militant view. And so appeared the Ghost Shirts, believed to protect their wearers from bullets. All the elements of tragedy were now in position: pride, desperation, mystical belief and a superior power bent on revenge. It took place at Wounded Knee, in South Dakota, on 29 December 1890, the day after a large party of Lakota Ghost Dancers, clad in their Shirts, had agreed to surrender. They were intercepted by 500 troops of the Seventh Cavalry. No one seems sure exactly what happened: a deaf Lakota couldn't hear the order to disarm, a Shaman began the Ghost Dance, a gun went off, or some braves opened fire: whatever, nearly all of the Lakota men, women and children died. A blizzard prevented recovery of the bodies for several days: they were found frozen and contorted in a horrible realisation of Jack's dance.

There had been a prologue of odd and curious resonances days before. Since the Big Horn, Sitting Bull had been in exile in Canada until surrendering to confinement and reservation, apart from that freakish interlude when he was allowed to join Buffalo Bill's Wild West Show, earning $50 for riding around the arena once, as well as whatever would be offered for his autograph or signed photo. And we imagine the world of celebrity a recent phenomenon. This was rather like sending Osama Bin Laden off from Guantánamo on a string of cabaret engagements. Sitting Bull was back at the Standing Rock reservation when the Ghost Dance began. The old chief was also a shaman: he was said to have foreseen victory at the Big Horn in a vision brought on by trance dancing and knife cuts; and now there had been a vision of his own death, at the hands of his own people. As the unrest spread, worries about Sitting Bull's influence led to the despatch of police to detain him. It went badly awry; there was a skirmish between the police and Sitting Bull's supporters during which the old chief was shot dead. The police were, of course, all Lakota Sioux. And there was the white horse, as familiar a magical symbol as a Jack. Sitting Bull had been presented with a circus horse by Buffalo Bill (who at one point was going to negotiate with his ex-employee). When gunfire broke out, the horse recognised its old circus cue and went into its routine of tricks; as its master died, it was prancing, kneeling and rearing. I'm not sure whether there is a word to describe this conjunction of events and signs, but it is also said, almost inevitably, that the horse seemed immune to the flying bullets during this dance. The *New York Times*, reporting Sitting Bull's Death, said that the police bullets 'had made a good Indian of him'. Jack died, indigent, in 1932, his prophecies unfulfilled, if you discount the earthquake that destroyed San Francisco in 1906.

WILTON

The blockbuster has a lengthy and often forgotten history. One of the first was *The Unfortunate Traveller: Or The Life of Jacke Wilton* by Thomas Nashe, which appeared in 1594. It is a rollicking picaresque (the earliest) tale starring young Jack and his thrilling adventures in France, Germany and Italy, and, in a fine early example of 'faction', features Erasmus, Martin Luther, Thomas More and more. Jack is a knavish page who lives on his wits, gets whipped for his pains, experiences fair and most foul, ends up at the Field of the Cloth of Gold, and marries his true love, an Italian courtesan.

The book also seethes with parody and satire: Nashe (1567–1601) was one of those several extraordinary Elizabethans with more wit, gusto and talent than was entirely good for them. He seems, like most of them, to have enjoyed little better than the opportunities presented by a good feud for full-on literary attacks with all available weaponry; and his was considerable. Principal among those to be withered was Gabriel Harvey, a familiar figure of formidable but stately intellect and social insecurity ripe for Nashe's darts. Some trace the habit of poking fun at certain blameless if unexciting English towns to Nashe's 1596 broadside suggesting that Harvey should go back where he came from: 'Have with You to Saffron Walden'. Nashe also makes the first written mention that survives of the famous rhyme from '**Jack and the Beanstalk**' (qv): 'Fy, fa, fum, I smell the blood of an Englishman.' Given his connections with the Earl of Oxford, his collaboration with Marlowe and Jonson and the appearance of a suspiciously similar phrase in *King Lear*, you will no doubt be wondering if Nashe has been proposed as the real hand behind Shakespeare. Indeed: he is supposed to have worked on *Henry VI Part One*; in 1589, he also referred to an earlier version of *Hamlet*, now lost. Once again, my fierce academic respect for the truth, however, compels me to reveal that he died in 1601, which is a touch early. Worry not, though, it won't stop them. I remember, and not for the first time, the late Enoch

Powell declaring at lunch at the *Daily Telegraph* that Shakespeare was an alias and invention, since there was suspiciously little mention of what must have been a glittering figure at court and social events. But one hack present had the answer to that: 'I expect he was very busy writing all those plays.'

WOLFMAN JACK

Nostalgia doesn't mean you had to be there. Brits can feel nostalgia for 1950s small-town America because they used to watch television's version of it. And so, too, with the Wolfman, Wolfman Jack, the bandido disc jockey broadcasting from just across the Rio Grande with enough wattage to reach New York on a clear night, or Moscow. The outlaw stations, or border blasters, parents to the British pirates of the 1960s, had been broadcasting across the US with a power forbidden within it since the 1920s. Their pioneer was John Romulus Brinkley (1885–1942), just about medically qualified (the Eclectical Medical School, Kansas City), and the energetic promoter of a cure for impotence involving the placing of goats' testicles in the male human testicle sac or the female abdomen. Doc Brinkley started a radio station in Kansas to advertise his services, but experienced difficulties with both the medical and radio authorities, largely because his cure was completely bogus, he often operated while drunk and his patients were dying. Hence the move south of the border and the continued offer of pills and injections over the airwaves, the accumulation of wealth, the loss of it (and a leg) and a final departure to join his patients.

The Wolfman's tale is a little happier. Robert Smith (1938–95), from New York, arrived on XERF in 1959, howling out some terrific patter between some terrific rock 'n' roll records at times when all good teenagers should have been reading a good book or fast asleep rather than listening under the bedclothes or cruising round town in a hot rod. Added to the delicious rebellious illicitness of it all was the

Wolfman's carefully cloaked identity. At his peak, in the 1960s, he was broadcasting from three stations. But the Mexican government had become uneasy with the activities of his fellow broadcasters, evangelical stations which were preaching a gospel much too hot for the Catholic host country. The stations were closed down, and Wolfman Jack's magic moments would have passed but for one of his nostalgic former young listeners, George Lucas, who made *American Graffiti* in 1973 and Jack famous all over again. The second time around was different, though: Jack was seen, and everywhere; a little light had been let in on the magic. He died from a heart attack after broadcasting from a Planet Hollywood restaurant, and his passing was announced by the vice-president of Wolfman Jack Enterprises. Let us better remember him courtesy of this transcription quoted by Don Waller in the *Guardian*: 'Dis heah's de Wolfman comin' atcha! Skinny-dippin' in the oil of joy on the Big X. AAWWWRRIIGHT, baay-bee! Aaaa-oooooooohhh! Ah ya wit me out deah? Ah ya readeh? 'Cause we gonna try ta do it faw ya, honey! We gonna blow ya mahn, babe-eh! OOOOOWWWWOOOOOoooooooo . . . Ya gonna love it ta death!'

WORTHING

What name did one of our greatest playwrights and wits, a man of the most acute sensitivity to social nuance, choose as the exact contrast to a name that stands for all that is most sober and respectable and, well, dull, in his play of almost the same name? Being Oscar Wilde, of course, and obsessed with paradox, he reversed the qualities for Jack Worthing, the responsible country squire, and his imaginary naughty brother, Ernest, the London libertine, thus mocking the earnestness he saw as the enemy of the aesthetic. So when Gwendolen is criticising Jack – 'there is very little music in the name Jack, if any at all, indeed. It does not thrill. It produces absolutely no vibrations' – she means exactly the opposite. I rest my case. And handbag.

X

XAVIER

Francisco de Asis Javier Cugat Mingall de Bru y Deulofeu was born in the town of Gerona, in Catalonia, on 1 January 1900. Rather better known as Xavier Cugat, or Coogie, or 'The King of the Rumba', he is a man to whom legend attached, as it tends to do if you dress your musicians in bright red, have an accompanying dance troupe called The Gigolos and conduct while cradling a chihuahua in your arms. That birth date, for example, was said to be felt so auspicious in Spain that his father, a leftist activist, was released from prison on account of it. Shortly thereafter the family left for Cuba, where they moved in across the street from a violin-maker. By the age of 12, he was first violinist with the Cuban Symphony Orchestra, which accompanied Caruso when he came to perform in Havana. The great singer took a shine to Coogie, who left to accompany him and began a picaresque journey and career which saw him drawing cartoons in Hollywood before being the right man at the right time to cash in on the American dance affair with the Latin beat in the 1920s and '30s. He was helped by his friend, Rudolph Valentino, and began a series of lengthy engagements which took in the Coconut Grove in Los Angeles, Al Capone's little place, Chez Paris in Chicago and more than a decade at New York's Waldorf-Astoria (see **Jack Astor**).

Coogie might have invested in a talking picture in Spanish without realising there was as yet no sound equipment in Latin America, but he was shrewd enough to give North America an easy fusion of tropical rhythms. Cole Porter heard him rehearsing at the Waldorf-Astoria and asked him to play his new song, 'Begin the Beguine'; there followed 'Peanut Vendor', 'Maria Elena' and 'Tico Tico'. He was also a frequent performer in films, especially with Esther Williams, to whose splashy extravaganzas he was supremely suited (Esther still wears a little badge at parties which reads, 'Yes, I still swim'). Coogie, who died in 1990, had five extremely lively marriages and divorces. He was the author of two books, *I, Cugat* and *My Wives*.

By now, you're probably wondering what he has to do with Jack. Well, that fine song, 'Jack, Jack, Jack (or Cu-Tu-Gu-Ru)' lends its name to one of his most popular albums. Yes, all right, all right, I am struggling slightly here, as Jacks are not big on anonymity. There was a masked heavyweight wrestler from Tipton a few years back, Jack Xavier, whose real name was Lorenzo Divattimo, but he's gone a bit quiet. Other Jacks, of course, have much featured in popular song, although it often seems to be because of the convenience of the rhyme with 'back'. Even so, Percy Mayfield's 'Hit the Road Jack', when performed by Ray Charles, is one fine thing.

'Grocer Jack (Excerpt from a Teenage Opera)', a hit in Britain for Keith West in 1967, is interesting. Simple, sentimental, featuring a breathy, lispy children's chorus that could make the less controlled contemplate violence, it is nevertheless so memorable that it comes into the category of song defined by scientists as an 'earworm': one which, as the name suggests, wriggles into the brain and refuses to leave. Mark Twain wrote a short story about a man who becomes obsessed with a piece of advertising doggerel. Continually hearing the note A in his head drove Schumann mad. In my case, access was eased by my father, who, being, as we have seen, a grocer called Jack, insisted on singing it repeatedly in his self-mocking way.

The term comes from the German *Ohrwurm*; coincidentally or not, the composer of 'Grocer Jack' is a German, Mark Wirtz, born in Cologne, who arrived in Britain in the '60s, learnt English, formed a band called Marc Rogers and the Marksmen, and then became a producer for EMI, which was when, one night, he dreamt about a grocer called Jack, taken for granted until his untimely death. It was the first song of the *Teenage Opera*, so called only because an American producer acquaintance of Wirtz used the word 'teenage' as an all-purpose adjective of approval.

Keith West was a friend of Wirtz and lead singer with a psychedelic band optimistically entitled Tomorrow. Further extracts failed to wriggle. Wirtz moved to the United States, gave up music, and then had another crack at Jack in 1996. He tells me: 'The few that have heard the complete work have hailed it as a masterpiece.' Anyone reckless enough to release it should get in touch with Mark, who is now concentrating on fulfilling his ambition to confound received opinion and become the first German to achieve world acclaim as a stand-up comic.

The only cure so far discovered for an earworm is to drive it out by sending another one in after it. Manfred Mann's recording of 'My Name Is Jack' reached number eight in the British singles chart in 1968. It was written by John Simon, who, I suggest, is really a Jack. Try, for bemusing diversity of taste and talent, this list of people he has produced for and worked with: The Band, Big Brother and the Holding Company, Leonard Cohen, Simon and Garfunkel, Peter, Paul and Mary, The Mamas and the Papas, and, wait for it, Tiny Tim. Perhaps this explains the curious attraction of 'My Name Is Jack', or not. Jack was the name chosen by Simon for the young boy he spotted when he was looking at film footage to inspire his soundtrack for *You Are What You Eat*, a legendary documentary on the American underground of the 1960s, which is, according to review, a classic, an exercise in tedium, nearly unwatchable, and an illustration of the maxim that 'you should never trust a hippie with a camera'.

'Jack', a small boy, aged four or five, was indeed living at The Greta Garbo Home for Wayward Boys and Girls, the jokey-hippie name of a San Francisco crashpad. Crashpad? A word now as antique as 'heavy', 'right-on', 'happening' and 'jokey-hippiness': somewhere cheap and temporary to stay ($25 a week), what used to be a flophouse. In former times, The Greta Garbo, at the junction of Sutter and Laguna, had been the rather grander Kirkland Hotel. Jack, says Simon, was charging around The Greta (named, it seems, for a large poster of the solitary one in the foyer), oblivious to the weirdness of his fellow residents (and, presumably, his parents), hippies of the heaviest duty. The Greta is no more, although the song has always been big in Japan.

Next, and I'm sorry to do this to you, is 'The Lumberjack Song', that *cri de coeur* from a hard-working, cross-dressing tree feller with otherwise regular habits, written by Michael Palin, Terry Jones and the great Fred Tomlinson (whose Singers were the backing Mounties). Apart from being an earworm, the Monty Python piece has also completely removed that lovely old word 'lumberjack' from common usage: for some reason, they prefer to be called loggers now.

YEATS

Another Jack the Painter who pleases some of the people but not all of the critics. John Butler Yeats (1871–1957) preferred to be known as Jack B. Yeats, mostly perhaps because he was not fond of his father, John Butler Yeats, also a painter, but also a failed barrister, family man and manager of money. Jack's elder brother was William Butler Yeats (see under MacBride, which he would really have hated). Jack, the youngest of the four Yeats children, is described as the least troubled, which is comparative, as he had a breakdown from 1915 to 1917. This, of course, coincides with the upheavals in Ireland, and Jack had also had some of his own. His mother's family, the marvellously named Pollexfens, had a shipping business in Sligo, and Jack spent much of his childhood there, away from the family home in London. After early success as an illustrator and watercolourist, he was persuaded to return to Ireland increasingly as a part of the Irish artistic revival led by his brother. He produced some acclaimed illustrations from the west of Ireland, working with J.M. Synge, author of *The Playboy of the Western World*. But a permanent move to Ireland in 1910 and into oils did not go easily: he was judged far better at figures than landscape. One of his most famous works, though, dates from this period, inspired by the politics of the time: *In Memory* shows a flower girl commemorating a gun-runner shot by the British Army. His reputation and skill as a painter has thus become inextricable from the founding and finding of the Republic. Not that this has stopped those less sensitive to Hibernian times and tides from having a go: Brian Sewell, for example, has referred to the 'smudges and smears' of a 'famous rotten painter', comparing his later work with Jackson Pollock, which, from anyone else, would be a compliment. I prefer the judgement of Samuel Beckett, playwright, seer and, as it happens, not a bad cricketer: 'He brings light, as only the great dare to bring light, to the issueless predicament of existence.' He also produced the first cartoon-strip version of Sherlock Holmes in 1894.

YELLEN

Goodness me, but the world would be a much unhappier place without Jewish writers of American popular songs. The Gershwins, Berlins, Kerns, Arlens, Hammersteins and Harts brought or inherited the haunting lilts and thoughts of central and eastern Europe and seemed to adapt them to their brave new world without a skip or a miss. Jack Yellen was one such. Originally Jacek Jelen from Poland, Jack wrote the words to, among much else, 'Ain't She Sweet?', 'Happy Feet', 'Hard-Hearted Hannah' and 'I'll Be Seeing You'. With Milton Ager (yup, Jewish), Jack wrote 'Happy Days Are Here Again', adopted by Roosevelt as the anthem for his New Deal. You get a further idea of Jack's range with 'Yiddishe Momme' and 'All Aboard for Dixieland', 'How's Every Little Thing in Dixie?', 'Listen to That Dixie Band' and 'Are You From Dixie?' As his fellow lyricist, L. Wolfe Gilbert ('Ramona', 'Hello, Aloha, How Are You?'; yup, born in Odessa), once put it, 'Jack, I bet you came from the south of Poland.'

YELLOW

Another name for Yellow Fever, probably taken from the quarantine flag flown over hospitals and ships, is Yellow Jack. Still virulent among unvaccinated populations, Yellow Fever has been killing people around the world at least since an epidemic of it ravaged

Europe in the sixth century. An outbreak during the Spanish American War led Walter Reed, a US Army surgeon, to build on the work of the Cuban physician, Carlos Finlay, who had suggested that the mosquito was the carrier. During Reed's research two extremely courageous volunteers were deliberately infected, and died. One was Jesse William Lazear, a fellow Army doctor, who had allowed himself to be bitten by infected mosquitoes without telling his colleagues. The second was Clara Maass, who had volunteered to nurse in Cuba and the Philippines during the Spanish-American War, and to be injected a second time to see if her earlier deliberately induced bout of fever had immunised her. Her sacrifice had helped; the ensuing outcry also ensured that testing on humans followed testing on animals, to consequent and continuing controversy. Poor Clara was just 25.

YOUNGBLOOD

Make of this what you will: the four Jacks in the Professional Football Hall of Fame – Youngblood, **Christiansen**, **Lambert** and **Ham** – all played in defence, while the two Jackies – **Slater** and **Smith** – were offensive players. I also propose to admit one last Jackie, following a séance attended by the British writer and entertainer Ken Campbell, at which the late Laurence Olivier made his presence felt, and was asked who, in his opinion, was the world's finest living actor. His lordship, apparently, had no hesitation: '**Jackie Chan**'.

YOUR BODY

Steve 'Silk' Hurley, the übercool Chicago House DJ, has had one big hit: 'Jack Your Body', the anthem of Jacking, the House dance. This puts Steve in the same category as, for example, Edison Lighthouse ('Love Grows (Where My Rosemary Goes)'), Slim Dusty ('A Pub with No Beer'), Freddie Bell and the Bellboys ('Giddy Up a Ding Dong'),

Dora Bryan ('All I Want for Christmas Is a Beatle'), The Singing Nun ('Dominique'), Jasper Carrott ('Funky Moped') and Windsor Davies & Don Estelle ('Whispering Grass'). Those not familiar with Jacking should push the chairs out of the way, draw the curtains or warn the neighbours, put on 'Jack Your Body' and move the torso forward and backward in a rippling motion, as if a wave were passing through it, in time to the beat. If you have a partner readily available (probably best not the neighbour), grind your pelvises together.

Z's Pizza

Where the land is grand, the corn is as high as an elephant's eye, and the wind comes sweeping down the plain, there lies the city of Kingfisher, settled in a day on Monday, 22 April, during the great Oklahoma Land Run of 1889, when, at high noon, cavalry bugles sounded on the Texas and Arkansas borders of the territory and eager Americans raced in by horse, wagon and foot to stake their claims in one of the most remarkable pieces of property distribution anywhere, any time. And there in Kingfisher (population, 4,500), hard by the old Chisholm cattle trail, on North Main, is Jack Z's Pizza restaurant. Jack is Jack Deane, 41, a dedicated pizza man: he worked for Pizza Hut and liked pizza so much he decided to start his own enterprise. The Z is from 'pizza'. Jack's special is the Slobberknocker, which has pretty much every topping on it, including banana and peppers. Jack is looking to roll out his concept across the Great Plains and beyond. I wouldn't bet against him, either: Sam Walton, the founder of Wal-Mart, was a Kingfisher man. Jack's proud of his name, and the grandfather he's named after, 'really one wonderful guy'. Jack allows that people called Jack tend to be a 'little quirky', with a good sense of humour. That's why, if you should find yourself in Kingfisher, and you have a copy of this book with you, take it along to Jack's, and, if he likes the look of you, he might cut you a deal. Especially if your name is Jack.

ACKNOWLEDGEMENTS

A book such as this would have taken most of a lifetime to write without the wonders of the World Wide Web. It's fashionable, I know, to be a bit snooty about those of us who consult closely with Doctor Google and Professor Wikipedia; but, if this condescension can be justified at all, it would apply only to the sort of uncorroborated and unimaginative borrowing which is lazy, dull and no fun at all. The Doctor and the Professor encourage learning and curiosity, and should be celebrated for the marvels that they are (and, in the case of the Professor, who provides his services free, rewarded with donations). I hope, too, that I have made it clear in the text that my approach to a book such as this is to resist the uncorroborated unless it is irresistible and then to present it as not entirely reliable. If I have been led astray, blame me, not the messengers.

These also include the indispensable *Oxford English Dictionary* and *Oxford Dictionary of National Biography*, made (freely) available online by Somerset County Council's libraries. Equally admirable and vital, if (understandably) requiring a subscription, was the great London Library, which provided me with many of the books I briskly raided, as well as further online reference works, including the *American National Biography*, and the impressively dense academic work collated by JSTOR. The *Australian Dictionary of Biography* and the *Dictionary of Canadian Biography* are also recommended. I am extremely grateful, too, to the second hand booksellers of Britain, whose impressively efficient services are available online at AbeBooks and Amazon.

All of this was joined by the remarkable array of electronic international newspaper cuttings provided by the LexisNexis service, made available to me by my generous employer in other journalistic activities, *The Independent*. A special word, too, for the splendid obituary writers of *The Independent*, *The Times*, the *Daily Telegraph* and *The Guardian*: their work is the place to go for the telling anecdote and vignette.

I must thank my publishers, Mainstream, and particularly Bill Campbell, who encouraged my idea. Thanks also to two fine editors, Helen Bleck and Claire Rose; as usual, any mistakes are all my own; without them, and Mainstream's scrupulous proofreaders, there would have been many more. My agent, Annabel Merullo, provided persuasive support. My family, too, Liv, Cristian and Luis, should be praised for greeting yet another fascinating Jack story with only the occasional sigh, raised eyebrow and bit of glazing.

Anyone wishing a more relaxed journey through Jacks and their works will find these titles most useful:

INTRODUCTION

The Kinship of Jack, Parts I & II, Society for Name Studies in Britain and Ireland, 2003

The Pedigree of Jack, Edward W.B. Nicholson, Alexander and Shepheard, 1892

Quirkology: The Curious Science of Everyday Lives, Richard Wiseman, Pan Macmillan, 2007

What's in a Name?: Everything You Wanted to Know, Leonard R.N. Ashley, Geneaological Publishing, 1989

Naming Your Baby: The Definitive Dictionary of First Names, Julia Cresswell, A&C Black, revised edition, 2007

JACK AND JILL (ET AL.)

The Oxford Dictionary of Nursery Rhymes, Iona and Peter Opie (eds), OUP, 1951

Curious Myths of the Middle Ages, Sabine Baring-Gould, Rivingtons, 1866

JACK ARMSTRONG

Cerealizing America: The Unsweetened Story of American Breakfast Cereal, Scott Bruce and Bill Crawford, Faber & Faber, 1995

JACK BOOT

The Story of the German Soldier, John Laffin, Cassell, 1965 and a paper kindly provided to the author by Lieutenant Colonel Mike McCabe

JACK BRADLEY

Flags of Our Fathers, James Bradley with Ron Powers, Bantam, 2000

JACK BUCHANAN

Top Hat and Tails: The Story of Jack Buchanan, Michael Marshall, Elm Tree, 1978

JACK BYRON

Downstream: Across England in a Punt, Tom Fort, Century, 2008

JACK CADE

Jack Cade's Rebellion of 1450, I.M.W. Harvey, Clarendon, 1991
Lord of London, Eric Simmons, Muller, 1963

JACK COHEN

Tiger by the Tail, Ian MacLaurin, Macmillan, 1999

JACK COMER (ET AL.)

Brewer's Rogues, Villains and Eccentrics: An A–Z of Roguish Britons Through the Ages, William Donaldson, Cassell, 2002
Hit 'em Hard: Jack Spot, King of the Underworld, Wensley Clarkson, HarperCollins, 2002

JACK DASH

Good Morning Brothers! A Militant Trade Unionist's Frank Autobiography, Jack Dash, Mayflower Books, 1970

JACK DEMPSEY

A Flame of Pure Fire: Jack Dempsey and the Roaring '20s, Roger Kahn, Thomson Learning, 1999

JACK DONOHOE (ET AL.)

Hero on a Stolen Horse: The Highwayman and his Brothers-in-Arms the Bandit and the Bushranger, Hilary and Mary Evans, Frederick Muller, 1977

JACK DUCKWORTH (ET AL.)

Coronation Street: Celebrating 30 Years, Graeme Kay, Boxtree, 1990

JACK GREENWELL

Barca: A People's Passion, Jimmy Burns, Bloomsbury, 1998

JACK HARRISON

100 Greats: Hull Rugby League Club, Raymond Fletcher, Tempus, 2002

JACK HOBBS

Jack Hobbs: Gentleman and Player, Pat Landsberg, Harrap, 1953
Jack Hobbs: Profile of the Master, John Arlott, John Murray, 1981

JACKS

A History of Playing Cards, Roger Tilley, Studio Vista, 1973
Encyclopaedia of Superstitions, E. and M.A. Radford, Rider & Company, 1948
Encyclopaedia of Superstitions, Folklore, and the Occult Sciences of the World, Cora Linn Daniels and Charles MacClellan Stevans, University Press of the Pacific, 1903

JACK IN THE GREEN

The Jack in the Green: A May Day Custom, Roy Judge, Folklore Society, 1979
A Social History of England, Asa Briggs, Weidenfeld & Nicolson, 1983
The Rise and Fall of Merry England: The Ritual Year 1400–1700, Ronald Hutton, OUP, 1994
The Golden Bough: A Study in Magic and Religion, J.G. Frazer, Macmillan, 1890
1,000 Curiosities of Britain, Egon Jameson, Herbert Joseph, 1937

JACK JUDGE

Jack Judge: The Tipperary Man, Verna Hale Gibbons, Sandwell Community Library Service, 1998

JACK KAHANE

Obelisk: A History of Jack Kahane and the Obelisk Press, Neil Pearson, Liverpool University Press, 2008

JACK KEROUAC

On the Road, Jack Kerouac, Viking Press, 1957
What Happened to Kerouac?, Richard Lerner and Lewis McAdams, DVD, Delta Music, 1986

JACK KETCH

Hangmen of England, Brian Bailey, W.H. Allen, 1989

JACK LAMBTON

The Creevey Papers: A Selection from the Correspondence and Diaries of the Late Thomas Creevey, MP, Sir Hubert Maxwell (ed.), John Murray, 1904

JACK LLEWELLYN DAVIES

J.M. Barrie and the Lost Boys: The Real Story Behind Peter Pan, Andrew Birkin, Constable, 1979

JACK DE MANIO

All Our Todays: Forty Years of Radio 4's Today Programme, Paul Donovan, Jonathan Cape, 1997

BLIND JACK METCALF

The Life of John Metcalf, commonly called Blind Jack of Knaresborough, York, 1795
Lives of the Engineers, Vol. 1, Part III, Chpt V, Samuel Smiles, 1861

JACK MYTTON

The Life of John Mytton, Esq., C.J. Apperley, Routledge, 1837

NAVY JACK

The Last Shot: The Incredible Journey of the CSS Shenandoah and the True Conclusion of the American Civil War, Lynn Schooler, HarperCollins, 2005

JACK O' CLOCKS

'The Clock Jacks of England', William Wooding Starmer, *Proceedings of the Musical Association*, 44th session, 1917-18

J.H. PLUMB

England in the Eighteenth Century, J.H. Plumb, Penguin, 1950

J.B. PRIESTLEY

The Shell Guide to England, John Hadfield (ed.), Michael Joseph, 1970
You Won't Believe This But . . ., Barry Cryer, Virgin, 1996

JACK PURVIS

Gods, Mongrels and Demons, Angus Calder, Bloomsbury, 2003

JACK THE RIPPER

Thomas Bulling and the Myth of the London Journalist, Thomas C. Westcott, available at www.forum.casebook.org

JACK ROSENTHAL

By Jack Rosenthal: An Autobiography in Six Acts, Jack Rosenthal, Robson Books, 2005

JACK RUBY

Reclaiming History: The Assassination of President John F. Kennedy, Vincent Bugliosi, W.W. Norton &Co., 2007

JACK SLIPPER

Slip-Up: The Classic Newspaper Story of All Time, Anthony Delano, Andre Deutsch, 1977

JACK STRACHEY

Lives of the Great Songs, Tim de Lisle (ed.), Penguin, new edition, 1995

JACK STRAW

The Peasants' Revolt of 1381, R.B. Dobson (ed.), Macmillan, 1970

JACK TAR

Storm and Conquest: The Battle for the Indian Ocean 1808–10, Stephen Taylor, Faber & Faber, 2007
Nelson's Blood: The Story of Naval Rum, Captain James Pack, Kenneth Mason, 1982

JACK 'SNUFFY' TRACY

The One and Only Phyllis Dixey, Philip Purser and Jenny Wilkes, Futura, 1978

SIEGFRIED SASSOON

Siegfried Sassoon and the Great War: The Making of a War Poet, Dennis Silk, Salisbury Printing Company, 1998
The Complete Memoirs of George Sherston, Siegfried Sassoon, Faber & Faber, 1937
The War Poems, Siegfried Sassoon, Faber & Faber, 1983

JACK STRAUS

The Biggest Game in Town, Al Alavarez, Houghton Mifflin, 1983

JACK SIMMONS AND JACK BOND
Anything but Murder, David Lloyd, Collins Willow, 2000

JACK SPRAT
King John, W.L. Warren, Methuen, 1961
The Big Over Easy, Jasper Fforde, Hodder & Stoughton, 2005
The Eyre Affair, Jasper Fforde, Viking, 2002
Lost in a Good Book, Jasper Fforde, Hodder & Stoughton, 2002

SPRING-HEELED JACK
www.mikedash.com

UNION JACK
The Union Jack: The Story of the British Flag, Nick Groom, Atlantic Books, 2006

JACK VAHEY
Soldiering and Scribbling, Archibald Forbes, Kessinger Publishing, 2004
Hell Riders: The Truth about the Charge of the Light Brigade, Terry Brighton, Viking, 2004

JACK WILKES
Four Portraits: Boswell, Gibbon, Sterne and Wilkes, Peter Quennell, Hutchinson, 1945
The Extraordinary Mr Wilkes, Louis Kronenberger, Doubleday, 1974

Lastly, I should also like to thank all the people in this book, Jacks and the rest, into whose remarkable lives I have so brusquely trespassed; and to apologise for the abrupt treatment and breezy summaries offered in return for such liberties. You should know that I stand amazed by it all, never more so than by the sheer gusto you have put into living. I must also apologise to and for any Jacks who have been unaccountably overlooked in my highly specialised approach to thoroughness and consistency. Next edition?